STUDIES IN PHILOSOPHY

STUDIES IN PHILOSOPHY

BRITISH ACADEMY LECTURES

By

G. F. STOUT, C. C. J. WEBB
H. A. PRICHARD, G. E. MOORE
R. B. BRAITHWAITE, J. L. AUSTIN
H. B. ACTON, K. R. POPPER
JOHN WISDOM, AND A. N. PRIOR

Selected and Introduced by
J. N. FINDLAY

London
OXFORD UNIVERSITY PRESS
NEW YORK · TORONTO
1966

Saint Dominic College Library
St. Charles, Illinois

Oxford University Press, Ely House, London W.1

GLASGOW NEW YORK TORONTO MELBOURNE WELLINGTON
CAPE TOWN SALISBURY IBADAN NAIROBI LUSAKA ADDIS ABABA
BOMBAY CALCUTTA MADRAS KARACHI LAHORE DACCA
KUALA LUMPUR HONG KONG

Selection, Introduction, and new material
© Oxford University Press, 1966

*For copyright reasons this book may
not be issued on loan or otherwise
except in its original soft cover.*

*Printed in Great Britain by
Richard Clay (The Chaucer Press), Ltd.,
Bungay, Suffolk*

CONTENTS

Introduction *By* J. N. FINDLAY	1
The Nature of Universals and Propositions *By* G. F. STOUT (*1921*)	5
Our Knowledge of One Another *By* C. C. J. WEBB (*1930*)	25
Duty and Ignorance of Fact *By* H. A. PRICHARD (*1932*)	41
Proof of an External World *By* G. E. MOORE (*1939*)	65
Moral Principles and Inductive Policies *By* R. B. BRAITHWAITE (*1950*)	93
Ifs and Cans *By* J. L. AUSTIN (*1956*)	115
The Philosophy of Language in Revolutionary France *By* H. B. ACTON (*1959*)	143
On the Sources of Knowledge and of Ignorance *By* K. R. POPPER (*1960*)	169
The Metamorphosis of Metaphysics *By* JOHN WISDOM (*1961*)	213
Some Problems of Self-Reference in John Buridan *By* A. N. PRIOR (*1962*)	241
Index	260

INTRODUCTION

BY J. N. FINDLAY

The present volume consists of ten brilliant and characteristic philosophical lectures given at the British Academy during the last half-century: eight were Henriette Hertz Trust Annual Philosophical Lectures and two Dawes Hicks Lectures on the History of Philosophy. In general, they illustrate the strong British penchant, which goes back to the later Middle Ages, for exact, cautious, logical thinking, but they include a few lectures of another tendency. They are certainly the products of a very remarkable, creative period in the history of philosophical thought and amply justify the foundations which caused them to be given.

The Henriette Hertz Trust Lectures began in 1914, but the first lecture chosen is that of G. F. Stout on 'The Nature of Universals and Propositions'. Stout now appears as a philosopher of very considerable stature, remembered for his deeply original analyses of states of mind and of the constitution of the objective world for knowledge, which are oddly hidden away in works professing to deal with matters of empirical psychology. The present lecture is devoted to the fascinating contentions, which influenced many, that 'of two billiard balls, each has its own particular roundness separate and distinct from that of the other', and that 'the distributive unity of a class or kind is an ultimate and unanalysable type of unity'. The lecture can fairly be called a nobly abstract piece of work, bringing the clear light of argument into a dark corner of traditional philosophy, which some would still like to leave draped in cobwebs.

The second lecture chosen is C. C. J. Webb's 'Our Knowledge of One Another', a remarkably lucid treatment of a problem that was to become *the* problem of philosophy in ensuing decades. Webb is among the first to emphasize that the problems raised by the mutual recognition of persons are no less primary and independent than those raised by sense-perception, self-awareness, etc. He strongly discounts any form of inferential theory, and practically makes a world of communicating persons a presupposition of all understanding and discourse. The 'wisdom' crystallized in the idealistic tradition which Webb espoused was only to be regained with difficulty after lengthy, tortured oscillations between solipsism and behaviourism.

In the third lecture, 'Duty and Ignorance of Fact', H. A. Prichard devotes infinite care and subtlety to the consideration of the question: 'If I have an obligation does it depend on the existence of certain facts of the situation or on my having certain thoughts about certain facts of the situation?' He reaches the conclusion that we can *know* the second alternative to be true, despite its highly paradoxical character. The lecture is one of the most deservedly famous specimens of British analysis, and raises a whole class of issues to a higher and more exact level of discussion.

Even more famous than Prichard's lecture is the next lecture chosen, G. E. Moore's 'Proof of an External World'. Moore here elaborately pretends to remove a traditional 'scandal' of philosophy, that the existence of 'things outside of us' must be accepted on faith and cannot be proved. He removes the scandal and proves his proposition by the delightful expedient, worthy of a Zen Buddhist, of showing the audience his two hands, 'making certain gestures, and saying the words "Here is one hand and here is another".' The complex argument of the paper has been much misunderstood, and has been taken for an endorsement of an 'ordinary language' view of philosophy, according to which the facts that it is linguistically correct to say that these are hands, and to call hands 'physical objects' or 'objects external to my mind' is sufficient to refute any idealistic thesis. Moore never embraced this linguistic view, and his proof depends on our simply *knowing*, being absolutely sure of whatever may be meant by the gesture and words in question, a meaning which includes such abstruse claims as that hands are 'logically independent' of perception. The article is far from being one of Moore's best, but it none the less illustrates a dialectical skill and an exact use of language which well deserve to be called 'incomparable'.

The next lecture I have chosen is R. B. Braithwaite's 'Moral Principles and Inductive Policies', which exploits the remarkable analogy, so often overlooked by the scientifically minded, between the principles which validate hypotheses and laws in science and those which validate moral judgements and principles. The reasonableness of the one, it appears, is much the same sort of thing as the reasonableness of the other, and what undermines the one may well utterly undermine the other. Braithwaite does not carry the analogy very far, but has certainly shown that there is a morality of science, and by implication, perhaps, some sort of science of morals.

J. L. Austin's 'Ifs and Cans', the next lecture chosen, is an admirable specimen of his 'linguistic phenomenology', a study of the world in and through the medium of words. Austin shows with detailed care, what Wittgenstein only asserted in quite general terms, how different are the concepts which really live and are at work in our words from the artificially tidied-up concepts of philosophers. In a footnote he shows, quite in passing, that an arguable indeterminism seems to be implied by what we ordinarily say. This lecture too, in a manner very different from Moore's, could well be called 'incomparable'.

The next lecture chosen, H. B. Acton's 'Philosophy of Language in Revolutionary France', both recalls to interesting life the analytic and linguistic programme of the French *idéologues*, and also uses them to make ironic comment on contemporary linguistic fashions in philosophy.

The next lecture, K. R. Popper's 'Sources of Knowledge and Ignorance', has been chosen, not only for its brilliance and originality, but also because it represents a strand of philosophizing widely influential yet different from the pure analysis mainly current in recent British thought. It sees knowledge and science in an historical and social context, it carries a valuable message, and it asks fundamental questions which it has become the fashion to ignore. If its final outcome is somewhat problematic, it is not less valuable for being so.

In the next lecture, John Wisdom's 'Metamorphosis of Metaphysics', we have an interesting development of a view which Wittgenstein sometimes toyed with but on the whole discouraged: that there was a specific, legitimate metaphysical game (or games), mainly concerned with the stressing of underemphasized analogies and differences which was not fundamentally changed when we passed from philosophies commonly classified as 'traditional' to their 'logico-analytic successors'. The latter, to quote Wisdom, only really differed 'in air and in guise' from the former. This 'rehabilitation of metaphysics', also stated in many other articles of Wisdom's, and sometimes suggesting a novel version of Hegelianism, is certainly an interesting product of our period.

A. N. Prior's 'Some Problems of Self-Reference in John Buridan' has, finally, been selected because it has brought to life a whole brilliant world of scholastic analysis and argument and related it to the arguments and analyses of the present.

There are very many excellent Academy lectures on philosophy which have not been included in the present collection. It would not be difficult, in fact, to collect a second series of lectures as good as those here published. Enough specimens will, however, have been provided to illustrate the vigour and variety and characteristic virtues of recent British thought, and its continued contribution, despite changes of fashion, to philosophical themes that may well be called 'perennial'.

THE NATURE OF UNIVERSALS AND PROPOSITIONS

BY G. F. STOUT

There are various types or forms of unity which may all be regarded as partial phases of the unity of the universe. There is the unity of the complex of qualities qualifying the same thing or concrete individual. There is the unity of space and time or space-time. There is the teleological unity, exemplified in a living organism. And there are others which I need not enumerate. It is only with one of these that I am here directly concerned—the unity of a class or kind as including its members or instances. What I am going to mean by the term 'universal' is either this unity itself, if it is taken as ultimate, or if it is not taken as ultimate, whatever principle is supposed to account for it: I mean what Mr. Bosanquet names the abstract universal in distinction from other forms of unity which he names concrete universals. The so-called abstract universal is, no doubt, when considered by itself, relatively superficial and shallow. None the less, it is vitally important, inasmuch as it is presupposed in all other forms of unity, so that without it there can be no thought. Hence the view taken of it by a philosopher essentially contributes to determine his whole philosophical position.

I hold myself that the unity of a class or kind is quite ultimate, and that any attempt to analyse it leads to a vicious circle. But this is not the traditional view, and it is not the view taken by leading philosophers of the present day such as Mr. Bradley, Mr. Bosanquet, Mr. Bertrand Russell, Mr. McTaggart, and Mr. W. E. Johnson in his recent admirable work on Logic. According to these writers, qualities and relations, as such, are universals. They are so inasmuch as the same relation may severally and separately relate distinct sets of terms, and the same qualities may be common to many distinct particular things. A plurality of particular things, sharing a common character, is a logical class, signified by a general term. The diverse particulars are the denotation, and the common character is the connotation of the general or distributive term applicable to each member of the class. Thus, the unity of a class or kind is regarded as derivative, not ultimate. It is constituted by the identity of some character, simple or complex, characterizing the things denoted by the general name. The identity of the character is interpreted strictly and literally. There is no plurality of particular qualities corresponding to the plurality of particular things. The common quality is regarded as indivisibly single. Two billiard balls are both round and smooth. So far as they are both round, the roundness of the one is the roundness of the other, and so far as they are both smooth, the smoothness of the one is the smoothness of the other. Abstract nouns, as standing for the quality in its singleness, without reference to any multiplicity of things qualified by it, are thus regarded as singular terms, like proper names. If we ask how, for example, shape can be identical both in square things and round things, the best answer is that of Mr. Johnson, who distinguishes between indeterminate and determinate characters. Shape is a single indeterminate character capable of being variously determined as square, round, or triangular. Similarly for relations. My nose is above my chin, and Smith's nose is above Smith's chin. His nose is distinct from mine, and the same is true of our chins. But there is the single identical relation of 'above and below' which relates both my nose to my chin and his nose to his chin. The question whether relations are or are not characters predicable of things is not here relevant. In order, however, to explain my language in what follows, I may say that I hold them to be predicable characters. I agree entirely with Mr. Johnson's treatment of the question in his chapter on Relations. 'My nose is above my chin' means 'my nose is to my chin as above to below, the nose being above and the chin below'.

This whole doctrine which I have roughly outlined, of the singleness of characters, whether qualities or relations, seems to me fundamentally wrong. A character characterizing a concrete thing or individual is as particular as the thing or individual which it characterizes. Of two billiard balls, each has its own particular roundness separate and distinct from that of the other, just as the billiard balls themselves are distinct and separate. As Jones is separate and distinct from Robinson, so the particular happiness of Jones is separate and distinct from that of Robinson. What, then, do we mean when we say, for instance, that roundness is a character common to all billiard balls? I answer that the phrase 'common character' is elliptical. It really signifies a certain general kind or class of characters. To say that particular things share in the common character is to say that each of them has a character which is a particular instance of this kind or class of characters. The particular instances are distributed among the particular things and so shared by them. It is true that the term 'class' tends in ordinary usage to be applied to classes of things, whereas such words as 'kind' or 'sort' are naturally applied also to qualities and relations. My point is that these terms all express the same ultimate form of unity, the distributive unity which comprehends what are for that reason called members of a class, instances or examples of a sort or kind. To define a general term exclusively by reference to classes of things, therefore, involves a vicious circle. There is no generality in substances which is not entirely derivative. It is wholly constituted by the generality of the adjectives which qualify them, and the generality of adjectives does not consist ultimately in possessing common adjectives.

Abstract nouns are, on my view, not singular but general terms. Shape, for example, stands for 'all shapes as such', and squareness stands for all square shapes as such. On the other hand, the shape of the table at which I am writing is a singular term. Abstract nouns supply the appropriate verbal form for naming qualities and relations when they are to be themselves characterized by other qualities and relations, as when we say that 'human happiness is transient'. Adjectives and verbs supply the appropriate verbal form for attributing characters to things.

The statement found in some text-books of Logic that adjectives are not names of qualities but of the things they qualify is, of course, nonsense.

The position that characters are as particular as the concrete things or individuals which they characterize, is common to me and the nominalists. But I differ from them essentially in maintaining that the distributive unity of a class or kind is an ultimate and unanalysable type of unity. The nominalists, on the contrary, say that it can be explained through the relation of resemblance. This view seems to me entirely indefensible. Distributive unity is signified by such words as 'all', 'every', 'any', 'some', and the indefinite article. Can the meaning of these words be stated adequately in terms of resemblance? This is plainly impossible. Consider the example 'all triangles'. It may be said that this means all shapes that resemble each other in a certain respect. But such formulas presuppose that the word 'all' has a meaning of its own that cannot be reduced to relations of similarity. It is precisely the concept of distributive unity which remains unexplained. The nominalist entirely fails to show how we can think of a class or kind as a whole without setting out before our mind each one of its members or instances so as to discern relations of similarity between them. Yet he cannot help tacitly assuming that this is not required for our apprehension of the class as a whole. Berkeley, for example, says that we take a given particular triangle as representing all other figures which resemble it in a certain respect. But this is nonsense, unless we can think of all the other figures as one total object without severally apprehending each of them or indeed any one of them.

What again is meant by resemblance in a certain respect? In what respect must figures resemble each other to be classed as triangles? Shall we say 'by being enclosed by three lines'? The answer is a good one if we suppose that three-sidedness is a single quality indivisibly present in the plurality of things which it qualifies. But nominalism is based on a denial of this position. Hence in the mouth of the nominalist the answer can only mean that the figures must resemble each other inasmuch as they are all triangles—inasmuch as they are all members of the class 'triangular figures'. This is plainly a vicious circle, when what requires to be explained is precisely the meaning of the words 'class' or 'kind'.

How, then, it may be asked, are relations of resemblance connected with the distributive unity of a class or kind? My own view is briefly as follows. A relation considered as subsisting between terms presupposes some complex unity within which both the terms and relations fall. This complex unity is the *fundamentum relationis*. For example, a relation of 'above and below' as subsisting between *a* and *b* presupposes a spatial complex including both *a* and *b* and the spatial relation between them. In like manner, resemblance presupposes a complex unity of the peculiar type which I call the distributive unity of a class. The same holds for dissimilarity so far as this admits of degrees, as between colours, and does not amount to disparity which makes comparison impossible, as between colours and sounds. The unity of the complex as a whole ought not to be confused with relations between terms. Thus the resemblance is always between members of a class of things or particular instances of a kind of quality. The unity of the class or kind as a whole is not a relation at all. It is what, with Mr. Johnson's permission, I should like to call a 'tie'—a *fundamentum relationis*.

Agreeing with the nominalist that characters are as particular as the things or substances they characterize, the inference I draw from this thesis is not that there really are no universals, but that the universal is a distributive unity. I have now to defend this thesis and consider some of the implications.

It will be convenient to begin with characters which consist in transient state, acts, or processes, e.g. a sneeze, the flight of a bird, the explosion of a mine. These are so obviously particular that they present a special difficulty for those who hold that qualities and relations are, as such, universals. The difficulty is so pressing that it has driven more than one recent writer to assert that transient states or acts are substances, not characters of substances. Mr. McTaggart, for example, after defining a substance as that which has qualities or relations but is not itself a quality or relation, writes as follows (*Nature of Existence*, p. 73): 'A sneeze would not usually be called a substance, nor would a party at whist, nor all red-haired archdeacons. But each of the three complies with our definition, since each of them has qualities and each is related without being a quality or relation.' Mr. McTaggart's definition is defective. If we are not to ignore a fundamental and relevant distinction we must add to it that a substance must be a particular existence and not a universal. This excludes the red-haired archdeacons. We may pass the whist party, considered as a group of men sitting at a table and playing a game. A sneeze is certainly particular. But it is equally certain that it is not a substance, even according to McTaggart's definition. It may indeed have characters predicated of it: it may be violent and inconvenient. But it is also a character predicable of something else, the particular man who sneezes. It has its being only in its concrescence with the other qualities and relations of the concrete individual while he is sneezing. The sneeze cannot continue to exist in however altered a form apart from the sneezer, as a hand or eye may when severed from the body. Similarly, when Mr. Johnson says that a flash of lightning is a substance, I admit that this is true of the lightning, while it flashes but not of the flashing of the lightning.

We may then assume that at least a large and important group of characters are as particular as the substances which they characterize. Is this true of all qualities and relations? It must be so, because there is no distinction of substances as separate particulars which does not involve a corresponding distinction of their characters as separate particulars. I apprehend two billiard balls as separate substances, inasmuch as each is taken to be in a separate place. One is here and the other there on the surface of the billiard table. How can I know or suppose this unless I know or suppose that the roundness, smoothness, and whiteness of the one ball is locally separate from the roundness, smoothness, and whiteness of the other, and that the relation of contact between the one ball and the cloth is locally separate from the contact between the other ball and the cloth?

It has been objected that what is really the same indivisible quality may none the less appear separately in different times and places. There is here, I think, a serious confusion between two senses of the word 'appear'. We say that something may appear to be what it is not. So used, appearing is synonymous with seeming. But we also say not that something appears or seems to exist, or to be this or that, but simply that it appears, meaning that it is an actual apparition, that it is actually presented or given in experience. In this sense, nothing can really appear except what really is, and really is as it appears. I may, in double vision, have two images of a single candle flame. There then appear or *seem* to be two candle flames, whereas in fact there is only one. But the visual presentations not only appear or seem to exist and be separate. Both they and their separation really appear, are really presented or given, and must therefore really exist. It is only because the images really exist and are really separate that there appear or seem to be two flames. Now, when it is said that, for instance, the brightness of one light appears separately from the brightness of another, what is meant is simple appearance and not seeming. This must be so, because the separate appearance is taken as explaining how the qualities may seem to be separate though they are not, just as the double image explains why the single candle flame seems to be double. But the explanation refutes itself. If the qualities of separate things really appear separately, and if their separateness really appears, then they really are separate, and do not merely seem to be so.

I may restate my general argument in another way. Whatever view may be held of the distinction of a substance from its qualities, it is almost universally admitted that the substance is nothing *apart from* its qualities. Mr. McTaggart makes this proposition the basis of an argument to show that substances cannot be diverse without being in some respect dissimilar. In this he may be right. But the same principle seems also to lead to a conclusion which he would reject, that qualities are distinct particulars, just as substances are. If substance is nothing apart from its qualities, to know the substance without knowing its qualities is to know nothing.

It follows that we cannot distinguish substances from each other without discerning a corresponding distinction between their qualities. It follows also that if the distinction of the substances is not preconditioned by any discerned dissimilarity between their qualities, the qualities must be primarily known as separate particulars, not as universals. The universals will be involved only inasmuch as they are particulars of the same general sort or kind. Now in looking, let us say, at a sheet of white paper, I am able to discern the several parts of the paper without discerning qualitative unlikeness between each part and every one of the others. Even if I am aware of qualitative unlikeness between one part and some other part I can clearly recognize that this is not the primary ground of the distinction between them. Whether I suppose the unlikeness to be great or almost imperceptible or quite absent, diversity is still discernible. Indeed, if it were not presupposed there could be no question of likeness or unlikeness. Nor can we say that each part is distinguishable by its distinctive relations to other parts. For in order that one particular may be known as related in the required way to other particulars, it is a logical precondition that it shall itself be known as one particular among others.

In this argument I have assumed that a thing is nothing apart from its characters, and that therefore there can be no knowledge of it which is not knowledge of its characters. But Mr. Bertrand Russell and, I believe, Mr. Moore reverse this reasoning. According to them, knowledge of a thing as in any way characterized, is only knowledge about it, and presupposes a logically prior and independent knowledge of the things themselves, which they call acquaintance. Hence they would argue that inasmuch as things can be known independently of any knowledge of their characters, it cannot be true, as I have assumed, that they are nothing apart from their characters. Mere acquaintance with a thing is supposed to involve no apprehension of anything which could possibly be predicated of it. What is known in this way cannot be expressed in words. I am acquainted with a colour presentation while it is being presented, and with a toothache while I am feeling it. If, however, I am aware of the toothache as being painful or intense, or as felt, or as existing, or as mine, or as beginning, persisting, or ceasing, or as in any way distinct from or connected with anything else, or even as being 'something or other', such awareness is knowledge *about* the toothache and not merely acquaintance with it. Acquaintance with the toothache consists in the fact that it is felt, not in knowledge of this or any other fact. Acquaintance with a colour presentation consists in the fact that it is presented, not in knowledge of this fact or of any other.

I do not at all doubt that what is here called acquaintance really exists. Without it there can be no knowledge; for if we were not acquainted with some things we could not know anything. It is what I have called actual appearance as distinguished from seeming. It constitutes the radical meaning of the word 'experience' which gives distinctive significance to all its other applications. It is what, following Mr. Bradley, I have been accustomed to call immediate experience. But it cannot, I think, be properly regarded as knowledge. It is true that I can know about a toothache while I am actually experiencing it, as I cannot know about it while I am not experiencing it. And we may perhaps call this way of knowing, knowledge by acquaintance. Still, the knowledge is only knowledge *about*, and is distinct from the acquaintance which conditions it. How, indeed, can we know anything, if it is supposed that we know absolutely nothing about it?

Let us, however, for the sake of argument, concede that acquaintance, as such, is knowledge. There is still no ground for regarding it as a knowledge merely of things, apart from their qualities and relations. It is true, indeed, that we do not know *about* the qualities and relations when we are merely acquainted with them. We do not know that they exist or what they are. We do not distinguish them from each other or from the things they characterize. If reasons of this sort prove that we do not know the qualities, they prove equally that we do not know the thing qualified. For in mere acquaintance, we do not know that the thing exists or what it is: we do not distinguish it from other things or from its qualities. If we can know the thing in this blind way, then in the same blind way we can know its characters. If we inquire what in mere acquaintance we are acquainted with, mere acquaintance itself, being blind and dumb, can supply no answer. The answer must be sought in analytic judgements which involve knowledge about. But these judgements never reveal a mere thing apart from its characters, but always the thing as in some way characterized. Both for mere acquaintance with things and for knowledge about them the principle holds good that a substance, being nothing apart from its adjectives, cannot be known apart from them.

At this point we are confronted by the ultimate question, What is the distinction between a substance, on the one hand, and its qualities and relations, on the other? To me only one view appears tenable. A substance is a complex unity of an altogether ultimate and peculiar type, including within it all characters truly predicable of it. To be truly predicable of it is to be contained within it. The distinctive unity of such a complex is *concreteness*. Characters of concrete things are particular, but not concrete. What is concrete is the whole in which they coalesce with each other. This view of substance as a complex unity, when coupled with the doctrine that qualities and relations are universals, leads naturally, if not inevitably, to the denial of an ultimate plurality of substances. This is the line of thought which we find in Mr. Bradley and Mr. Bosanquet. Reality must be concrete and individual; the individual cannot be constituted by any mere union of universals. Yet if we inquire what so-called finite individuals are, we find nothing but qualities and relations, which, as such, are taken to be universals. Hence, the true individual transcends the grasp of finite thought. There can be only one substance, the absolute and individual whole of being; all finite existences including finite selves are merely adjectives of this. If taken as ultimate they are mere appearances.

On the other hand, those who maintain that there is an ultimate plurality of substances, and yet hold that characters are, as such, universals, seem logically bound to deny that a substance is the complex unity of all its qualities and relations. Thus Mr. McTaggart, who occupies this position, asserts in his *Unity of Existence*, chap. v, that the complex unity is itself only a complex adjective, and therefore presupposes a subject ultimately distinct from itself. I have elsewhere criticized this view on the ground that it makes the whole being of substance consist in its relatedness to something else, to the characters which characterize it. Mr. McTaggart now replies that when, for instance, 'Smith is said to be happy', the fact that he is happy is the primary fact, and the fact that he is related to the quality of happiness is only derivative (p. 70). But this leaves my difficulty untouched. What Mr. McTaggart calls the primary fact, the happy Smith, is, according to him, a complex containing two existences ultimately quite distinct from each other, the substance, on the one hand, and, on the other, all characters predicable of it. But two distinct existences within a complex can be connected only by a relation; and the relation in this case can be no other than what is directly expressed in such propositions as 'Smith is happy'.

Mr. McTaggart also directly attacks the alternative view that the substance is the complex unity comprehending what for that reason are called its characters. Unfortunately, his argument starts with a misunderstanding. 'It has', he says, 'been maintained that we shall, if we take the right view, be able to dispense with the conception of substance and use only the conception of qualities.' This is certainly not what I take to be the right view. For me, the concrete complex containing all the characters of a thing is not a character but the thing itself. To say that the inclusive complex must itself be a predicable character, is like saying that a triangle must be the side of a triangle, that the class 'horses' must be a horse. What remains of Mr. McTaggart's argument, after we have allowed for such misunderstanding, amounts only to this, that a proposition such as 'Smith is happy' cannot, without absurdity, be formulated in the language of my theory. We cannot, he urges, assert of the complex comprising all characters predicable of Smith that this complex is happy. We cannot. But this rendering of 'Smith is happy' is not mine. Mine would rather be: 'The concrete unity including the character of being known by the name of Smith also includes the character of being happy.' This, I take it, is precisely what is meant by asserting that Smith is happy. The formula given by McTaggart itself needs to be translated in terms of my theory. So translated it would run: 'The complex including all the characters of Smith includes, besides these, another character of Smith, that of being happy.' This is nonsense. But in my view there is no reason why it should be sense.

There still remains one question which I have not yet considered, though it is of vital importance to my general argument. If I am right, what is meant by a character common to a class of things is a general kind of character of which a particular instance characterizes each member of the class. It follows that the logical divison of a wider class into mutually exclusive subclasses according to the same *fundamentum divisionis* is possible only through a corresponding division of a wider class of characters into subclasses of characters. This view is, of course, quite incompatible with the position of those who regard a common character as a single quality or relation indivisibly belonging to each and all of the things it characterizes. Have they any alternative explanation? I know of no other than that which is offered in chap. xi of Mr. Johnson's *Logic*, on 'The Determinable'.

Mr. Johnson begins by comparing the propositions 'Red is a colour' and 'Plato is a man'. He inquires whether Red is asserted to be a member of a class called 'colours', as Plato is asserted to be a member of the class 'men'. He simply takes for granted without discussion, that redness at any rate, if not colour, is a singular term, standing for a single quality and not for a general kind of qualities. He thus, from my point of view, partially begs the question at issue from the outset. In his way of dealing even with the problem as he himself formulates it, there seems to be a similar *petitio principii*. He decides that 'colours' does not stand for a class of which redness is a member. The sole reason which he gives is that whereas Plato, for example, is recognized as a man through the quality of humanity common to him and other men, it is not true that red is recognized as a colour through a quality distinct from itself and common to it and other colours such as blue and yellow. But this is merely to assert, what is in any case evident, that inasmuch as substances are not qualities, classes of substances are not classes of qualities. On any view, the division of substances into classes is in some way dependent on a corresponding distinction between their adjectives. It presupposes that, in some sense, a plurality of things share in a common character. The only question is, what is meant by their sharing in a common character? I take this to mean that each is characterized by a particular instance of a general kind or class of characters. We may if we choose apply the term class exclusively to general kinds of substances. But the real question is whether the words 'kind' and 'class' stand for the same ultimate type of distributive unity, which is found in substance, only because and so far as it is found in their characters, and cannot therefore be ultimately different for substances and for characters.

This is not Mr. Johnson's view. Does he offer any tenable alternative? Instead of the distinction between general and particular, and between more and less general, he would in dealing with characters substitute the distinction of the determinable and the completely or relatively determinate. 'To predicate *colour* or *shape* of an object,' he says, 'obviously characterizes it less determinately than to predicate of it *red* or *circular*; hence the former adjective may be said ... to be indeterminate as compared with the latter.'

There is certainly a sense in which this distinction is valid and useful. If I know or consider merely the fact that something is a colour, this does not determine what special sort of colour it is. This is determined only by further propositions in which

18 NATURE OF UNIVERSALS AND PROPOSITIONS

it is asserted to be red or to be blue. So understood, the distinction is relative to the knowing mind. It is what Mr. Johnson calls 'epistemic'.[1] In this sense I am myself prepared to use the terms determinable and determinate. But in this sense the distinction is applicable to substances as well as adjectives. If I consider something merely as being an animal this leaves undetermined the question whether it is a mouse or a man.

Mr. Johnson, of course, means far more than this. For him the relation of determinable is constitutive, not merely epistemonic. It is a relation between qualities as such; and for qualities it takes the place of the distinction between degrees of generality which is supposed to hold only for substances. According to Johnson, colour is not a general kind of quality comprising redness as a sub-kind. On the contrary, colour and redness are both singular, each standing for a single positive quality. Colour, he tells us, 'though it is indeterminate, is, metaphorically speaking, that from which the specific determinates, red, yellow, green, &c., emanate; while from shape emanate another completely different series of determinates such as triangular, square, octagonal, &c. Thus our idea of this or that determinable has a distinctly positive context, which would be quite inadequately represented by the word indeterminate.' On this view the proposition 'red is a colour' means that a single positive quality red is related to another positive quality colour by a peculiar relation appropriately named that of a determinate to its determinable. Now it seems to me that Mr. Johnson has not only failed to show that there is such a relation but that he has also, in the course of his argument, suggested a cogent reason for denying it. He points out very clearly that red is not recognized as a colour through any quality distinct from itself and shared in common by it and all colours, as redness is shared by all red things. As he puts it, 'the several colours . . . are given the same name colour, not on the ground of any partial agreement, but on the ground of a special kind of difference which distinguishes one colour

---

[1] The proper form is 'epistemonic', but the barbarism is convenient.

from another.' I would add that there is a peculiar kind of resemblance as well as of difference. The point is that red and yellow do not resemble each other in one character and differ in another. The respect in which they are alike, i.e. colour, is also the respect in which they are dissimilar. The same holds for squareness and roundness. As the late Professor Cook Wilson used to say, 'square shape is not squareness plus shape; squareness itself is a special way of being a shape'.

Are considerations of this sort inconsistent with my view that redness is a subclass of the more general class 'colour' as red things is a subclass of coloured things? There would be an inconsistency only if it could be shown that a red thing is distinguished from a yellow thing not merely by its colour but by some other character. But, as Mr. Johnson himself expressly points out, this is not so. In the logical division of a class of things into subclasses, the *fundamentum divisionis* is always a determinable adjective predicated of every member of the class divided; and the subclasses are always distinguished by determinates of this determinable. It is true, indeed, that a concrete thing is, or implies, the concrete union of many characters which are not related to each other as determinable and determinate. Hence it is possible to select this or that indeterminate adjective, simple or complex, as a basis of division. Thus we divide books according to their size or according to their binding. But a subclass is never distinguished by the presence or absence of a fresh adjective which is not indeterminately applicable to all members of the wider class. When we divide books into bound or unbound the *fundamentum* is the status of books as regards binding; the term unbound has a positive meaning as applied to books which it would not have if applied to coals or candles.

There is nothing in these statements which is not fully accounted for if we suppose that the distinction of general and particular and of degrees of generality in things is constituted by, and therefore presupposes, a precisely corresponding distinction of general and particular, and of degrees of generality in adjectives. On the other hand, Mr. Johnson's view is not really self-consistent. Assuming as he does that redness is a singular term, and denying that colour is a class including redness as a member, he is bound to regard colour also as a singular term. As such it can only stand for a single quality, just as redness stands for a single quality. What, then, can be meant by saying that red, green, or blue are colours? What is asserted cannot be that each is identical with colour. For they would, then, be identical with each other. We seem compelled to say that redness is in part identical with colour and in part different. It must be a complex including the indeterminate quality colour which is equally present in blue and green, and also a determining quality which distinguishes it from blue and green. But as Mr. Johnson has himself shown, this is untrue. There is no determining quality which makes the determinable determinate. We must, therefore, give up the initial assumption that redness and colour are singular terms.

They are general, i.e. distributive terms. Redness, considered as a completely determinate general term, stands for the distributive unity of particular reds. To be a particular red is to be *either* this, that, or the other particular instance of redness. Redness in general is comprised within a more comprehensive unity called 'colour in general', which also comprises yellowness and blueness. Every particular instance of redness is a particular instance of colour. Colour in general is nothing but the distributive unity of its specific sub-kinds, just as these are ultimately the distributive unity of their particular instances. To be a particular colour is to be a particular example *either* of this, that, or the other special kind of colour. The words 'either, or' mark the distributive tie, and exclude the conception of colour as a single though indeterminate quality.

The distinction of the determinable and its determinates, though it presupposes generality, has none the less, as I said before, its own place and value if we regard it not as constitutive but epistemonic. In particular, it is important in considering the nature of propositions. I have included this topic in my title. But I have left myself so little time, that I must be content with a brief indication of what I intended to say about it.

A proposition, whatever else it may be, is something proposed or set before the mind as the object of certain subjective processes—questioning, doubting, asserting, supposing, and also practical deliberation and decision. Belief and will do not necessarily consist in such processes. I may be aware of myself as sitting at a table and writing, without mentally asserting that this is so, and without at all questioning whether it is so or not. There is knowledge about things without any explicit mental act of judging. Similarly, I may voluntarily shake hands with a friend without any thought of doing otherwise, and therefore without choosing or deciding to shake hands. What is thus taken for granted constitutes a vast and vague background from which propositions emerge here and there.

Nothing takes shape as a proposition, either theoretical or practical, unless it is in some way suggested, however transiently, that from some general point of view it may or might be otherwise. If the thought of its being otherwise is prolonged there is questioning or practical hesitation. If it is still further prolonged, and developed in detail, there is doubt or deliberation. Thus we may say that a proposition is apprehended as a possible alternative. What, then, is an alternative? There are two meanings of the word, distinct though inseparable. In one sense an alternative is such only relatively to the variable knowledge and interest of the individual. But this presupposes that the objective universe is so constituted as to present alternatives to the knowing and willing mind. Their existence is ultimately implied in the existence of general classes or kinds of generalities as the distributive unity of particular instances and subclasses. To have shape is to have this, that, or the other special sort of shape. This holds good whether or not someone knows which special shape the thing in fact has. Even when the thing is known or believed to be square, it is still true that it is either square or round or octagonal or so forth. But a mind interested in knowing what the specific shape is, and already knowing it to be square, need not and does not concern itself with the existence of other alternatives, unless it is suggested, for example, by the words or behaviour of other persons. Otherwise the proposition that the thing is square will not occur to it at all. In mere supposition, the mind attends to the nature and implications of an alternative as such, ignoring, either provisionally or entirely, the question whether it is realized or to be realized. Consider the following. 'If I get this post I shall have no time for research work.' 'If I had been appointed to that post I should have had no time for research work.' 'If there had been no carbon there would have been no organic life.' 'If there were no incompatible qualities the logical law of contradiction would have no application.' These are all propositions about what, from some more or less general point of view, is an alternative possibility. They are propositions which have a proposition as their subject. They rarely occur where the alternative is already known or fully believed to be realized, or where it has already been practically decided that it shall be realized. On the contrary, they occur frequently where it is known that the alternative is not, and is not to be, realized. They are then called fictions.

This view implies that there really are alternative possibilities. Now, in the most natural and common use of language the real and possible are correlated and opposed in such wise that it is as absurd to say that the possible *quâ* possible is real, as it is to say that what is above is, as such, below. None the less, possibilities as such are not mere inventions of the understanding, or mere appearances. They really exist. Their existence is not merely possible. When a man has to choose between death and apostasy these alternatives are really contained in the general situation with which he is confronted. But only one of them is realized. Which of them it shall be depends on the man himself. Only determinism gone mad could deny that, to this extent, there is free-will.

The meaning of the adjectives 'true' and 'false', in their ordinary use, presupposes the conception of the proposition as an alternative. Alternatives are such only in relation to some real fact. One of them, and when they are fully distinguished, not more than one, is identical with the real fact. A proposition is true when it is identical with the realized alternative. To assert, deny, doubt, or suppose that this alternative is realized, is to assert, deny, doubt, or suppose what is true. The unrealized alternatives are false propositions.

Of course the distinction between truth and falsity holds also for the inarticulate domain of what is merely taken for granted. But it is only so far as alternatives are apprehended as such, i.e. as propositions, that we become aware of the distinction: then only can we consider and examine competing claims to truth. Even at this stage our assertions, denials, and doubts are, on the most important matters, conditioned and controlled by a vast background of what is merely taken for granted. If in this background there is anything which is incapable, from any point of view, of being apprehended as an alternative, then, though it may be transcendently important, we can never be aware of it as a proposition so as to express it in language and discuss it.

A word in conclusion on the metaphysical bearings of the logical doctrine of universals.

I have already indicated how the philosophy of those who maintain the unity of the universe is affected by the view that universals are qualities and relations. But it plays an equally important part with Mr. Russell, for whom there is no universe, but only an indefinite aggregate of disjointed items, each conceivably capable of existing by itself. As an integral part of this theory, he disjoins particulars and universals as two intrinsically independent realms of existence. He finds it possible to do this because, for him, qualities and relations are, as such, universals. Inasmuch as they are universals, they cannot in any way form part of the being of the particular things which they qualify or relate. On the other hand, inasmuch as they are qualities and relations, they cannot contain the particular things. Characters cannot contain what they characterize. It follows that the domain of concrete things and individuals in its own intrinsic being falls entirely apart from the domain of universals in their intrinsic being. From this point of view, we can understand Mr. Russell's distinction between acquaintance with things and knowledge about them, and his still more perplexing distinction between knowledge about and knowledge by description.

Plainly, the nature of general and abstract ideas is a topic which has the same philosophical importance now that it had for Berkeley; and however defective his treatment of it was, some things which he said deserve to be repeated even now —though with a difference.

OUR KNOWLEDGE OF ONE ANOTHER

BY CLEMENT C. J. WEBB

I think that it will be generally allowed that the nature of our self-consciousness, on the one hand, and that of our perception of the external world on the other, are wont to receive in philosophical discussion a larger share of consideration than the nature of our mutual recognition of one another as persons with whom social intercourse is possible. The explanation of this comparative neglect of the problem of our knowledge of one another is probably to be sought, at any rate in part, in the fact that in our acquaintance with our fellow human beings we may, on a first inspection, seem merely to be combining the two other kinds of cognition to which I have referred. That I am not alone I am, it may be suggested, certified by perceptions of the same kind as those which inform me of the existence of external objects other than my fellow human beings; while in my interpretation of these perceptions as in this instance revealing not merely external objects but objects significant of feelings, thoughts, purposes of the same nature as my own, yet not my own, I am but supposing the consciousness which I have of myself to be as it were repeated, although with variations; which variations themselves, however, are only apprehended through an imaginative reproduction of them as feelings, thoughts, purposes belonging to myself. I do not suppose that the assumptions I have just described are usually worked out in detail; if they were, the difficulties which they involve, and to some of which I propose in this lecture to invite your attention, would more often disturb acquiescence in them. But I think that the assumptions are implied in what I believe to be a not uncommon failure to realize that the problem presented by the mutual recognitions of persons is of no less philosophical importance, no less primary and relatively independent than those of self-consciousness and of perception; that it might even be plausibly contended that this mutual recognition is presupposed both by self-consciousness and by perception of the external world; and that, though this thesis should turn out to be untenable, yet that light may be thrown alike on our self-consciousness and on our perception of the external world by a study of that awareness of other persons which we enjoy in our experience of social intercourse.

It is perhaps worth pointing out, in order to clear the ground, that only to superficial reflection will it seem possible to account for this awareness itself by a process which it is natural enough to employ in ascertaining whether what has the appearance of a living man is truly such or, say, a waxwork figure. There was such a figure of a policeman at the door of Madame Tussaud's Exhibition in my youth, and one was dared to make sure by a pinch whether this were a real or an artificial guardian of the peace. Would he react to the pinch as a real one would—that is, as one would react oneself if so assaulted? But this process, used as a method of testing the reality of a claimant to the status of another person, presupposes our possession of the idea of another person, who can feel and act as I feel and act. It could not create this idea, nor indeed suggest itself at all, were this idea not already present in one's mind. If we suppose it to be the source of this idea, we are forgetting that one cannot perceive one's own body so as to become aware of its shape except in a mirror; and that, as is hinted by the legend of Narcissus and by Aesop's fable of the dog with the meat, a first experience of beholding one's own reflected image would be far from suggesting its true interpretation. Rather it would lead to such vain enhances or futile attacks as those stories tell of. But, leaving on one side this by no means unimportant consideration, the attempt to account for our awareness of other persons as an inference from the resemblance of their bodily shape and movements to our own implies that our initial position is that of a 'solipsist', aware only of himself and needing, before he can attain to consciousness of any reality other than himself, to infer a cause beyond himself of what at first appear to him to be merely states or feelings of his own. I have a recollection of hearing the late Lord Balfour remark in the course of a philosophical discussion that he found it very difficult to deny 'solipsism' to be our original condition, but no less difficult to see how, if it were so, we could ever get out of it. The second difficulty appears to me insuperable, but as to the former I cannot believe that solipsism is a position that anyone was ever really in. A purely feeling consciousness, for which the contrast of self with what is other than self does not exist, there may be, though it is not to such a consciousness that we could attribute an act of inference. But, for the term 'solipsist' to be applicable to it, this contrast must be supposed already present, at least ideally. If, however, I attempt, for the sake of argument, to imagine a being conscious of himself and of states of himself as such, but of nothing beyond himself with which to contrast these, I can (though with difficulty and without conviction) persuade myself to picture him as seeking in something other than himself the cause of changes in his own experience, some archetype, so to say, of what as a state of himself he already *ex hypothesi* distinguishes from himself; but that he should take this something other than himself to be a reduplication of that which, also *ex hypothesi*, is essentially unique, the *solus ipse*, insistence on whose uniqueness for each subject is the very point of the doctrine which we are criticizing, this I cannot bring myself even to imagine.

But the impossibility of the whole doctrine is perpetually being forced upon us as we try to describe it by the difficulty which we find in expressing it intelligibly. An original or native solipsism is surely a chimera. The only fact to which the name can be legitimately given is a speculation arising in the mind of one who, though already possessed of the conception of other selves, asks himself whether it could not be dispensed with, and forces his imagination to make an effort to dispense with it.

If, however, we dismiss as on every ground unsatisfactory the attempt to explain our knowledge of one another as an inference from the shape and movements of certain external objects to their association with a consciousness such as each of us has of his own self, what account are we to give of that knowledge? For, despite the difficulties which I have mentioned as besetting that which I have rejected, it seems plain both that we do, as a matter of fact, regard a certain sort of shape and certain kinds of movement as inseparably conjoined with the capacity for social intercourse which constitutes our experience of persons; and that it is only by 'putting ourselves in their place', by interpreting the behaviour of others by feelings, thoughts, and purposes, such as we ourselves experience in ourselves, that the mutual understanding involved in social intercourse is attained.

So far as regards the former of these apparent facts, we must, no doubt, note that we are quite familiar with cases in which the communication of thoughts, feelings, purposes, may and does take place, through letters, 'broadcasting', books, painting, music, where the parties do not perceive each other's bodily form; nay, where one party may actually no longer exist in the body at all, but 'being dead, still speaks' (as we say) through his works to those who are alive. In such cases it is assuredly not from our perception of an external object shaped and moving in certain ways that we infer the person. On the contrary, we infer from the apprehension of thoughts and emotions not our own that such external objects exist or have existed as we have learnt from our own experience, confirmed by that of others, are regularly associated with thinking and feeling. Indeed, the hypothesis that in some instances thoughts and emotions may be communicated to us by incorporeal spirits, though it may be judged gratuitous and improbable, cannot be ruled out as logically inadmissible. In the majority of alleged instances of such communication, however, it is to be observed that perception of external objects still plays its part; there are written or spoken words, or other sights or sounds, serving as the means of communication; and it is precisely where even these are lacking, where a thought seems to occur or an emotion to arise, which the person to whom this happens takes to be 'put into his mind' by someone else, that this supposition of origination by the activity of another person would be generally allowed to be most precarious and unverifiable.

Normally, at any rate, the perception of a certain kind of external object is necessary to prompt us to engage in social intercourse by indicating the presence of a person capable thereof. But this perception by itself would have no effect in bringing about such intercourse without the establishment of a *rapport* between the communicating parties which is a direct relation, not analysable into relations of any other kind or explicable in terms of any others. The invention of writing and of other means of human communication and expression has introduced into the mechanism of such communication various modifications which not only substitute, as the primary provocative to social intercourse, for the perception of a human body the perception of the object serving as the means of communication, but also render possible, as we have seen, the apprehension by one person of thoughts, feelings, and purposes, of another person, which have not been communicated by that other especially to him, and that even where no mutual *rapport* between the author and the recipient of the communication is possible. A study of the effect of these developments on the consciousness of personal fellowship would be of great value; but what I am now concerned to point out is that they all presuppose the existence of what I have called a mutual *rapport* between persons, such as is exemplified in an ordinary conversation, and cannot be exhaustively accounted for as an inference from the perception by each interlocutor of the other's body and its movements. Upon the reality or necessity to the life of man as a rational and social being of this *rapport* I would insist; but, while decidedly distinguishing it from any process (however closely associated with it) which should be capable of explanation in terms of a purely natural science, pledged to leave what is spiritual out of its calculations, I have no such interest as might be suspected in maintaining the actuality or even the possibility of what is usually called 'telepathy', still less of conversations with discarnate spirits. The reality and necessity of a direct relation between human minds or souls is quite compatible with the presence in the constitution of human nature of conditions inconsistent with the occurrence of such alleged phenomena. Until, however, the presence of such conditions is satisfactorily ascertained, the question of their occurrence must remain a matter of empirical evidence.

I now turn from the perception of external objects to the self-consciousness which, according to the 'inferential' theory of our knowledge of one another, is also presupposed by that knowledge. The consciousness of self may be, as Descartes held, the bed-rock of certainty, to which when we are come, we can question and doubt no farther; but it is not with this consciousness of self that our experience begins. Of all the truths that Plato taught, none is more irrefragable than the truth intimated in his parable of the large and small letters that we come to a knowledge of our own inner being through acquaintance with the societies in which the spiritual nature whereof individual souls are instances has expressed itself, and by which these individual souls have themselves been moulded. The history of moral reflection as presented in literature, wherein appreciation of goodness and badness in others long precedes such introspection as we find, for example, in the *Confessions* of St. Augustine; the language in which, when introspection and self-examination have come into use, we talk of the soul's interior life; the method instinctively pursued in self-criticism of trying 'to see ourselves as others see us'—all confirm this doctrine of Plato's; and we may recall the same philosopher's description in the *Theaetetus* of thinking as a silent converse of the soul with herself, patterned as it were upon such discussions as he has detailed for us in his own Socratic dialogues.

The lesson of all this is that we can no more derive our knowledge of one another from our self-consciousness than from our perception of external objects, or from a mere combination of the two. For our knowledge of one another would seem to be anterior in time to our consciousness of self as such; and indeed a more plausible case might be made out for deriving our self-consciousness from our consciousness of other persons than vice versa. The child, as has often been remarked, is apt to speak of himself in the third person before he acquires the habit of using the first; and sometimes the first realization of the unique selfhood implied in calling oneself 'I' may with children of a reflective disposition come as a sudden and, for the moment, overwhelming experience. I can recollect something of the kind as happening to me when five or six years old; and the like is related of himself as a very young child by Jean Paul Richter.[1] Again, the tendency of children and primitive men to personify objects which we should regard as impersonal has been frequently noted; and this observation might be employed in support of a contention that our perception of material things is so far from forming a premiss of the inference whereby we reach the knowledge of other persons, that that perception itself originates rather in our primary apprehension of other persons by the dropping out of it, in certain cases, in which it has been frequently disappointed, of the expectation of a personal response.

I could not, however, myself go so far in reaction from the theory which I began this lecture by criticizing. I think indeed that in all probability the apprehension of one's fellows is, of the three kinds of apprehension which we have been considering, the first to predominate in human experience; that reflection on oneself as separate from one's fellows or on *things* as being of a different nature from theirs is subsequent to our recognition of them. But these distinctions, when recognized, are recognized and not created. Self-consciousness and perception of an external world are alike fundamentally diverse from one another and from awareness of other persons, however intimately associated and intertwined with one another these three modes of consciousness may be. Nowhere, to my mind, has the impossibility of deriving our perception of an external world from any experience which

[1] Quoted in the review of his biography in Carlyle's *Critical and Miscellaneous Essays*, ed. 1888, i. 30.

does not already involve it been more convincingly demonstrated than in the remarkable articles published on this subject some twenty years ago in *Mind*[2] by Mr. Joseph, my immediate predecessor in the delivery of a lecture on this foundation; and the recognition of self-consciousness as the fundamental feature of all experience is, one may fairly say, the characteristic note of modern philosophy. No manipulation of unextended feelings will yield the consciousness of an extended world; no genuine 'solipsist' (did such exist) could discover *another* self. But it is because he *is* a self that a man can be aware of others that are selves; as it is because he *is*, or if we prefer to say so, *has* a sensitive material organism that he can perceive other material objects, including indeed those other sensitive material organisms, the establishment of physical contact wherewith is the normal condition of spiritual relations between persons for which such contact can never by itself fully account; but including also objects the contact with which does *not* prove to be the occasion of these relations, and which we thus come to distinguish as not *persons* but only *things*.

I should then maintain on the one hand that, while our consciousness of self is *sui generis*, while it is, as Descartes showed, beyond the reach of question or doubt, because even doubting presupposes a doubter; while it is the recognition of that unity of apperception which, as Kant taught, is presupposed in all the processes of synthesis which constitute our experience; yet, on the other hand, this consciousness of self is mediated to us by the apprehension of others as our *fellows*. We could not apprehend them as such, if we were not that to them which we apprehend them as being to us, namely *socii*; nor could we be their fellows if *we* were not *selves*, whose nature is revealed to us in the mirror which they, as it were, hold up to us; and when, through the mediation of social intercourse there has been developed in us an *explicit* consciousness of self, this is the recognition of a distinction between ourselves and others which is already in existence and without which social intercourse could not have been.

[2] Vol. xix, pp. 305 and 457; xx, p. 161.

Again, I suppose that the first external object of which each of us was aware was the body of his mother or nurse, and this it was which mediated to us our primary experience of social intercourse. Were there not really a body, an external object, and had not the infant a body external to it in space and in physical contact with it, we should not have been aware of it; while it is only at a far more advanced stage of our mental development, and only gradually then, that the differentiation between the *merely* external object or thing and the human or animal body, the external object which is capable of mediating social or quasi-social intercourse, becomes the sharp distinction which it is for us today.

It would take me too far afield or carry me into regions with which I can claim no familiar acquaintance were I to do more than point out here that a certain support is lent to the thesis here defended, which gives to our awareness of our fellows a primacy of the kind above described among our modes of apprehending reality, both by the results of modern investigation of what is called 'crowd-psychology' and also by the theories, based in the main on the study of mental pathology, which go by the name of the 'new psychology'. For the former suggest that we still bear about us, and unmistakably display on certain occasions, the traces of the development of individual personality within the bosom of a group, the members of which were directly conscious of their unity therein; while the latter find the key to the understanding of the structure and growth of the human mind in what they are wont to describe as *libido*, or, as we may prefer to say (in order to avoid a word with associations that inevitably colour its use in a wider than its original sense), in love-relationships, such as would first arise in their most elementary form within the community of the primitive family.

I pass now to some considerations regarding the relation of our knowledge of one another to that form of human experience the study of which has for some considerable time chiefly occupied my own attention. I mean our religious experience.

Religious experience I take to be a normal function of the human spirit; and by religious experience I understand the consciousness of Something to which all else that we experience, ourselves included, *totum quod sumus et in quo sumus*, is related as to its background, its meaning, or its cause, and related, since we are thus ourselves included, not merely remotely and inferentially but directly and intimately; which therefore excites in us a sentiment of awe and reverence, which may range from a cowering fear like Caliban's up to the 'perfect love' of St. John, which 'casts out fear, because fear hath torment', but of which this is the peculiar and distinguishing object, not to be confounded with other objects of fear or love which are not, to use the convenient term lately made current by Professor Rudolf Otto, 'numinous'. The famous lines composed by Wordsworth 'a few miles above Tintern Abbey' describe, no doubt, the religious experience of a great poet, and an experience in mediating which what we call the beauty of nature played an exceptionally preponderant part; and I am speaking of religious experience as existing in some fashion and degree in the child or savage as well as in the mature or the civilized man, and as capable of mediation by many other forms of being than those which especially communicated to the writer of those lines the consciousness which they describe. Yet, for reasons which I will shortly give, I will remind you that this was the consciousness of

> A Presence that disturbs me with the joy
> Of elevated thoughts; a sense sublime
> Of something far more deeply interfused,
> Whose dwelling is the light of setting suns,
> And the round ocean and the living air,
> And the blue sky, and in the mind of man;
> A motion and a spirit, that impels
> All thinking things, all objects of all thought,
> And rolls through all things.

I quote these familiar words because it would be hard to find any better expression of the truths which I wish here to insist upon in regard to religious experience: the truth that it is the experience of a unitary principle in all experience and in the multitude of objects of experience, and may be mediated by any part of that experience or by the totality of its parts; and the truth that it is an experience which, as Wordsworth says, 'disturbs' him who enjoys or suffers it, as being an experience of what intimately concerns him, and touches him, so to say, to the quick.

'The mind of man', 'all thinking things', 'all objects of all thought';—the different kinds of experience which we have already discussed, the apprehension of our fellows, the consciousness of self, our perception of the external world, all mediate the experience of something which is other than them all, yet can reveal itself in any of them all. The many forms of nature-worship; the Indian faiths for which God is above all the *Ātman* or true Self; the type of religion most familiar to ourselves, wherein, where a multitude or even two or three are gathered together, another more august *socius* is discovered in the midst of them, in their common relation to whom they find the principle of their social unity; these illustrate the 'varieties of religious experience' corresponding to the different modes of its mediation. It is the third variety which is relevant to our present inquiry.

In that variety the object of the religious consciousness is commonly envisaged as 'another person'—as the object, that is to say, of the kind of knowledge with which this lecture is concerned—but always, I think, with a difference. In this connexion I should like gratefully to acknowledge the assistance in the discrimination of religious from social experience which I have received from the treatment of the subject in Professor Alexander's Gifford Lectures on *Space, Time, and Deity*.[3] We cannot count, as he has pointed out, on the same kind of response in the case of God as certifies us that we are in spiritual relations with another finite person; and a man's religion has often been wrecked on the discovery which was made by the priests of Baal of old, that 'there is neither voice nor any to answer nor any that regards' his prayers. It is not given to

[3] Vol. ii, pp. 380, 381.

many to welcome, as Goethe welcomed, the express affirmation of Spinoza that in loving God we must not seek for a reciprocation of our love. But neither is it necessary to accept that affirmation. Without expecting the kind of answer of which the priests of Baal were disappointed, we may be assured that our worship is not in vain. May I here adopt some words from the passage in Professor Alexander's book to which I have already referred—although in so doing I shall omit others in their immediate context which imply certain peculiarities of their writer's theology which I do not accept or find to be necessarily involved in the statement which I shall quote? 'Though we speak,' says Professor Alexander, 'as we inevitably must, in human terms of God's response to us, there is no direct experience of that response except through our own feeling that devotion to God or worship carries with it its own satisfaction.' 'God [Professor Alexander says "the universe"] does not answer our prayers by overt external actions, as our fellows respond to our social approaches to them, but in the strength and sustainment which he [or "it", as my author puts it] gives to our minds.' 'In both cases', he adds, 'it is intercourse with the object which discovers it to us, but religious intercourse is different from social intercourse, and is only called such by a metaphor. In this respect our faith in God is nearer to simple sensation [I should prefer to say 'perception'] than our assurance of other minds. The assurance of the reality of God we cannot call surer than our assurance of each other's minds; both are equally sure; but it is simpler. Moreover, being infinite, God has the wider and deeper attachment in the nature of things, as Berkeley realized.'

These last words of my quotation from Professor Alexander suggest the distinction of religious from social experience, of our knowledge of God from our knowledge of one another, which arises from the different relation in which they respectively stand to the two other kinds of experience with the relation of which to our knowledge of one another the earlier part of this lecture was concerned.

The perception of the external world, itself mediated through sensations from which, nevertheless, taken apart from such perception merely as feelings of the perceiving individual, I believe it to be impossible to derive our knowledge of external objects extended in space—this perception in its turn mediates to each of us the knowledge of other persons, though, here again, that knowledge cannot, I hold, be derived from the perception apart from a spiritual *rapport* (as I have called it) for which the perception by itself does not account. But it is not the perception of external objects as such, but only the perception of *certain* objects—human bodies and their movements, sounds recognized as proceeding from human bodies, papers or the like inscribed with marks attributed to human agency and interpreted as signs of human feelings, apprehensions, purposes, or thoughts—it is only the perception of *such* objects that mediates to us the knowledge of other persons. We may, as we saw, be mistaken in the first instance as to whether a particular object before us is of this kind, the criterion being what Professor Alexander calls 'an overt external action' (itself of course an object of perception) by which 'our fellows respond to our social approaches'. The discrimination of perceptions in connexion with which such a response is to be expected is, as we saw, only gradually effected in the course of the development whether of the race or of the individual. On the other hand, a perceived object may mediate a consciousness of the numinous—to use Otto's word—and here the test of what may be called a social response is, as we have noted, not usually to be had. Moreover, though not all objects of perception do, nor do any always, mediate this consciousness, *any objects may* do so; since that of which we are aware in our religious experience is immanent in all reality, and (I put it vaguely, in order to avoid raising further questions which, however important, are remote from our present purpose) at the back of all reality.

Turning from our perception of the external world to our self-consciousness, I recognize my fellows indeed in virtue of my being what each of them is, a self: but I recognize them as being selves other than my own self: my relation to them, though it is to be carefully borne in mind that it is not adequately described as one of mutual exclusion (since communication to the other of what is in the mind of each is of its very essence) yet *does* involve mutual exclusion, in so far as from first to last I am not you and you are not I. Such, however, is not the character of the relation between the self and God. No one who believes in God regards God's privity to the thoughts and intents of his heart, however the thought of it may make him ashamed and afraid, as an invasion of his personality, such as he would resent did he discover a like privity on the part of a fellow man to whom he has not chosen to reveal those thoughts and intents. Even at a lower level of spiritual development, where one would hardly speak of the object of the religious consciousness as 'God', I take it that this object is never treated as a *mere* thing nor as a *mere* fellow being; but that there is attributed to it what I may perhaps be allowed to call a mystical intimacy with us, which 'disturbs' him who experiences it, though not necessarily 'with the joy of elevated thoughts' (for the feeling may be very far from joyful and the thoughts by no means such as we should call 'elevated'), but yet with a sense of something which closely touches the springs of individual personal life.

In conclusion I would add a few words about a matter which is naturally suggested by the considerations which I have been laying before you, and which brings into relation with them a problem of great importance and difficulty, which I can but mention now and not discuss. We saw that we are capable of perceiving external objects because we are ourselves material organisms, or, if we prefer to say so, because we have material bodies which are organic to us; and that we are capable of enjoying social intercourse with other persons because we are ourselves persons or self-conscious selves. Are we to go on to say that we are capable of a knowledge of God because we are ourselves divine? There is much in the symbolical phraseology of the great historical religions to authorize such a statement. The Christian apostle adopts the Stoic poet's declaration that we are God's offspring; the Scriptures which Jews and Christians alike accept as inspired represent man as created in God's image and quickened to life by the imparting of God's own breath; while the human soul was in the Orphic theology an immortal god fallen into a lower sphere of being. Again, the realization of the soul's true divinity is the aim set before us by many, perhaps by most, of the teachers of the faiths which have arisen in India and the Far East; an aim in their recommendation of which they are at one with not a few Western philosophers. It is indeed characteristic of these faiths, as I remarked before, that the description of the object of religion as the *Ātman* or Self predominates over the representation of that object as another person or persons—while in the West the latter representation prevails, and the other mode of expression is found only in the language of a comparatively few mystically inclined devotees. It would be, I think, on all hands acknowledged that a capacity in the human soul to become in some measure a partaker of the divine nature—the phrase occurs in the New Testament—is implied in its susceptibility to religious experience; but the degree to which the distinction between the subject and the object of religious experience is to be regarded as a vanishing factor in the spiritual development of the former or as belonging to the essence of religion, and as never to the end to be ignored without an impoverishment and ultimate loss of spiritual life—this remains a point of serious divergence between different religious traditions and between different schools of philosophy engaged in the interpretation of the experience which these traditions enshrine. It belonged, I think, to the subject upon which I undertook to address you to refer to this divergence; but to pursue it farther is the business of another inquiry.

DUTY AND IGNORANCE OF FACT

BY H. A. PRICHARD

The question which I propose to consider is essentially dull and tiresome; it worries us little, if at all, in practical life; and it is apt to be ignored, or, at least, only casually treated, by those whose business is theory. Nevertheless, at any rate for theory, it is important.

As it first presents itself, the question is: 'If a man has an obligation, i.e. a duty, to do some action, does the obligation depend on certain characteristics of the situation in which he is, or on certain characteristics of his thought about the situation?' The question is vague because of the vagueness of the term 'thought', but at the outset this does not matter. Consideration of it, however, will force us to consider another question, viz.: 'Can an obligation really be an obligation to do some *action*, and, if not, what should be substituted for the term "action"?' And, should a substitute prove necessary, the main question will have to be modified accordingly.

To appreciate the importance, and even the meaning, of the question, we have first to see how it arises.

We have all from time to time thought that we ought, and again that we ought not, to do certain actions. And, if we were asked to give a general account of these actions, we should be inclined to say that, though not all of one sort, yet they all fall under one or other of a limited number of kinds of action which are set out in current moral rules, i.e. current general statements each stating that a man ought or ought not to do an action of a certain kind. Further, at any rate until certain difficulties have occurred to us, we think these rules true. We think, for instance, that a man ought to speak the truth, to carry out the orders of his government, not to steal, and not to hurt the feelings of another. And this is not surprising, since these rules are simply the result of an attempt to formulate the various general characteristics of the particular acts we have thought duties which have led us to think them duties.

Elucidation, however, is needed of the general character of the meaning of a moral rule, and therefore also of the thought which it is used to express.

It is, no doubt, not easy to say what we mean by 'an action' or by 'doing something'. Yet we have in the end to allow that we mean by it originating, causing, or bringing about the existence of something, viz. some new state of an existing thing or substance, or, more shortly, causing a change of state of some existing thing. This is shown by the meaning of our phrases for various particular actions. For by 'moving our hand' we mean causing a change of place of our hand; by 'posting a letter' we mean bringing about that a letter is in a pillar-box; and so on. We may be tempted to go farther, and say that we mean by 'an action' the *conscious* origination of something, i.e. the originating something knowing that we are doing so. But this will not do; for no one, for instance, thinks himself denying that he has hurt a man's feelings when he says that he did not know that he was hurting them and, indeed, thought that he was not. Correspondingly, we mean by 'doing an action of a certain kind' bringing about something of a certain kind, viz. a state of a certain kind of a thing of a certain kind. Consequently the meaning of a moral rule can be stated in the form: 'A man ought, or ought not, to bring about a thing of a certain kind'. Thus by 'A man ought to honour his parents' we mean: 'A man ought to bring about in his parents the knowledge that he holds them in honour'.

But this is not all. We ordinarily think that in doing certain actions we bring about the things which we do directly, while in doing certain others we do so indirectly, i.e. by directly bringing about other things which in turn cause them. Thus we think that in moving our head we bring about a change of place of our head directly, whereas in giving a friend the family news we bring about his receipt of the news indirectly, i.e. by bringing about directly certain other changes which in turn cause it. No doubt on reflection we may find it difficult to defend the thought that, e.g., in moving our head we directly cause our head to change its place; and we may be reduced to thinking that, in moving our head, what we bring about directly is some new state of certain cells of our brain of which we are wholly unaware in doing the action. But such a reflection does not conflict with our thought that we bring about certain things indirectly. Nor does it lead us to deny the distinction between bringing something about directly and bringing something about indirectly, since, so long as we think that we bring about certain things indirectly, we inevitably imply that there are certain things which we bring about directly, even if we do not know what they are. It is as impossible for all bringing about to be indirect as for all knowledge to be indirect. And, if we now turn to the phrase for the act of a certain kind referred to in some moral rule, we find that in every case it stands for bringing about something of a certain kind indirectly. We mean, for instance, by 'honouring a parent' causing a parent to find himself held in honour by causing something else to cause it; we mean by 'speaking the truth' causing another to know our thought by causing certain sounds which cause him to have this knowledge; and so on. We can therefore say generally that the meaning of a moral rule has the form: 'A man ought, or ought not, to bring about a thing of a certain kind indirectly'.

To bring about something indirectly is, however, to bring it about in a less strict sense than is to bring about something directly. For, where we bring about something by causing something else to cause it, the result is not wholly due to us. And, where we bring about something x indirectly, what we bring about in the strict sense is the thing which causes x. Correspondingly we use the term 'action' both in a strict sense in which it means bringing about something directly, and also in a looser sense in which it means bringing about something whether directly or indirectly. And where, e.g., some action of ours is referred to as giving some relation the family news, we must allow that our action in the strict sense is some such act as transferring certain ink to certain places on a piece of paper; and in support of this admission we might point out that, in the strict sense of 'action', our action must cease with the cessation of our activity. We have, therefore, to allow that if a moral rule is stated in terms of 'doing something' and of 'bringing about something' in the strict sense, its meaning will be of the form: 'A man ought to do such an act or acts, i.e. bring about such a thing or things, as will cause a thing of the kind A to assume a state of the kind x'.

Further, in stating some moral rule, we are plainly in two respects speaking elliptically. Thus, in asserting that a man ought to support his indigent parents, we clearly do not mean that a man ought at *any* time to support his indigent parents. We are thinking, and expect to be understood as asserting, that the duty exists only when two conditions are satisfied. The first is, of course, that the man has parents who are indigent and willing to receive the means of support; and the second is that he is able to support them. For we never think that an action can be a man's duty unless he is able to do it. But since to support parents is to bring about something indirectly, the realization of the second condition involves the existence of a certain combination of things capable of having certain changes of state effected in them, such that, on the one hand, the man can produce the changes directly, and also such that, on the other hand, if these changes are produced, they will result in the parents having the means of support. In asserting a moral rule, however, we take for granted that a man has permanently the capacity of bringing about certain things directly, and therefore we think of the realization of the second condition as consisting simply in the fact that the situation in which the man is is such that some one, or some group, of the things which he can bring about directly would, if produced, effect his parents' possession of the means of subsistence. Consequently, to generalize, we can say that any moral rule, when modified so as to express fully the thought which it is used to express, will be of the following form: 'When the situation in which a man is contains a thing of the kind A capable of having a state of the kind x effected in it, and when also it is such that some state or combination of states which the man can bring about directly will cause a state of the kind x in A, the man ought to bring about that state or combination of states'.

Again, once the thought is expressed in this form, it becomes obvious that, in having the thought, we are implying that when a man has an obligation to do some act in the strict sense, corresponding to the rule, what renders him bound to do the action is the special character of the situation in which he is in the two respects just indicated, this being what gives rise to the fact that, if he were to do the action, he would indirectly be causing a state of the kind in question. Plainly, therefore, if we were to put forward a particular set of rules as exhaustive, we should be implying that the question whether we are bound to do some particular action, in the strict sense, will turn on whether the existing situation contains any of the various pairs of conditions which bring the act under one or other of the rules. Clearly also, even if we did not think such rules as we could offer exhaustive, we should still think that the question could only be settled in the same kind of way, although we could not settle it.

Now when we reflect on this general idea or thought underlying our assertion of a set of moral rules, viz. that where we have an obligation to do some action in the strict sense, it depends on certain characteristics of the situation, we find it in two related respects very attractive. For, first, being the thought that any obligation depends solely on certain characteristics of the situation, it is on its negative side the thought that the obligation is wholly independent of our knowledge and thought about the situation. And we welcome this negative side, since we do not like to think that the question whether some action is a duty turns not on the nature of the situation but on that of our attitude towards it in respect of knowledge and thought. Moreover, the thought seems implied in much of our procedure in practical life. For frequently when in doubt, as we often are, whether some action in the narrow sense is a duty, our doubt seems to arise from doubt about the actual facts. Thus when I see someone who shows symptoms of having fainted and it occurs to me that, if I shouted, I might revive him, I may doubt whether I am bound to shout; and, when I do, my doubt sometimes seems to arise partly from doubt whether he has really fainted, and partly from doubt whether shouting would revive him. And if I try to resolve my doubt about the duty by resolving my doubt about the facts, I at least seem to be implying that the question whether I am bound to shout turns on what the facts really are. Second, the thought implies that if some action is a duty, it would bring about some state referred to in a moral rule, such as the recovery of a sick man, and would not be merely an act which we think would be likely to do so; and we welcome this implication because we should like to think that, if we have done some duty, we have achieved some change to which a moral rule refers, e.g. that we have helped a man out of a trouble, and not merely done something which we thought would do this but which possibly has in fact damaged a man who was in no trouble at all.

Yet there is no denying that if we try to defend this thought we become involved in very awkward consequences. There are various admissions which we shall have to make which we thoroughly dislike when we come to reflect on them.

The most awkward of these emerges as soon as we ask: 'How am I to *know* that some moral rule is applicable to me here and now?' The rule being of the form recently stated, the question becomes: 'How am I to *know* that the situation satisfies the two conditions necessary for the application of the rule, viz. first, that it contains a particular thing of the kind A capable of having a state of the kind x effected in it, and, second, that it is such that some act or acts which I can do would cause this A to assume a state of the kind x?' And as regards the first condition, we shall have to admit that the situation may often satisfy it, without my knowing, or even being able to discover, that it does so. We may perhaps insist that sometimes I know that there is someone to whom I have made a promise, or again that I have parents who are in difficulties; but we cannot deny that sometimes I am uncertain whether there is someone to whom I have made a promise, or whether my parents are in difficulties, or again whether a man whom I meet is ill, at any rate with an illness which anything I can do would be likely to diminish. And we shall have to allow that in most of these latter cases I have no means of resolving my doubt. We shall therefore have to admit that for this reason alone I may often have a duty without knowing, or even being able to discover, that I have. Again, as regards the second condition, there are, undeniably, absolutely no occasions on which, where some particular state which I can bring about directly would cause an effect of the kind x, I either *know*, or even can come to *know*, that it would, although of course I may have a strong opinion about the matter. For plainly I never either do or can *know* that any particular action which I can do in the narrow sense would have a certain effect. Thus, unquestionably, I neither do nor can know that giving some man a certain drug would cause his recovery; and if in fact I give him the drug, and afterwards find that he has recovered, even then I cannot *know* that I have cured him, though I may think it very likely. Again I never *know* that by uttering certain sounds I shall cause a man to know what I think; and I know that however much I may try to speak the truth, I may fail. Consideration, then, of the second condition forces us to admit that there is absolutely no occasion on which a moral rule applies to me on which I can know that I have the duty in question. In fact, reflection on these conditions compels us to admit that no moral rule can express knowledge, and that, to express knowledge, we must substitute a hypothetical statement in which we replace the word 'when' of a moral rule by 'if'. To express knowledge, its form will have to be: '*If* the situation in which a man is contains a thing of the kind A capable of having a state of the kind x produced in it, and also *if* it be such that one of the things which he can bring about directly will cause A to assume such a state, then he ought to bring about that thing.' The need of this substitution is obvious, since for the reasons given an individual is sometimes uncertain whether the first, and always uncertain whether the second, condition is realized. Indeed, on this view that an obligation, if there be one, depends on certain features of the situation, we are driven to the extreme conclusion that, although we may have duties, we cannot know but can only believe that we have; and therefore we are even rendered uncertain whether we, or anyone else, has ever had, or will ever have, a duty.

Here we may note the answer which this view requires us to give to a question which is often raised. Obviously at different times opposite views have been taken of the rightness or wrongness of certain kinds of action, in consequence of different views concerning matters of fact. Thus while some men must in the past have been sincerely convinced that it was a duty to torture heretics, most men are now equally convinced that a man ought not to do so; and the explanation obviously lies in a difference of opinion about the effects of torture. And the question is often asked: 'Where there is such a difference of view concerning the rightness or wrongness of a certain kind of action, which party is right?' To this question, on the view we are considering, the answer can only be: 'We do not know; no one knows; and no one ever will know. Even those, e.g., who considered it a duty to torture heretics may have been right.'

That we can never know that we have a duty is not, however, the only conclusion to which we are driven on this view. There are others related to it. One is that, though we may have duties we can never, strictly speaking, do a duty, if we have one, *because* it is a duty, i.e. really, in consequence of *knowing* it to be a duty. And the reason is, of course, simply that we can never have the knowledge. At best, if we have a duty, we may do it because we think without question, or else believe, or again think it possible, that the act is a duty. Another conclusion is that some past act of mine may have been a duty although in doing it I believed that the act was one which I ought not to do. Thus my shouting on seeing a man may have been in fact a duty, because he was faint and shouting would revive him, and yet I may have shouted to satisfy a grudge, believing that he was asleep and that my shouting would disturb him, and in spite of thinking that I ought not thus to disturb him. A third is that I may do some act which is in fact a duty, although in doing it I do not even suspect that it will have the effect which renders it a duty. This would happen, e.g., if I shouted simply to attract the attention of a passer-by and without noticing the man's condition at all. Similar conclusions, too, have to be drawn with regard to acts of the kinds which we think we ought not to do.

These conclusions being all unwelcome, we naturally want to discover what modification of the form of a moral rule would enable us to escape them, and then to consider how we fare if we accept it. Now what the conclusions all followed from was the thought underlying the assertion of a set of moral rules that if some particular action is a duty, the obligation depends on certain facts of the situation. And to this thought there is only one alternative, viz. the thought that the obligation depends on our being in a certain attitude of mind towards the situation in respect of knowledge, thought, or opinion. This thought can be described as the subjective view of the basis of an obligation, not in the sense of the view that no acts are really right or really wrong, but in the sense of the view that the ground of an obligation lies in some state of the man's own mind. And in contrast the opposed view can be designated the objective view.

The question, therefore, at once arises: 'What have we to represent this state or attitude as being, if we are to render this alternative view at least plausible?' The most obvious suggestion is, of course, to represent it as our thinking certain things likely or probable, and to represent the alternative view as being that if, e.g., I am bound to shout, it is because I think it likely that the man in front of me has fainted and that, if he has fainted, shouting would cure him, i.e. have his revival as an effect. But, when we come to consider this view, we find that we do not like it either.

It has, no doubt, at least one definite advantage over the view which it is to replace. It does not preclude us from thinking that it is possible to *discover* our duties, since, when we think something likely, we either know, or at least by reflecting can discover, that we do. The question whether I am thinking something likely is no more one about which I can be mistaken than is the question whether I have a certain pain. Consequently, also, the view does not preclude us from thinking that it is possible for us to do some action, knowing that we ought to do it. For the same reason it saves us from having to allow that we are, and must always remain, uncertain whether we have or shall ever have a duty.

On the other hand, it of course inevitably implies that any obligation I may have depends not on the fact that the action would have a certain character, if I were to do it—that of producing a certain effect—but on my thinking it likely that it would. It implies, e.g., that where I am bound to shout my obligation depends not on the fact that if I were to shout I should be reviving a man who has fainted, but on my thinking it likely that I should. And a paradox involved comes to light if we imagine ourselves omniscient beings, who in consequence knew the circumstances. For if we were such beings, the analogous view would be that, if we were bound to shout, what would render us bound to shout would not be the fact that shouting would cure the man, but our knowing that it would; and it would therefore imply that this knowledge, so far from being the knowledge of the ground of the obligation, was itself the ground of the obligation, and that our knowledge of the ground of the obligation consisted in our knowing that we knew that shouting would cure the man.

Again, to defend the view, we shall have to modify it at least to the extent of maintaining that if, for instance, I am bound to shout, what renders me so bound is not simply my thinking it likely but my thinking it at least in a certain degree likely that shouting would cure the man. For no one would maintain that I am bound to shout if I think the likelihood remote beyond a certain degree. But then we are faced by the question: 'What degree is necessary?' And we have to answer that we can formulate it only within certain limits which differ

DUTY AND IGNORANCE OF FACT

in different cases according to the degree of benefit to the other man which I think likely to accrue from my shouting. We shall, therefore, also have to allow that I shall not always be able to discover whether I ought to shout, since there will be border-line cases in which I shall be unable to discover whether the degree to which I think the act likely to confer a certain benefit is sufficient to render it a duty. And therefore we shall have to allow that even on this view I may have a duty without being able to discover that I have it.

Again, the view, at any rate unless further modified, implies not only that in similar circumstances it may be one man's duty but not another's to do some action, owing to some difference in their thought about the facts, but also that the same thing is true of a single individual at different moments. For I may at first think it just, but only just, possible that shouting would cure a man, and then on further consideration think that there is a very good chance that it will; and, if so, while at first I shall not be bound to shout, afterwards I shall. And, again, the converse may happen.

Also, we have to distinguish from thinking likely what for lack of a better phrase we may call thinking without question. For on seeing a man who has fainted, instead of thinking it likely, I may from lack of reflection think without question that shouting would cure him, not being uncertain that it would, and therefore not thinking it likely, but at the same time not being certain. And on the view in question, unless it be modified, we shall have to hold that when this happens I am not bound to shout, in spite of thinking without question that shouting would cure him, since I am not thinking it likely.

It will, however, probably occur to us that these last two difficulties can be met by a further modification. This is to maintain (1) that I am bound to shout only if I think it likely that shouting would effect a cure *after* having considered the circumstances fully, i.e. after having considered as fully as I can whether he is ill and whether shouting would cure him if he is, and so having obtained the best opinion I can about the circumstances, and (2) that whenever I have not done this I am bound to do something else, viz. to consider the circumstances fully.

This modification, it must be allowed, does remove the difficulties. Nevertheless the idea that, where we have not done so, we ought to consider the circumstances fully, is itself not free from difficulty. This becomes obvious as soon as we ask: '*Why*, for instance, when it first strikes me that shouting might cure the man, am I bound to consider fully whether it would?' For the answer which we are at first inclined to give is: 'Because, if I consider the matter fully, I may come to think shouting in a certain degree likely to cure him, and, if I do, I shall then be bound to shout'. And yet this answer cannot be right. For plainly the duty of doing one action cannot possibly depend on the duty of doing another the duty of doing which cannot arise unless the former action has been actually done. It may or may not be some doctor's duty to accept a particular hospital post, but if it is, it cannot be because, if he accepts it, he will then be bound to operate on certain of the patients. Moreover, if the answer were right, I could always escape having a duty to shout merely by abstaining from considering the circumstances, and yet no one thinks this possible. The truth is that our having a duty to consider the circumstances cannot be based on the possibility of our having a future duty of another kind if we were to consider them. Rather, to vindicate such a duty, we must represent the two so-called duties as respectively an element and a possible element in a *single* duty, viz. to consider the circumstances, and then if, but only if, as a result, we reach a certain opinion, do a certain future action. And if we do this we can explain the need of this complicated and partially hypothetical phrase for what is after all a single duty by the fact that the duty is one of the full nature of which we are at the time inevitably ignorant owing to our ignorance of the facts.

Again, if the view is to correspond with what we ordinarily think, still further modifications may seem necessary for various reasons, of which one is that we ordinarily think, for instance,

DUTY AND IGNORANCE OF FACT

that before it can be a duty for me to shout I must also have considered what is likely to be the effect of shouting on any one else who may be within range.

But, in order to consider the main issue, we need not inquire what, if any, further modifications are needed. For, even if they are needed, the fundamental issue will remain the same, viz.: 'If I have an obligation, does it depend on the existence of certain facts of the situation or on my having certain thoughts about certain facts of the situation?'

Here it may be noted that the issue is not avoided by those who would deny the truth of any set of moral rules on the ground that, if we think them true, we are involved in the absurdity of admitting that we may at any moment have conflicting duties, i.e. two or more duties only one of which we can carry out. For, in order to avoid this admission, they have to maintain that where some action is a duty it is because it would possess some such character as that of producing something good in a greater degree than any other of the acts which the man is able to do. And, in maintaining this, they will be faced with the same question in a slightly different form, viz.: 'Does the obligation depend on the fact that the action would possess this character in a greater degree than any other, or does it depend on the fact that the man, after full consideration, thinks it likely that it would?'

The issue, then, being as stated, the first thing to do appears to consist in ascertaining which of the alternative views better corresponds with the thought of our ordinary life.

There are two ways in which this thought appears to imply the objective view. First, we frequently think without question both that the situation contains some thing in a certain state, and also that some action which we could do would produce a change in it of a certain kind, and then think without question that we ought to do the action. Thus, when we do not reflect, we frequently think without question that a man whom we meet has some malady and that giving him some drug would relieve it, and, where we do, we think without question that we ought to give the drug. And here we seem implying that what renders us bound to do the act is just the fact that the situation is of a certain sort, together with the fact that the act would have a certain effect in that situation. Second, we often seek to change the mind of someone else about a duty by trying to convince him that he is mistaken about the facts; and, in doing so, we seem implying that the question whether he has the duty depends on the nature of the facts. Thus, where A thinks he ought to vote for X rather than Y, B may try to convince A that he ought to vote for Y by arguing that X and Y will, if elected, act otherwise than as A expects. Again, we may argue with a friend that he ought to send his child to school M rather than school N, which he considers the better, on the ground that M is really the better. And if someone were to maintain that he ought to torture a certain heretic, as the only way of saving his soul, we should presumably try to convince him that he was mistaken by convincing him that torture would not have this effect.

On the other hand, at any rate a large portion of our ordinary thought is in direct conflict with the objective view. Consider, e.g., our attitude to the question: 'Ought we to stop, or at least slow down, in a car, before entering a main road?' If the objective view be right, (1) there will be a duty to slow down only if in fact there is traffic; (2) we shall be entitled only to think it likely—in varying degrees on different occasions—that we are bound to slow down; and (3) if afterwards we find no traffic, we ought to conclude that our opinion that we were bound to slow down was mistaken. Yet, provided that after consideration we think that there is even a small chance of traffic, we in fact think that there is definitely a duty to slow down, and that the subsequent discovery that there was no traffic would not prove us mistaken. Again, imagine that we are watching a car approaching along a road which we know forks, and of which one fork has, we know, just suffered a landslide, and that we have no idea which road the driver is intending to take, or whether he knows about the landslide.[1] The objective view would require us to think that there is a

[1] I owe the illustration to Mr. R. G. Collingwood.

duty to stop the car only if it is going to destruction, so that, if we are anxious to do what we ought, we can only insure ourselves against the possibility of failure to do what we ought by stopping the car, knowing that, after all, we may be doing something we are not bound to do. Yet plainly we in fact think without any doubt whatever that we are bound to stop the car, unless we have reason for being quite confident that the car is about to take the safe fork. Again, no nurse thinks that she is bound to light a fire in her patient's room only if in fact there will be a frost next morning. She thinks she is bound to do so, unless she thinks there is practically no chance of a frost. Indeed the objective view is in direct conflict with all the numerous cases in which we think without question that we ought to do something which we are thinking of as of the nature of an *insurance* in the interest of someone else.

Moreover the extent to which our ordinary thought involves the subjective view is usually obscured for us by our tendency to think that the terms 'likely' and 'probable' refer to facts in nature. For we are apt, for instance, to express our thought that someone has probably fainted, and that shouting would probably revive him, by the statements: 'He has probably fainted' and 'Shouting would probably revive him'. We are then apt to think that these statements state the existence of certain facts in nature called probabilities, in the spirit which leads some physicists to regard electron-waves as waves of probability[2]; and we are then apt to think that an obligation to shout arises from these probabilities. It needs, however, but little reflection to realize that there are no such things as probabilities in nature. There cannot, e.g., be such a thing as the probability that someone has fainted, since either he has fainted or he has not. No doubt it is extremely difficult to formulate the precise nature of the fact which we express, for instance, by the statement: 'X has probably fainted'. But at least we must allow that, whatever its precise nature may be, the fact must consist in our mind's being in a certain state or

[2] Cf. *The Mysterious Universe*, p. 122 (Sir James Jeans).

condition. And, once this is realized, it becomes obvious that most of our ordinary thought involves the subjective view.

Again, even when we try to change someone else's mind about a duty, we do not really imply the subjective view. This is shown by our thinking that when our attempt to change his opinion about the facts is over, then, whether we have or have not succeeded, the question whether he is bound to do the action will turn on the nature of *his opinion* about the facts. Thus we think that, provided the would-be torturer remained, in spite of all we had said, in a very high degree confident that torturing, and torturing only, would save the heretic, he would be bound to inflict the torture. No doubt we also think that we should take steps to prevent him; but here there is no inconsistency. And in fact we not infrequently think ourselves bound to do some action which will prevent someone else doing something which he is bound to do. Indeed, if this were not so, few would fight conscientiously for their country.

Undoubtedly, then, the subjective view better corresponds with our ordinary thought. Yet, as should now be obvious, it is exposed to various difficulties. Of these the chief are two. The first is that on this view knowledge of the existence of borderline cases precludes us from thinking that we can always discover our duties. Still in this respect it is more satisfactory than the objective view, since the latter implies that we can never discover a duty. The second and more fundamental difficulty is that it represents the duty of doing some action as depending not on the fact that the action would have a certain character if we were to do it but on our thinking it likely that it would. And to maintain this seems impossible.

We thus seem to have reached an impasse. For both of the alternative views lead to fundamental difficulties, and yet there is no third alternative.

Before, however, we consider the matter further, we ought to consider a difficulty which is common to both views, and which, if it proves well founded, will force us to modify both.

In considering the problem, we have throughout been taking for granted that an obligation is necessarily an obligation to do some *action*, and, strictly speaking, an action in the strict sense. But we ought at least to ask ourselves whether this assumption, obvious though it seems, is true.

Unquestionably an obligation must be an obligation to perform some *activity*. An obligation can only be an obligation to be *active*, and not to be *affected*, in a particular way. And to assert that an obligation is always an obligation to do some *action*, in the strict sense of action, e.g. to move my arms, is really to assert that the activity of the kind which an obligation is an obligation to perform consists in *doing* something, as distinct from an activity of some other kind, such as thinking or imagining. But, as was said earlier, by 'doing something' in the strict sense, we mean bringing about something directly, i.e. bringing about something in the strict sense. Therefore to assert that an obligation is an obligation to do something is really to assert that the activity of the kind which an obligation is an obligation to perform consists in bringing about something. And in making the assertion we are implying that there is a special *kind* of activity and, indeed, a special kind of *mental* activity, for which the proper phrase is 'bringing about something'. For if we thought that what we call bringing about x really consists in performing an activity of some other kind of which x will be an effect, we should have to allow that what we call the obligation to bring about x is really the obligation to perform some particular activity of this other kind of which x would be an effect, and that, therefore, an obligation, so far from being an obligation to *do* something, is always an obligation to perform an activity of this other kind. In asserting, then, that an obligation is an obligation to *do* something, we are implying that there is a special kind of activity consisting in doing something, i.e. bringing about something.

On reflection, however, we become forced to admit that, though we think that on certain occasions we do bring certain things about, yet we do not think that there is any such thing as a special kind of activity consisting in bringing about something. We can realize this in the following way. It will, of course, be allowed that where we think of some past action of ours as one in which we indirectly brought about some particular thing, as where we think of ourselves as having cured someone's illness, we think it fair to ask: '*How* did we do the action?' We take the question to have the intelligible meaning: 'What was that by the direct production of which we indirectly produced what we did?'; and we can give some sort of answer. But we can also ask a question verbally similar, where we think of some past action as one in which we directly brought about something. Where, e.g., I think of myself as having moved my hand, I can ask: '*How* did I move it?' In such a case, of course, the question cannot be of the same kind, because *ex hypothesi* I am not thinking of the action as one in which I caused some particular thing by causing something else, and so I cannot be asking: 'By directly causing what, did we cause what we did?' Nevertheless we do think the question legitimate; and we can give some sort of answer. If, e.g., I ask: 'How did I move my hand?' I should in most cases answer: 'By setting, or exerting, myself to do so'. And in doing so I should be implying that what I called moving my hand really consisted in setting myself to move it, and that I referred to this activity as moving my hand because I thought that this activity had a change of place of my hand as an effect. Again, in another case my answer might be: 'By setting myself to move my other hand', the case being one in which I set myself to move one hand and in fact moved the other. And here also I should be implying that what I called moving my hand really consisted in a particular activity of another sort of which the change of place of my hand was an effect. The general moral can be stated thus: In no case whatever, where we think of ourselves as having brought about something directly, do we think that our activity was of a sort consisting of bringing about something. On the contrary we think of the activity as having been of another sort, and mean, by saying that we brought about directly what we did, that this activity of another sort had the change in question as a direct effect.

The same conclusion can be reached by considering what we really mean by saying 'I can do so and so', when we use 'do' in the strict sense. It may first be noticed that if in ordinary life we are asked whether we can do some action in the strict sense, we cannot always give a definite answer. No doubt if we were asked: 'Can we make a noise identical in pitch with the highest C of the piano?' we should unhesitatingly answer 'No'; and if we were asked: 'Can we make a loud noise?' we should unhesitatingly answer 'Yes'. But if we were asked: 'Can we make a noise similar in pitch to the middle C of the piano?' we should have to answer: 'I don't know', though we might possibly add: 'But I *think* I can'. It may next be noticed that even where we unhesitatingly answer 'Yes', we are, if pressed, inclined to hedge to the extent of saying: 'Well at least I can do the action, e.g. shout, *if* I choose'. Such a statement, however, as we see when we reflect, is very odd. It cannot be meant literally, and can at best be only an idiom. For while it is sense to say: 'If I choose to make a loud noise, I *shall* in fact make it', it cannot be sense to say: 'If I choose to make it, I *can* make it'. And no one would maintain that our *ability* to do something, as distinct from our *doing* it, can depend on our choosing to do it. Indeed the statement really presupposes the thought that I *can* choose to make a loud noise, and is in fact only a brachylogical way of saying: 'Since I can choose to make a loud noise, and since choosing to make it would in fact have a loud noise as an effect, I can make it'. At the same time 'choose' cannot be an accurate phrase for what we mean, since 'choose' means choose between alternatives, and in fact we have no alternatives in mind. 'Will', the verb corresponding to 'volition', might perhaps be suggested as the proper substitute; but the term would be merely artificial. What seems wanted is one or other of the two phrases which have been already used, viz. 'setting myself to', or 'exerting myself to', so that 'choosing to make a loud noise' becomes 'setting or exerting myself to make a loud noise'. And, if this is right, what is in our minds when we say: 'I can make a loud noise' is not the thought that there is a special kind of activity of which I am capable consisting in bringing about a loud noise, but rather the thought that a special kind of activity of which

I am capable, consisting in setting myself to bring about a loud noise, would have a loud noise as an effect.

Two conclusions are at once obvious. The first is that the true answer to any question of the form: 'Can I do so and so?' must be: 'I don't know'. This is, of course, clear in certain cases. Plainly we never *know* that if we were to set ourselves to thread a needle, we should thread it; or that if we were to set ourselves to draw a line through a point on a piece of paper, we should succeed. But in the last resort this is the only answer ever possible, since we never *know* that we have not become paralysed. Even in the case of moving our arms or making a noise we do not *know* that, if we were to set ourselves to do it, we should do anything, though, of course, we may think it very likely both that we should do something, and also that we should move our arms, or make a noise, in particular. The second conclusion is that whatever we are setting ourselves to do, we never in so setting ourselves *know* that we are doing what we are setting ourselves to do, i.e. bringing about what we are setting ourselves to bring about, or indeed that we are doing anything at all. In other words, it follows that where we are setting ourselves to do something, we never *know* what we are doing, and at best can only find out afterwards what we have done. And for this reason alone we cannot sustain the view to which reference was made earlier that 'doing something' means not simply bringing about something, but bringing about something knowing that we are doing so. For, apart from other objections, if it did, we in using the phrase should be implying that there is a special kind of activity consisting in bringing about something of the special nature of which we are aware in performing the activity; and we do not think this. At the same time, the view has an underlying element of truth; for though bringing about something is *not*, setting ourselves to bring about something *is*, a special kind of activity of the special nature of which we are aware in performing it; and therefore the idea underlying the view is sound, though misapplied.

As regards an obligation, the moral is obvious. It is simply that, contrary to the implication of ordinary language and of moral rules in particular, an obligation must be an obligation, not to *do* something, but to perform an activity of a totally different kind, that of setting or exerting ourselves to do something, i.e. to bring something about.

It may be objected that, if an obligation were an obligation to perform a mental activity of a special kind other than that of bringing something about, the nature of that activity would have to be describable by itself, and not solely by reference to something else, as it is implied to be if we describe it as setting ourselves to bring something about. But to this two replies can be given. The first is that we find no difficulty in allowing the appropriateness of this procedure in analogous cases. Thus we have no difficulty in allowing the existence of such a kind of thing as a desire, although we are perfectly aware that to desire is necessarily to desire something, e.g. the eating of an apple or the prosperity of our country, so that no desire can be described simply in terms of a certain state of mind. Again, we readily allow that there is such a thing as a state of wondering, or, again, of being angry, although we are quite aware that to wonder is to wonder, for instance, whether rain is coming, and to be angry is to be angry with someone for what he has done. The second reply is simply that if we try to describe the nature of the activity which we perform when we think we are bringing about something without reference to bringing about something, we find that we totally fail.

If, however, we allow, as we now must, that an obligation must be an obligation not to do something but to set ourselves to do something, we have to modify accordingly not only the original question but also both the alternative views of the basis of an obligation.

The effect, however, as regards the relation between the alternatives, is simply to intensify their difference. For, given the modification, on either view an obligation will be an obligation not to bring about something directly but to set ourselves to do so. And if there be an obligation to set ourselves to bring about some particular thing y directly, then, on the objective view, the obligation will depend in part on an additional fact the existence of which we shall be unable to discover, viz. that setting ourselves to bring about y would bring it about directly, while on the subjective view it will depend in part on an additional thinking something likely, viz. our thinking setting ourselves to bring about y likely to bring it about.

The question, therefore, arises whether this modification renders it any easier to decide between the alternatives. And the answer appears to be that in one respect it does. For once it has become common ground that the kind of activity which an obligation is an obligation to perform is one which may bring about nothing at all, viz. setting ourselves to bring about something, we are less inclined to think that, for there to be an obligation to perform some particular activity, it must have a certain indirect effect. To this extent the modification diminishes the force of the objective view without in any way impairing that of its rival. Yet undoubtedly it does nothing to remove what is, after all, the outstanding difficulty of the subjective view—a difficulty compared with which the others are only difficulties of detail, i.e. difficulties concerning its precise nature. This difficulty of the view in its original form lies in its representing the obligation to do some action as depending not on the fact that the action would have a certain character, if we were to do it, but on our thinking it likely that it would. This dependence seems impossible. For an obligation to do some action seems a characteristic of the action; and therefore, it would seem, it must depend on the fact that the action would have a certain characteristic, if it were done, and not on our thinking it likely that it would. And if here we substitute for 'do some action', 'set ourselves to do some action', there is a difficulty of precisely the same kind.

It is, however, worth considering whether, after all, this difficulty is insuperable, and whether it may not simply arise from a mistake. We are apt to think of an obligation to do some action as if it were, like its goodness or badness, a sort of quality or character of the action. Just as we think that when we say of some action which we could do that it would be good, or, again, bad, we are stating that, in a wide sense of the term 'character', it would have a certain character, so we are apt to think that when we say of it that we are bound, or bound not, to do it, we are stating that it would have a certain character, for which the proper term would be 'ought-to-be-doneness' or 'ought-not-to-be-doneness'. And this tendency is fostered by our habit of using the terms 'right' and 'wrong' as equivalents for 'ought' and 'ought not'. For when we express our thought that we ought, or ought not, to do some action by saying that the act would be right, or wrong, our language inevitably implies that the obligation or disobligation is a certain character which the act would have if we were to do it, a character for which the only existing words are 'rightness' in the one case and 'wrongness' in the other. And when we think this, we inevitably go on to think that the obligation or disobligation must depend on some character which the act would have. But, as we recognize when we reflect, there are no such characteristics of an action as ought-to-be-doneness and ought-not-to-be-doneness. This is obvious; for, since the existence of an obligation to do some action cannot possibly depend on actual performance of the action, the obligation cannot itself be a property which the action would have, if it were done. What does exist is the fact that you, or that I, ought, or ought not, to do a certain action, or rather to set ourselves to do a certain action. And when we make an assertion containing the term 'ought' or 'ought not', that to which we are attributing a certain character is not a certain activity but a certain man. If our being bound to set ourselves to do some action were a character which the activity would have, its existence would, no doubt, have to depend on the fact that the activity would have a certain character, and it could not depend on our thinking that it would. Yet since, in fact, it is a character of ourselves, there is nothing to prevent its existence depending on our having certain thoughts about the situation and, therefore, about the nature of the activity in respect of the effects. Indeed, for this reason, its existence must depend on some fact about ourselves. And while the truth could not be expressed by saying: '*My setting myself to do so-and-so* would *be* right, because *I think* that it would have a certain effect'—a statement which would be as vicious in principle as the statement: '*Doing so-and-so* would *be* right because *I think* it would be right'—there is nothing to prevent its being expressible in the form: '*I* ought to set myself to do so-and-so, because *I* think that it would have a certain effect'. We are therefore now in a position to say that the fundamental difficulty presented by the subjective view is simply the result of a mistake.

This being so, there remains only one thing to do. This is to consider, in some instance where we have considered the circumstances as fully as we can, whether we ought to perform some particular activity, and then ask: 'Does the answer to this question turn on the nature of our *thought* about the situation, and therefore about the effect of the activity, or on the nature of the *situation* and therefore on that of the effect of the activity?' This must be our remaining task, once general difficulties have been cleared away. For there is no way of discovering whether some general doctrine is true except by discovering the general fact to which the doctrine relates; and there is no way of discovering some general fact except by apprehending particular instances of it. And here there is little that need be said. For we have only to carry out this procedure to find not that we are *inclined to think*, or even that we are of the opinion that, but that we are *certain*, i.e. *know*, that the answer turns not on the nature of the situation but on that of our thought about it. This certainty is attainable most readily if the instance taken is similar to those already considered in which our doubts about the nature of the situation are considerable. But it is attainable in any instance, provided that we really face the question.

We therefore cannot but allow that the subjective view is true, in spite of what at first seems its paradoxical character, and that, therefore, in order to defend any moral rule whatever, we must first modify its form accordingly.

PROOF OF AN EXTERNAL WORLD

BY G. E. MOORE

In the preface to the second edition of Kant's *Critique of Pure Reason* some words occur, which, in Professor Kemp Smith's translation, are rendered as follows:

> It still remains a scandal to philosophy . . . that the existence of things outside of us . . . must be accepted merely on *faith*, and that, if anyone thinks good to doubt their existence, we are unable to counter his doubts by any satisfactory proof.[1]

It seems clear from these words that Kant thought it a matter of some importance to give a proof of 'the existence of things outside of us' or perhaps rather (for it seems to me possible that the force of the German words is better rendered in this way) of 'the existence of *the* things outside of us'; for had he not thought it important that a proof should be given, he would scarcely have called it a 'scandal' that no proof had been given. And it seems clear also that he thought that the giving of such a proof was a task which fell properly within the province of philosophy; for, if it did not, the fact that no proof had been given could not possibly be a scandal to *philosophy*.

Now, even if Kant was mistaken in both of these two opinions, there seems to me to be no doubt whatever that it is a matter of some importance and also a matter which falls properly within the province of philosophy, to discuss the question what sort of proof, if any, can be given of 'the existence of things outside of us'. And to discuss this question was my object when I began to write the present lecture. But I may say at once that, as you will find, I have only, at most, succeeded in saying a very small part of what ought to be said about it.

---

[1] B xxxix, note: Kemp Smith, p. 34. The German words are 'so bleibt es immer ein Skandal der Philosophie . . ., das Dasein der Dinge ausser uns . . . bloss auf *Glauben* annehmen zu müssen, und wenn es jemand einfällt es zu bezweifeln, ihm keinen genugtuenden Beweis entgegenstellen zu können'.

The words 'it... remains a scandal to philosophy... that we are unable...' would, taken strictly, imply that, at the moment at which he wrote them, Kant himself was unable to produce a satisfactory proof of the point in question. But I think it is unquestionable that Kant himself did not think that he personally was at the time unable to produce such a proof. On the contrary, in the immediately preceding sentence, he has declared that he has, in the second edition of his *Critique*, to which he is now writing the Preface, given a 'rigorous proof' of this very thing; and has added that he believes this proof of his to be 'the only possible proof'. It is true that in this preceding sentence he does not describe the proof which he has given as a proof of 'the existence of things outside of us' or of 'the existence of the things outside of us', but describes it instead as a proof of 'the objective reality of outer intuition'. But the context leaves no doubt that he is using these two phrases, 'the objective reality of outer intuition' and 'the existence of things (*or* 'the things') outside of us', in such a way that whatever is a proof of the first is also necessarily a proof of the second. We must, therefore, suppose that when he speaks as if *we* are unable to give a satisfactory proof, he does not mean to say that he himself, as well as others, is *at the moment* unable; but rather that, until he discovered the proof which he has given, both he himself and everybody else *were* unable. Of course, if he is right in thinking that he has given a satisfactory proof, the state of things which he describes came to an end as soon as his proof was published. As soon as that happened, anyone who read it was able to give a satisfactory proof by simply repeating that which Kant had given, and the 'scandal' to philosophy had been removed once for all.

If, therefore, it were certain that the proof of the point in question given by Kant in the second edition, is a satisfactory proof, it would be certain that at least one satisfactory proof can be given; and all that would remain of the question which I said I proposed to discuss, would be, firstly, the question as to what *sort* of a proof this of Kant's is, and secondly the question whether (contrary to Kant's own opinion) there may not perhaps be other proofs, of the same or of a different sort, which are also satisfactory. But I think it is by no means certain that Kant's proof is satisfactory. I think it is by no means certain that he did succeed in removing once for all the state of affairs which he considered to be a scandal to philosophy. And I think, therefore, that the question whether it is possible to give *any* satisfactory proof of the point in question still deserves discussion.

But what is the point in question? I think it must be owned that the expression 'things outside of us' is rather an odd expression, and an expression the meaning of which is certainly not perfectly clear. It would have sounded less odd if, instead of 'things outside of us' I had said 'external things', and perhaps also the meaning of this expression would have seemed to be clearer; and I think we make the meaning of 'external things' clearer still, if we explain that this phrase has been regularly used by philosophers as short for 'things external to *our minds*'. The fact is that there has been a long philosophical tradition, in accordance with which the three expressions 'external things', 'things external to *us*', and 'things external to *our minds*' have been used as equivalent to one another, and have, each of them, been used as if they needed no explanation. The origin of this usage I do not know. It occurs already in Descartes; and since he uses the expressions as if they needed no explanation, they had presumably been used with the same meaning before. Of the three, it seems to me that the expression 'external to *our minds*' is the clearest, since it at least makes clear that what is meant is not 'external to *our bodies*'; whereas both the other expressions might be taken to mean this: and indeed there has been a good deal of confusion, even among philosophers, as to the relation of the two conceptions 'external things' and 'things external to *our bodies*'. But even the expression 'things external to our minds' seems to me to be far from perfectly clear; and if I am to make really clear what I mean by 'proof of the existence of things outside of us', I cannot do it by merely saying that by 'outside of us' I mean 'external to our minds'.

There is a passage (*K.d.r.V.*, A 373) in which Kant himself says that the expression 'outside of us' 'carries with it an unavoidable ambiguity'. He says that 'sometimes it means something which exists *as a thing in itself* distinct from us, and sometimes something which merely belongs to external *appearance*'; he calls things which are 'outside of us' in the first of these two senses 'objects which might be called external in the transcendental sense', and things which are so in the second '*empirically external* objects'; and he says finally that, in order to remove all uncertainty as to the latter conception, he will distinguish empirically external objects from objects which might be called 'external' in the transcendental sense, 'by calling them outright things which are *to be met with in space*'.

I think that this last phrase of Kant's 'things which are to be met with in space', does indicate fairly clearly what sort of things it is with regard to which I wish to inquire what sort of proof, if any, can be given that there are any things of that sort. My body, the bodies of other men, the bodies of animals, plants of all sorts, stones, mountains, the sun, the moon, stars, and planets, houses and other buildings, manufactured articles of all sorts—chairs, tables, pieces of paper, &c., are all of them 'things which are to be met with in space'. In short all things of the sort that philosophers have been used to call 'physical objects', 'material things', or 'bodies' obviously come under this head. But the phrase 'things that are to be met with in space' can be naturally understood as applying also in cases where the names 'physical object', 'material thing', or 'body' can hardly be applied. For instance, shadows are sometimes to be met with in space, although they could hardly be properly called 'physical objects', 'material things', or 'bodies'; and although in one usage of the term 'thing', it would not be proper to call a shadow a 'thing', yet the phrase 'things which are to be met with in space' can be naturally understood as synonymous with 'whatever can be met with in space', and this is an expression which can quite properly be understood to include shadows. I wish the phrase 'things which are to be met with in space' to be understood in this wide sense; so that if a proof can be found that there ever have been as many as two different shadows it will follow at once that there have been at least two 'things which were to be met with in space', and this proof will be as good a proof of the point in question, as would be a proof that there have been at least two 'physical objects' of no matter what sort.

The phrase 'things which are to be met with in space' can, therefore, be naturally understood as having a very wide meaning—a meaning even wider than that of 'physical object' or 'body', wide as is the meaning of these latter expressions. But wide as is its meaning, it is not, in one respect, so wide as that of another phrase which Kant uses as if it were equivalent to this one; and a comparison between the two will, I think, serve to make still clearer what sort of things it is with regard to which I wish to ask what proof, if any, can be given that there are such things.

The other phrase which Kant uses as if it were equivalent to 'things which are to be met with in space' is used by him in the sentence immediately preceding that previously quoted in which he declares that the expression 'things outside of us' 'carries with it an unavoidable ambiguity' (A 373). In this preceding sentence he says that an 'empirical object' 'is called *external*, if it is presented (*vorgestellt*) *in space*'. He treats, therefore, the phrase 'presented in space' as if it were equivalent to 'to be met with in space'. But it is easy to find examples of 'things', of which it can hardly be denied that they are 'presented in space', but of which it could, quite naturally, be emphatically denied that they are 'to be met with in space'. Consider, for instance, the following description of one set of circumstances under which what some psychologists have called a 'negative after-image' and others a 'negative after-sensation' can be obtained. 'If, after looking steadfastly at a white patch on a black ground, the eye be turned to a white ground, a grey patch is seen for some little time.' (Foster's *Text-book of Physiology*, IV. iii. 3, p. 1266; quoted in Stout's *Manual of Psychology*, 3rd edition, p. 280.) Upon reading these words recently, I took the trouble to cut out of a piece of white paper a four-pointed star, to place it on a black ground, to 'look steadfastly' at it, and then to turn my eyes to a white sheet of paper: and I did find that I saw a grey patch for some little time—I not only saw a grey patch, but I saw it *on* the white ground, and also this grey patch was of roughly the same shape as the white four-pointed star at which I had 'looked steadfastly' just before—it also was a four-pointed star. I repeated this simple experiment successfully several times. Now each of those grey four-pointed stars, one of which I saw in each experiment, was what is called an 'after-image' or 'after-sensation'; and can anybody deny that each of these after-images can be quite properly said to have been 'presented in space'? I saw each of them on a real white background, and, if so, each of them was 'presented' on a real white background. But though they were 'presented in space' everybody, I think, would feel that it was gravely misleading to say that they were 'to be met with in space'. The white star at which I 'looked steadfastly', the black ground on which I saw it, and the white ground on which I saw the after-images, were, of course, 'to be met with in space': they were, in fact, 'physical objects' or surfaces of physical objects. But one important difference between them, on the one hand, and the grey after-images, on the other, can be quite naturally expressed by saying that the latter were *not* 'to be met with in space'. And one reason why this is so is, I think, plain. To say that so and so was at a given time 'to be met with in space' naturally suggests that there are conditions such that *anyone* who fulfilled them might, conceivably, have 'perceived' the 'thing' in question— might have seen it, if it was a visible object, have felt it, if it was a tangible one, have heard it, if it was a sound, have smelt it, if it was a smell. When I say that the white four-pointed paper star, at which I looked steadfastly, was a 'physical object' and was 'to be met with in space', I am implying that *anyone*, who had been in the room at the time, and who had normal eyesight and a normal sense of touch, might have seen and felt it. But, in the case of those grey after-images which I saw, it is not conceivable that anyone besides myself should have seen any one of them. It is, of course, quite conceivable that other people, if they had been in the room with me at the time, and had carried out the same experiment which I carried out, would have seen grey after-images *very like* one of those which I saw: there is no absurdity in supposing even that they might have seen after-images *exactly* like one of those which I saw. But there is an absurdity in supposing that any one of the after-images which I saw could also have been seen by anyone else: in supposing that two different people can ever see the *very same* after-image. One reason, then, why we should say that none of those grey after-images which I saw was 'to be met with in space', although each of them was certainly 'presented in space' to me, is simply that none of them could conceivably have been seen by anyone else. It is natural so to understand the phrase 'to be met with in space', that to say of anything which a man perceived that it was to be met with in space is to say that it might have been perceived by *others* as well as by the man in question.

Negative after-images of the kind described are, therefore, one example of 'things' which, though they must be allowed to be 'presented in space', are nevertheless *not* 'to be met with in space', and are *not* 'external to our minds' in the sense with which we shall be concerned. And two other important examples may be given.

The first is this. It is well known that people sometimes see things double, an occurrence which has also been described by psychologists by saying that they have a 'double image', or two 'images', of some object at which they are looking. In such cases it would certainly be quite natural to say that each of the two 'images' is 'presented in space': they are seen, one in one place, and the other in another, in just the same sense in which each of those grey after-images which I saw was seen at a particular place on the white background at which I was looking. But it would be utterly unnatural to say that, when I have a double image, each of the two images is 'to be met with in space'. On the contrary it is quite certain that *both* of them are not 'to be met with in space'. If both were, it would follow that somebody else might see the *very same* two images which I see; and, though there is no absurdity in supposing that another person might see a pair of images exactly similar to a pair which I see, there is an absurdity in supposing that anyone else might see the *same identical pair*. In every case, then, in which anyone sees anything double, we have an example of at least one 'thing' which, though 'presented in space' is certainly not 'to be met with in space'.

And the second important example is this. Bodily pains can, in general, be quite properly said to be 'presented in space'. When I have a toothache, I feel it *in* a particular region of my jaw or *in* a particular tooth; when I make a cut on my finger smart by putting iodine on it, I feel the pain in a particular place in my finger; and a man whose leg has been amputated may feel a pain *in* a place where his foot might have been if he had not lost it. It is certainly perfectly natural to understand the phrase 'presented in space' in such a way that if, in the sense illustrated, a pain is felt *in* a particular place, that pain is 'presented in space'. And yet of pains it would be quite unnatural to say that they are 'to be met with in space', for the same reason as in the case of after-images or double images. It is quite conceivable that another person should feel a pain exactly like one which I feel, but there is an absurdity in supposing that he could feel *numerically the same* pain which I feel. And pains are in fact a typical example of the sort of 'things' of which philosophers say that they are *not* 'external' to our minds, but 'within' them. Of any pain which *I* feel they would say that it is necessarily *not* external to my mind but *in* it.

And finally it is, I think, worth while to mention one other class of 'things', which are certainly not 'external' objects and certainly not 'to be met with in space', in the sense with which I am concerned, but which yet some philosophers would be inclined to say are 'presented in space', though they are not 'presented in space' in quite the same sense in which pains, double images, and negative after-images of the sort I described are so. If you look at an electric light and then close your eyes, it sometimes happens that you see, for some little time, against the dark background which you usually see when your eyes are shut, a bright patch similar in shape to the light at which you have just been looking. Such a bright patch, if you see one, is another example of what some psychologists have called 'after-images' and others 'after-sensations'; but, unlike the negative after-images of which I spoke before, it is seen when your eyes are shut. Of such an after-image, seen with closed eyes, some philosophers might be inclined to say that this image too was 'presented in space', although it is certainly not 'to be met with in space'. They would be inclined to say that it is 'presented in space', because it certainly is presented as at some little distance from the person who is seeing it: and how can a thing be presented as at some little distance from me, without being 'presented in space'? Yet there is an important difference between such after-images, seen with closed eyes, and after-images of the sort I previously described—a difference which might lead other philosophers to deny that these after-images, seen with closed eyes, are 'presented in space' at all. It is a difference which can be expressed by saying that when your eyes are shut, you are not seeing any part of *physical* space at all—of the space which is referred to when we talk of 'things which are to be met with in *space*'. An after-image seen with closed eyes certainly is presented in *a* space, but it may be questioned whether it is proper to say that it is presented in *space*.

It is clear, then, I think, that by no means everything which can naturally be said to be 'presented in space' can also be naturally said to be 'a thing which is to be met with in space'. Some of the 'things', which are presented in space, are very emphatically *not* to be met with in space: or, to use another phrase, which may be used to convey the same notion, they are emphatically *not* 'physical realities' at all. The conception 'presented in space' is therefore, in one respect, much wider than the conception 'to be met with in space': many 'things' fall under the first conception which do not fall under the second—many after-images, one at least of the pair of 'images' seen whenever anyone sees double, and most bodily pains, are 'presented in space', though none of them are to be met with in space. From the fact that a 'thing' is presented in space, it by no means follows that it is to be met with in space. But just as the first conception is, in one respect, wider than the second, so, in another, the second is wider than the first. For there are many 'things' to be met with in space, of which it is not true that they are presented in space. From the fact that a 'thing' is to be met with in space, it by no means follows that it is presented in space. I have taken 'to be met with in space' to imply, as I think it naturally may, that a 'thing' *might be* perceived; but from the fact that a thing *might be* perceived, it does not follow that it *is* perceived; and if it is not actually perceived, then it will not be presented in space. It is characteristic of the sorts of 'things', including shadows, which I have described as 'to be met with in space', that there is no absurdity in supposing with regard to any one of them which *is*, at a given time, perceived, both (1) that it might have existed at that very time, without being perceived; (2) that it might have existed at another time, without being perceived at that other time; and (3) that during the whole period of its existence, it need not have been perceived at any time at all. There is, therefore, no absurdity in supposing that many things, which were at one time to be met with in space, never were 'presented' at any time at all, and that many things which *are* to be met with in space now, are not now 'presented' and also never were and never will be. To use a Kantian phrase, the conception of 'things which are to be met with in space' embraces not only objects of actual experience, but also objects of *possible* experience; and from the fact that a thing is or was an object of *possible* experience, it by no means follows that it either was or is or will be 'presented' at all.

I hope that what I have now said may have served to make clear enough what sorts of 'things' I was originally referring to as 'things outside us' or 'things external to our minds'. I said that I thought that Kant's phrase 'things that are to be met with in space' indicated fairly clearly the sorts of 'things' in question; and I have tried to make the range clearer still, by pointing out that this phrase only serves the purpose, if (*a*) you understand it in a sense, in which many 'things', e.g. after-images, double images, bodily pains, which might be said to be 'presented in space', are nevertheless *not* to be reckoned as 'things that are to be met with in space', and (*b*) you realize clearly that there is no contradiction in supposing that there have been and are 'to be met with in space' things which never have been, are not now, and never will be perceived, nor in supposing that among those of them which have at some time been perceived many existed at times at which they were not being perceived. I think it will now be clear to everyone that, since I do not reckon as 'external things' after-images, double images, and bodily pains, I also should not reckon as 'external things', any of the 'images' which we often 'see with the mind's eye' when we are awake, nor any of those which we see when we are asleep and dreaming; and also that I was so using the expression 'external' that from the fact that a man was at a given time having a visual hallucination, it will follow that he was seeing at that time something which was *not* 'external' to his mind, and from the fact that he was at a given time having an auditory hallucination, it will follow that he was at the time hearing a sound which was *not* 'external' to his mind. But I certainly have not made my use of these phrases, 'external to our minds' and 'to be met with in space', so clear that in the case of every kind of 'thing' which might be suggested, you would be able to tell at once whether I should or should not reckon it as 'external to our minds' and 'to be met with in space'. For instance, I have said nothing which makes it quite clear whether a reflection which I see in a looking-glass is or is not to be regarded as 'a thing that is to be met with in space' and 'external to our minds', nor have I said anything which makes it quite clear whether the sky is or is not to be so regarded. In the case of the sky, everyone, I think, would feel that it was quite inappropriate to talk of it as 'a thing that is to be met with in space'; and most people, I think, would feel a strong reluctance to affirm, without qualification, that reflections which people see in looking-glasses are 'to be met with in space'.

And yet neither the sky nor reflections seen in mirrors are in the same position as bodily pains or after-images in the respect which I have emphasized as a reason for saying of these latter that they are *not* to be met with in space—namely that there is an absurdity in supposing that *the very same* pain which I feel could be felt by someone else or that *the very same* after-image which I see could be seen by someone else. In the case of reflections in mirrors we should quite naturally, in certain circumstances, use language which implies that another person may see the same reflection which we see. We might quite naturally say to a friend: 'Do you see that reddish reflection in the water there? I can't make out what it's a reflection of', just as we might say, pointing to a distant hill-side: 'Do you see that white speck on the hill over there? I can't make out what it is.' And in the case of the sky, it is quite obviously *not* absurd to say that other people see it as well as I.

It must, therefore, be admitted that I have not made my use of the phrase 'things to be met with in space', nor therefore that of 'external to our minds', which the former was used to explain, so clear that in the case of every kind of 'thing' which may be mentioned, there will be no doubt whatever as to whether things of that kind are or are not 'to be met with in space' or 'external to our minds'. But this lack of a clear-cut definition of the expression 'things that are to be met with in space', does not, so far as I can see, matter for my present purpose. For my present purpose it is, I think, sufficient if I make clear, in the case of many kinds of things, that I am so using the phrase 'things that are to be met with in space', that, in the case of each of these kinds, from the proposition that there are things of that kind it *follows* that there are things to be met with in space. And I have, in fact, given a list (though by no means an exhaustive one) of kinds of things which are related to my use of the expression 'things that are to be met with in space' in this way. I mentioned among others the bodies of men and of animals, plants, stars, houses, chairs, and shadows; and I want now to emphasize that I am so using 'things to be met with in space' that, in the case of each of these kinds of 'things', from the proposition that there are 'things' of that kind it *follows* that there are things to be met with in space: e.g. from the proposition that there are plants or that plants exist it *follows* that there are things to be met with in space, from the proposition that shadows exist, it *follows* that there are things to be met with in space, and so on, in the case of all the kinds of 'things' which I mentioned in my first list. That this should be clear is sufficient for my purpose, because, if it is clear, then it will also be clear that, as I implied before, if you have proved that two plants exist, or that a plant and a dog exist, or that a dog and a shadow exist, &c., &c., you will *ipso facto* have proved that there are things to be met with in space: you will not require *also* to give a separate proof that from the proposition that there are plants it *does* follow that there are things to be met with in space.

Now with regard to the expression 'things that are to be met with in space' I think it will readily be believed that I may be using it in a sense such that no proof is required that from 'plants exist' there follows 'there are things to be met with in space'; but with regard to the phrase 'things external to our minds' I think the case is different. People may be inclined to say: 'I can see quite clearly that from the proposition "At least two dogs exist at the present moment" there *follows* the proposition "At least two things are to be met with in space at the present moment", so that if you can prove that there are two dogs in existence at the present moment you will *ipso facto* have proved that two things at least are to be met with in space at the present moment. I can see that you do not also require a separate proof that from "Two dogs exist" "Two things are to be met with in space" *does* follow; it is quite obvious that there couldn't be a dog which wasn't to be met with in space. But it is not by any means so clear to me that if you can prove that there are two dogs or two shadows, you will *ipso facto* have proved that there are two things *external to our minds*. Isn't it possible that a dog, though it certainly must be "to be met with in space", might *not* be an external object— an object external to our minds? Isn't a separate proof required that anything that is to be met with in space must be external to our minds? Of course, if you are using "external" as a mere synonym for "to be met with in space", no proof will be required that dogs are external objects: in that case, if you can prove that two dogs exist, you will *ipso facto* have proved that there are some external things. But I find it difficult to believe that you, or anybody else, do really use "external" as a mere synonym for "to be met with in space"; and if you don't, isn't some proof required that whatever is to be met with in space must be external to our minds?'

Now Kant, as we saw, asserts that the phrases 'outside of us' or 'external' are in fact used in two very different senses; and with regard to one of these two senses, that which he calls the 'transcendental' sense, and which he tries to explain by saying that it is a sense in which 'external' means 'existing *as a thing in itself* distinct from us', it is notorious that he himself held that things which are to be met with in space are *not* 'external' in that sense. There is, therefore, according to him, *a* sense of 'external', a sense in which the word has been commonly used by philosophers—such that, if 'external' be used in that sense, then from the proposition 'Two dogs exist' it will *not* follow that there are some external things. What this supposed sense is I do not think that Kant himself ever succeeded in explaining clearly; nor do I know of any reason for supposing that philosophers ever have used 'external' in a sense, such that in *that* sense things that are to be met with in space are *not* external. But how about the other sense, in which, according to Kant, the word 'external' has been commonly used—that which he calls 'empirically external'? How is this conception related to the conception 'to be met with in space'? It may be noticed that, in the passages which I quoted (A 373), Kant himself does not tell us at all clearly what he takes to be the proper answer to this question. He only makes the rather odd statement that, in order to remove all uncertainty as to the conception 'empirically external', he will distinguish objects to which it applies from those which might be called 'external' in the transcendental sense, by 'calling them outright things which are *to be met with in space*'. These odd words certainly suggest, as one possible interpretation of them, that in Kant's opinion the conception 'empirically external' is *identical* with the conception 'to be met with in space'—that he does think that 'external', when used in this second sense, is a mere synonym for 'to be met with in space'. But, if this is his meaning, I do find it very difficult to believe that he is right. Have philosophers, in fact, ever used 'external' as a mere synonym for 'to be met with in space'? Does he himself do so?

I do not think they have, nor that he does himself; and, in order to explain how they have used it, and how the two conceptions 'external to our minds' and 'to be met with in space' are related to one another, I think it is important expressly to call attention to a fact which hitherto I have only referred to incidentally: namely the fact that those who talk of certain things as 'external to' our minds, do, in general, as we should naturally expect, talk of other 'things', with which they wish to contrast the first, as 'in' our minds. It has, of course, been often pointed out that when 'in' is thus used, followed by 'my mind', 'your mind', 'his mind', &c., 'in' is being used metaphorically. And there are some metaphorical uses of 'in', followed by such expressions, which occur in common speech, and which we all understand quite well. For instance, we all understand such expressions as 'I had you in mind, when I made that arrangement' or 'I had you in mind, when I said that there are some people who can't bear to touch a spider'. In these cases 'I was thinking of you' can be used to mean the same as 'I had you in mind'. But it is quite certain that this particular metaphorical use of 'in' is not the one in which philosophers are using it when they contrast what is 'in' my mind with what is 'external' to it. On the contrary, in their use of 'external', you will be external to my mind even at a moment when I have you in mind. If we want to discover what this peculiar metaphorical use of '*in* my mind' is, which is such that nothing, which is, in the sense we are now concerned with, 'external' to my mind, can ever be 'in' it, we need, I think, to consider instances of the sort of 'things' which they would say are 'in' my mind in this special sense. I have already mentioned three such instances, which are, I think, sufficient for my present purpose: any bodily pain which I feel, any after-image which I see with my eyes shut, and any image which I 'see' when I am asleep and dreaming, are typical examples of the sort of 'thing' of which philosophers have spoken as '*in* my mind'. And there is no doubt, I think, that when they have spoken of such things as my body, a sheet of paper, a star—in short 'physical objects' generally—as 'external', they have meant to emphasize some important difference which they feel to exist between such things as these and such 'things' as a pain, an after-image seen with closed eyes, and a dream-image. But *what* difference? What difference do they feel to exist between a bodily pain which I feel or an after-image which I see with closed eyes, on the one hand, and my body itself, on the other—what difference which leads them to say that whereas the bodily pain and the after-image are 'in' my mind, my body itself is *not* 'in' my mind—not even when I am feeling it and seeing it or thinking of it? I have already said that one difference which there is between the two, is that my body is to be met with in space, whereas the bodily pain and the after-image are not. But I think it would be quite wrong to say that this is *the* difference which has led philosophers to speak of the two latter as 'in' my mind, and of my body as *not* 'in' my mind.

The question what the difference is which has led them to speak in this way, is not, I think, at all an easy question to answer; but I am going to try to give, in brief outline, what I *think* is a right answer.

It should, I think, be noted, first of all, that the use of the word 'mind', which is being adopted when it is said that any bodily pains which I feel are 'in my mind', is one which is not quite in accordance with any usage common in ordinary speech, although we are very familiar with it in philosophy. Nobody, I think, would say that bodily pains which I feel are 'in my mind', unless he was also prepared to say that it is *with* my mind that I feel bodily pains; and to say this latter is, I think, not quite in accordance with common non-philosophic usage. It is natural enough to say that it is with my mind that I remember, and think, and imagine, and feel *mental* pains—e.g. disappointment, but not, I think, quite so natural to say that it is with my mind that I feel *bodily* pains, e.g. a severe headache; and perhaps even less natural to say that it is with my mind that I see and hear and smell and taste. There is, however, a well-established philosophical usage according to which seeing, hearing, smelling, tasting, and having a bodily pain are just as much *mental* occurrences or processes as are remembering, or thinking, or imagining. This usage was, I think, adopted by philosophers, because they saw a real resemblance between such statements as 'I saw a cat', 'I heard a clap of thunder', 'I smelt a strong smell of onions', 'My finger smarted horribly', on the one hand, and such statements as 'I remembered having seen him', 'I was thinking out a plan of action', 'I pictured the scene to myself', 'I felt bitterly disappointed', on the other—a resemblance which puts all these statements in one class together, as contrasted with other statements in which 'I' or 'my' is used, such as, e.g., 'I was less than four feet high', 'I was lying on my back', 'My hair was very long'. What is the resemblance in question? It is a resemblance which might be expressed by saying that all the first eight statements are the sort of statements which furnish data for psychology, while the three latter are not. It is also a resemblance which may be expressed, in a way now common among philosophers, by saying that in the case of all the first eight statements, if we make the statement more specific by adding a date, we get a statement such that, if it is true, then it *follows* that I was 'having an experience' at the date in question, whereas this does not hold for the three last statements. For instance, if it is true that I saw a cat between 12 noon and 5 minutes past, today, it *follows* that I was 'having some experience' between 12 noon and 5 minutes past, today; whereas from the proposition that I was less than four feet high in December 1877, it does not *follow* that I had any experiences in December 1877. But this philosophic use of 'having an experience' is one which itself needs explanation, since it is not identical with any use of the expression that is established in common speech. An explanation, however, which is, I think, adequate for the purpose, can be given by saying that a philosopher, who was following this usage, would say that I was at a given time 'having an experience' if and only if either (1) I was conscious at the time or (2) I was dreaming at the time or (3) something else was true of me at the time, which resembled what is true of me when I am conscious and when I am dreaming, in a certain very obvious respect in which what is true of me when I am dreaming resembles what is true of me when I am dreaming resembles what is true of me when I am conscious, and in which what would be true of me, if at any time, for instance, I had a vision, would resemble both. This explanation is, of course, in some degree vague; but I think it is clear enough for our purpose. It amounts to saying that, in this philosophic usage of 'having an experience', it would be said of me that I was, at a given time, having *no* experience, if I was at the time neither conscious nor dreaming nor having a vision nor *anything else of the sort*; and, of course, this is vague in so far as it has not been specified what else would be *of the sort*: this is left to be gathered from the instances given. But I think this is sufficient: often at night when I am asleep, I am neither conscious nor dreaming nor having a vision nor *anything else of the sort*—that is to say, I am having no experiences. If this explanation of this philosophic usage of 'having an experience' is clear enough, then I think that what has been meant by saying that any pain which I feel or any after-image which I see with my eyes closed is '*in* my mind', can be explained by saying that what is meant is neither more nor less than that there would be a contradiction in supposing *that very same pain* or *that very same after-image* to have existed at a time at which I was having no experience; or, in other words, that from the proposition, with regard to any time, that *that* pain or *that* after-image existed at that time, it *follows* that I was having some experience at the time in question. And if so, then we can say that the felt difference between bodily pains which I feel and after-images which I see, on the one hand, and my body on the other, which has led philosophers to say that any such pain or after-image is '*in* my mind', whereas my body *never* is but is always 'outside of' or 'external to' my mind, is just this, that whereas there is a contradiction in supposing a pain which I feel or an after-image which I see to exist at a time when I am having no experience, there is no contradiction in supposing my body to exist at a time when I am having no experience; and we can even say, I think, that just this and nothing more is what they have meant by these puzzling and misleading phrases 'in my mind' and 'external to my mind'.

But now, if to say of anything, e.g. my body, that it is external to *my* mind, means merely that from a proposition to the effect that it existed at a specified time, there in no case follows the further proposition that *I* was having an experience at the time in question, then to say of anything that it is external to *our* minds, will mean similarly that from a proposition to the effect that it existed at a specified time, it in no case follows that any of *us* were having experiences at the time in question. And if by *our* minds be meant, as is, I think, usually meant, the minds of human beings living on the earth, then it will follow that any pains which animals may feel, any after-images they may see, any experiences they may have, though not external to *their* minds, yet are external to *ours*. And this at once makes plain how different is the conception 'external to our minds' from the conception 'to be met with in space'; for, of course, pains which animals feel or after-images which they see are no more to be met with in space than are pains which *we* feel or after-images which *we* see. From the proposition that there are external objects—objects that are not in any of *our* minds, it does *not* follow that there are things to be met with in space; and hence 'external to our minds' is not a mere synonym for 'to be met with in space': that is to say, 'external to our minds' and 'to be met with in space' are two different conceptions. And the true relation between these conceptions seems to me to be this. We have already seen that there are ever so many kinds of 'things', such that, in the case of each of these kinds, from the proposition that there is at least one thing of that kind there *follows* the proposition that there is at least one thing to be met with in space: e.g. this follows from 'There is at least one star', from 'There is at least one human body', from 'There is at least one shadow', &c. And I think we can say that of every kind of thing of which this is true, it is also true that from the proposition that there is at least one 'thing' of that kind there *follows* the proposition that there is at least one thing external to our minds: e.g. from 'There is at least one star' there follows not only 'There is at least one thing to be met with in space' but also 'There is at least one external thing', and similarly in all other cases. My reason for saying this is as follows. Consider any kind of thing, such that anything of that kind, if there is anything of it, must be 'to be met with in space': e.g. consider the kind 'soap-bubble'. If I say of anything which I am perceiving, 'That is a soap bubble', I am, it seems to me, certainly implying that there would be no contradiction in asserting that it existed before I perceived it and that it will continue to exist, even if I cease to perceive it. This seems to me to be part of what is meant by saying that it is a real soap-bubble, as distinguished, for instance, from an hallucination of a soap-bubble. Of course, it by no means follows, that if it really is a soap-bubble, it did in fact exist before I perceived it or will continue to exist after I cease to perceive it: soap-bubbles are an example of a kind of 'physical object' and 'thing to be met with in space', in the case of which it is notorious that particular specimens of the kind often do exist only so long as they are perceived by a particular person. But a thing which I perceive would not be a soap-bubble unless its existence at any given time were *logically independent* of my perception of it at that time; unless that is to say, from the proposition, with regard to a particular time, that it existed at that time, it *never* follows that I perceived it at that time. But, if it is true that it would not be a soap-bubble, unless it *could* have existed at any given time without being perceived by me at that time, it is certainly also true that it would not be a soap-bubble, unless it *could* have existed at any given time, without its being true that I was having any experience of any kind at the time in question: it would not be a soap-bubble, unless, whatever time you take, from the proposition that it existed at that time it does *not* follow that I was having any experience at that time. That is to say, from the proposition with regard to anything which I am perceiving that it is a soap-bubble, there *follows* the proposition that it is external to *my* mind. But if, when I say that anything which I perceive is a soap-bubble, I am implying that it is external to *my* mind, I am, I think, certainly also implying that it is also external to all other minds: I am implying that it is not a thing of a sort such that things of that sort *can* only exist at a time when somebody is having an experience. I think, therefore, that from any proposition of the form 'There's a soap-bubble!' there does really *follow* the proposition 'There's an external object!' 'There's an object external to *all* our minds!' And, if this is true of the kind 'soap-bubble', it is certainly also true of any other kind (including the kind 'unicorn') which is such that, if there are any things of that kind, it follows that there are *some* things to be met with in space.

I think, therefore, that in the case of all kinds of 'things', which are such that if there is a pair of things, both of which are of one of these kinds, or a pair of things one of which is of one of them and one of them of another, then it will follow at once that there are some things to be met with in space, it is true also that if I can prove that there are a pair of things, one of which is of one of these kinds and another of another, or a pair both of which are of one of them, then I shall have proved *ipso facto* that there are at least two 'things outside of us'. That is to say, if I can prove that there exist now both a sheet of paper and a human hand, I shall have proved that there are now 'things outside of us'; if I can prove that there exist now both a shoe and sock, I shall have proved that there are now 'things outside of us'; &c.; and similarly I shall have proved it, if I can prove that there exist now two sheets of paper, or two human hands, or two shoes, or two socks, &c. Obviously, then, there are thousands of different things such that, if, at any time, I can prove any one of them, I shall have proved the existence of things outside of us. Cannot I prove any of these things?

It seems to me that, so far from its being true, as Kant declares to be his opinion, that there is only one possible proof of the existence of things outside of us, namely the one which he has given, I can now give a large number of different proofs, each of which is a perfectly rigorous proof; and that at many other times I have been in a position to give many others. I can prove now, for instance, that two human hands exist. How? By holding up my two hands, and saying, as I make a certain gesture with the right hand, 'Here is one hand', and adding, as I make a certain gesture with the left, 'and here is another'. And if, by doing this, I have proved *ipso facto* the existence of external things, you will all see that I can also do it now in numbers of other ways: there is no need to multiply examples.

But did I prove just now that two human hands were then in existence? I do want to insist that I did; that the proof which I gave was a perfectly rigorous one; and that it is perhaps impossible to give a better or more rigorous proof of anything whatever. Of course, it would not have been a proof unless three conditions were satisfied; namely (1) unless the premiss which I adduced as proof of the conclusion was different from the conclusion I adduced it to prove; (2) unless the premiss which I adduced was something which I *knew* to be the case, and not merely something which I believed but which was by no means certain, or something which, though in fact true, I did not know to be so; and (3) unless the conclusion did really follow from the premiss. But all these three conditions were in fact satisfied by my proof. (1) The premiss which I adduced in proof was quite certainly different from the conclusion, for the conclusion was merely 'Two human hands exist at this moment'; but the premiss was something far more specific than this—something which I expressed by showing you my hands, making certain gestures, and saying the words 'Here is one hand, and here is another'. It is quite obvious that the two were different, because it is quite obvious that the conclusion might have been true, even if the premiss had been false. In asserting the premiss I was asserting much more than I was asserting in asserting the conclusion. (2) I certainly did at the moment *know* that which I expressed by the combination of certain gestures with saying the words 'There is one hand and here is another'. I *knew* that there was one hand in the place indicated by combining a certain gesture with my first utterance of 'here' and that there was another in the different place indicated by combining a certain gesture with my second utterance of 'here'. How absurd it would be to suggest that I did not know it, but only believed it, and that perhaps it was not the case! You might as well suggest that I do not know that I am now standing up and talking—that perhaps after all I'm not, and that it's not quite certain that I am! And finally (3) it is quite certain that the conclusion did follow from the premiss. This is as certain, as it is that if there is one hand here and another here *now*, then it follows that there are two hands in existence *now*.

My proof, then, of the existence of things outside of us did satisfy three of the conditions necessary for a rigorous proof. Are there any other conditions necessary for a rigorous proof, such that perhaps it did not satisfy one of them? Perhaps there may be; I do not know; but I do want to emphasize that, so far as I can see, we all of us do constantly take proofs of this sort as absolutely conclusive proofs of certain conclusions—as finally settling certain questions, as to which we were previously in doubt. Suppose, for instance, it were a question whether there were as many as three misprints on a certain page in a certain book. A says there are, B, is inclined to doubt it. How could A prove that he is right? Surely he *could* prove it by taking the book, turning to the page, and pointing to three separate places on it, saying 'There's one misprint here, another here, and another here': surely that is a method by which it *might* be proved! Of course, A would not have proved, by doing this, that there were at least three misprints on the page in question, unless it was certain that there was a misprint in each of the places to which he pointed.

But to say that he *might* prove it in this way, is to say that it *might* be certain that there was. And if such a thing as that could ever be certain, then assuredly it was certain just now that there was one hand in one of the two places I indicated and another in the other.

I did, then, just now, give a proof that there were *then* external objects; and obviously, if I did, I could *then* have given many other proofs of the same sort that there were external objects *then*, and could now give many proofs of the same sort that there are external objects *now*.

But, if what I am asked to do is to prove that external objects have existed *in the past*, then I can give many different proofs of this also, but proofs which are in important respects of a different *sort* from those just given. And I want to emphasize that, when Kant says it is a scandal not to be able to give a proof of the existence of external objects, a proof of their existence in the past would certainly *help* to remove the scandal of which he is speaking. He says that, if it occurs to anyone to question their existence, we ought to be able to confront him with a satisfactory proof. But by a person who questions their existence, he certainly means not merely a person who questions whether any exist at the moment of speaking, but a person who questions whether any have *ever* existed; and a proof that some have existed in the past would certainly therefore be relevant to *part* of what such a person is questioning. How then can I prove that there have been external objects in the past? Here is one proof. I can say: 'I held up two hands above this desk not very long ago; therefore two hands existed not very long ago; therefore at least two external objects have existed at some time in the past, Q.E.D.' This is a perfectly good proof, provided I *know* what is asserted in the premiss. But I *do* know that I held up two hands above this desk not very long ago. As a matter of fact, in this case you all know it too. There's no doubt whatever that I did. Therefore I have given a perfectly conclusive proof that external objects have existed in the past; and you will all see at once that, if this is a conclusive proof, I could have given many others of the same sort, and could now give many others. But it is also quite obvious that this sort of proof differs in important respects from the sort of proof I gave just now that there were two hands existing *then*.

I have, then, given two conclusive proofs of the existence of external objects. The first was a proof that two human hands existed at the time when I gave the proof; the second was a proof that two human hands had existed at a time previous to that at which I gave the proof. These proofs were of a different sort in important respects. And I pointed out that I could have given, then, many other conclusive proofs of both sorts. It is also obvious that I could give many others of both sorts now. So that, if these are the sort of proof that is wanted, nothing is easier than to prove the existence of external objects.

But now I am perfectly well aware that, in spite of all that I have said, many philosophers will still feel that I have not given any satisfactory proof of the point in question. And I want briefly, in conclusion, to say something as to why this dissatisfaction with my proofs should be felt.

One reason why, is, I think, this. Some people understand 'proof of an external world' as including a proof of things which I haven't attempted to prove and haven't proved. It is not quite easy to say *what* it is that they want proved—*what* it is that is such that unless they got a proof of it, they would not say that they had a proof of the existence of external things; but I can make an approach to explaining what they want by saying that if I had proved the propositions which I used as *premisses* in my two proofs, then they would perhaps admit that I had proved the existence of external things, but, in the absence of such a proof (which, of course, I have neither given, nor attempted to give), they will say that I have not given what they mean by a proof of the existence of external things. In other words they want a proof of what I assert *now* when I hold up my hands and say 'Here's one hand and here's another'; and, in the other case, they want a proof of what I assert *now* when I say 'I did hold up two hands above this desk just now'. Of course, what they really want is not merely a proof of these two propositions, but something like a general statement as to how *any* propositions of this sort may be proved. This, of course, I haven't given; and I do not believe it can be given: if this is what is meant by proof of the existence of external things, I do not believe that any proof of the existence of external things is possible. Of course, in some cases what might be called a proof of propositions which seem like these can be got. If one of you suspected that one of my hands was artificial he might be said to get a proof of my proposition 'Here's one hand, and here's another', by coming up and examining the suspected hand close up, perhaps touching and pressing it, and so establishing that it really was a human hand. But I do not believe that any proof is possible in nearly all cases. How am I to prove now that 'Here's one hand, and here's another'? I do not believe I can do it. In order to do it, I should need to prove for one thing, as Descartes pointed out, that I am not now dreaming. But how can I prove that I am not? I have, no doubt, conclusive reasons for asserting that I am not now dreaming; I have conclusive evidence that I am awake: but that is a very different thing from being able to prove it. I could not tell you what all my evidence is; and I should require to do this at least, in order to give you a proof.

But another reason, why some people would feel dissatisfied with my proofs is, I think, not merely that they want a proof of something which I haven't proved, but that they think that, if I cannot give such extra proofs, then the proofs that I have given are not conclusive proofs at all. And this, I think, is a definite mistake. They would say: 'If you cannot prove your premiss that here is one hand and here is another, then you do not know it. But you yourself have admitted that, if you did not know it, then your proof was not conclusive. Therefore your proof was not, as you say it was, a conclusive proof.' This view that, if I cannot prove such things as these, I do not know them, is, I think, the view that Kant was expressing in the sentence which I quoted at the beginning of this lecture, when he implies that so long as we have no proof of the existence of external things, their existence must be accepted merely on *faith*. He means to say, I think, that if I cannot prove that there is a hand here, I must accept it merely as a matter of faith—I cannot know it. Such a view, though it has been very common among philosophers, can, I think, be shown to be wrong—though shown only by the use of premisses which are not known to be true, unless we do know of the existence of external things. I can know things, which I cannot prove; and among things which I certainly did know, even if (as I think) I could not prove them, were the premisses of my two proofs. I should say, therefore, that those, if any, who are dissatisfied with these proofs merely on the ground that I did not know their premisses, have no good reason for this dissatisfaction.

MORAL PRINCIPLES AND INDUCTIVE POLICIES

BY R. B. BRAITHWAITE

The outstanding philosophic achievement of the half-century which has just drawn to a close has been an appreciation of the peculiar status of *a priori* judgements and of logically necessary or formally true propositions. The function of such judgements, dimly foreshadowed in Kant's doctrine of categories and forms of intuition, has been illuminated by the work of mathematical logicians and the genius of Dr. Ludwig Wittgenstein. Though many problems remain unsolved, the main outline is now clear: formally true statements assert nothing about the nature of the world; instead, their function is to state principles according to which empirical propositions are deduced from other empirical propositions, this deduction involving the use of a language or other mode of expression whose rules correspond to, and explain the logical necessity of, the formally true statements. Philosophers in the empiricist tradition have thus had the burden lifted from them of having to account for *a priori* truth, and have been strengthened in their desire to base all knowledge—all non-formal knowledge—upon experience, and upon experience alone.

This illumination has had an influence upon the perennial argument in ethics between naturalists and absolutists.[1] It has discredited the *a priori* concepts of the absolutists; but, by showing that statements are used in other ways than as expressive of facts, it has also cast doubt upon the possibility of a simple naturalistic analysis of ethical concepts. Empirically minded moral philosophers have therefore recently concentrated their attention upon the distinctive function of language

---

[1] This term is used to cover all moral philosophers whose ethical theories are objective but not naturalistic.

used in expressing moral judgements. Professor C. L. Stevenson has most admirably elucidated the intricate entanglement of 'emotive' with 'descriptive' meaning which occurs in ethical discourse, and the way in which emotive meaning modifies our attitudes, especially our attitudes of approval. These attitudes are, of course, not logically independent of the actions to which they give rise; and this dependence opens the road to an alternative empirical approach to the problems of ethics, namely, one starting from the fact of moral decision and of moral behaviour, and saying something about the principles which govern such decisions and behaviour. Such an approach, which will be attempted in this lecture, should be regarded as complementary rather than as contrary to the approach by way of language which Stevenson modestly calls a 'sharpening [of] the tools which others employ'.[2] It may, however, prove more sympathetic to those who feel that the principles of the good life are more important than those of ethical conversation, and that the problem before all of us is primarily how to exercise Practical Reason in making right decisions rather than Theoretical Reason in conducting their post-mortem examination.

The primary object of study in ethics will therefore be taken to be the principles that direct moral conduct. A man's acceptance of a moral principle will be regarded as making some sort of remark about his future conduct. Now there is another type of statements which also looks to the future, namely, scientific hypotheses and other inductive generalizations. The chief function of these in our thinking is predictive: by predicting the future they enable us to regulate our future conduct. So a good way of starting the inquiry may be to compare moral decisions with inductive beliefs.

There is another excellent reason for making the comparison. The problem of the justification of our inductive beliefs is analogous to that of the justification of our moral judgements in that both have presented similar difficulties to epistemologists. The difficulty of justifying induction has forced many philosophers to posit a notion of causality not analysable in

[2] *Ethics and Language* (1944), 1.

empirical terms and synthetic *a priori* propositions in which this causality can play a part. A similar reason appears to require something over and above the empirical in moral judgements. So perhaps a non-transcendental investigation of the former problem may throw light upon the latter.

The possibility of an empirical justification for induction has been argued by logicians since Hume opened the debate in 1739. Owing largely to the insight of C. S. Peirce, a solution in broad outline has been found acceptable by many contemporary philosophers, including myself. But before this solution can be transferred to its ethical analogue, the inductive problem will have to be restated. For the inductive problem is concerned with the justification of beliefs, whereas what we require for a comparison with ethics is a justification of actions.

To reformulate the problem is not difficult. It is not necessary to accept the whole doctrine, propounded by Bain,[3] that belief consists in a propensity to action and in nothing more whatever: all that is required is to admit that a propensity to future action forms an essential part of a belief in a general proposition relating to the future. Even this need not be admitted if we are willing to separate acting scientifically from thinking scientifically. What is wanted is to translate the language used by Peircean logicians about inductive beliefs into language appropriate to describe inductive action. Let us try to do this.

Man, like other animals, confronts the future with dispositions to behave in certain ways under certain circumstances. If circumstances of this sort befall him, he performs actions which he would not otherwise have performed. A few of his behaviour-dispositions he is born with; these are manifested either at birth or at some later time like the age of puberty; but most of his behaviour-dispositions he acquires by a process of learning. Behaviour-dispositions are not all fixed: they may change in accordance with second-order behaviour-dispositions, which themselves may be either innate or acquired.

One way in which man, like other animals, acquires new

[3] Alexander Bain, *The Emotions and the Will* (1859), 568; *Mental and Moral Science* (1868), 372. The doctrine is qualified in editions of 1872 and later.

behaviour-dispositions is of great importance. From having a behaviour-disposition which comes into play when a C-like event occurs, he learns to bring the behaviour belonging to this disposition into play *before* the C-like event occurs on the occasion of an event of a different kind—a B-like event—occurring. He learns to antedate the stimulus and to behave as he would have behaved had the C-like event occurred before it does in fact occur. This way of acquiring new behaviour-dispositions has been studied in its simplest form in what have been misleadingly called 'conditioned reflex' experiments: with man these new behaviour-dispositions can be acquired in much more sophisticated ways than the induction by simple enumeration practised by Pavlov's dogs.

Frequently in man behaviour in accordance with the new behaviour-disposition falls into two stages: a later stage of actions after the C-like event occurs, an earlier stage of actions elicited by the occurrence of the B-like event which are preparatory to the actions of the later stage. When the dinner-bell rings, I walk into the dining-room; if, like Pavlov's dogs, I am very hungry, my mouth waters; but I do not pick up knife and fork until the food is actually set before me. My whole chain of actions is appropriate to my finally eating food, but the earlier part of the chain is preliminary to the manifestation of my eating-disposition proper. This earlier stage may therefore be considered as a manifestation of a separate disposition—a disposition to act, on the occurrence of a B-like event, in a manner of preparedness to make appropriate responses to a C-like event, when that will happen.

Suppose that a B-like event has occurred, and that a man with this 'preparedness'-disposition is acting preparedly for a C-like event happening. Suppose that no C-like event happens. The man has already started to act in a manner appropriate to such an occurrence, since the preparedness itself is such an appropriate action; but, since what he is prepared for does not happen, there is in fact nothing to which his preparedness is appropriate. The man is, as we say, 'let down'. The situation is entirely different from that in which a man who is pursuing a course of action directed towards a certain goal finds during the course of this action that the attainment of his goal is prevented by adverse circumstances. In this case his goal-directed activity has been frustrated by *force majeure*; but the activity was appropriate to the original stimulus which elicited it; and, by virtue of what biologists call 'plasticity', the man can start again and try to attain his goal by a different and more effective route. But in the case which we are considering the proper stimulus is itself lacking: the man acts in a manner which is only appropriate if something happens which in fact does not happen. His activity, being 'uncalled for', becomes altogether pointless; and there is nothing for him to do but to cut his losses and to resume what he had been doing before he prepared himself for an eventuality which did not eventuate.

I have distinguished these preparedness-dispositions from dispositions to perform goal-directed activities. But most cases of goal-directed activity take place in stages, in which attainment of the subsidiary goal of the first stage is the stimulus eliciting the second stage, and so on. So the activity of pursuing the first subsidiary goal includes a preparedness for the second-stage activity when this first goal is attained; and, if circumstances prevent this attainment, the preparedness becomes pointless. If, in such a simple goal-directed action as carrying food to my mouth with a fork, the food falls off the fork before it reaches my mouth, my preparedness-action in opening my mouth becomes pointless—though it will regain its point when I try again more successfully. It is, however, worth separating out the preparedness-dispositions from the rest of the dispositions manifested in a complex course of action, because they have the peculiarity that since, unlike other dispositions, the situations to which their actions are appropriate are later in time than the actions themselves, manifestations of preparedness-dispositions can be rendered pointless, can be 'disappointed', in a way which is not possible for manifestations of other dispositions. There is a point in running to the station to catch a train even if you miss it, but no point at all if there is no train there to miss.

What I have described in terms of preparedness-dispositions is what, on the cognitive level (or in cognitive language, if one does not wish to admit a separate cognitive level), is described in terms of beliefs in general propositions which give rise to predictions that may turn out to be false. A course of action is a manifestation of a preparedness-disposition if the agent acts when a B-like event has occurred *as if* he believes that every B-like event is followed by a C-like event, his action being disappointed (as I have used this word) corresponding to a prediction based upon this belief being found to be false. In metaphorical language, the man is acting in reliance upon Nature living up to his expectations: if Nature lets him down, he is thwarted in a quite specific way.

Man, perhaps alone among the animals, can acquire second-order behaviour-dispositions enabling him, under certain circumstances, to exercise deliberate control over his first-order behaviour-dispositions. He has, within limits, powers both to acquire new first-order dispositions and to disacquire old ones: he has, within limits, liberty of choice as to what first-order dispositions he shall choose to have. Unless these choices are made arbitrarily, they will be made in accordance with some principle or policy.

It is here that evaluative notions enter. For a man, even if he always tries, will not always succeed in bringing his first-order dispositions, and consequently his behaviour, into line with his chosen policy. So we distinguish, with regard to any particular policy, between those dispositions which are in line with the policy and those which are not, calling the former by such adjectives as 'right' or 'rational' or 'good', and the latter by such adjectives as 'wrong' or 'irrational' or 'bad'. Since we are now concerned with what is in common in evaluating any disposition, the epithets 'valid' and 'invalid' will be employed as being the most neutral between ethics and logic. A policy will therefore be said to validate or to invalidate certain behaviour-dispositions; and to have that second-order disposition which consists in following the policy successfully will be to acquire (or to retain) behaviour-dispositions validated by the policy, and to disacquire (or to refrain from acquiring) behaviour-dispositions invalidated by the policy.

I have expressed myself in terms of a liberty of choice, within limits, because that is how the practical moral and logical problems present themselves to us *qua* would-be-moral-but-not-too-moral agents and *qua* would-be-rational-but-not-too-rational thinkers. But freedom to choose, and temptations to choose invalidly, are in fact irrelevant to the comparison of different sorts of validation. Even if no one ever made mistakes in arithmetic, it would be significant to say that no mistakes in arithmetic were made. And if all our wills were Kantian 'holy wills' and all our scientists were 'holy scientists', there would still be maxims in ethics and in inductive reasoning, though no categorical imperatives would be required to enforce obedience.

Positive policies which validate or negative policies which invalidate preparedness-dispositions will be called predictive policies: positive or negative policies which validate or invalidate other dispositions, or the non-preparedness parts of complex dispositions, will be called non-predictive policies. The problems of the former translated into the language of beliefs fall into the traditional province of inductive logic and scientific methodology: problems of the latter, also frequently treated in terms of beliefs, fall within the domain of traditional ethics.

The first and principal thesis maintained in this lecture is, then, that, if we think of the problems of inductive logic and of ethics in terms of how we would or might act in the future, the problems present a remarkable similarity in that the whole conceptual apparatus of policies validating or invalidating behaviour-dispositions is applicable to both.[4] To go on to discuss, as I wish to do, the justification for the selection of those policies which are to be adopted requires a summary account of the main features of the two different types.

[4] Among contemporary philosophers John Dewey has been the most vigorous in combating the separation of moral from scientific knowledge. But Dewey has tried to effect the integration by emphasizing the predictive function of moral judgements, which is exactly that feature of scientific judgements which I take moral judgements to lack.

Let us take predictive policies first. Though there are many derivative negative predictive policies (e.g. that invalidating all those preparedness-dispositions corresponding to hypotheses which the consensus of opinion of a certain group of scientists—or of a certain group of theologians—holds to be untenable), there is only one fundamental negative predictive policy, namely, that which treats as invalid any preparedness-disposition a manifestation of which is disappointed (in my sense of this word). This policy with respect to behaviour-dispositions corresponds to the policy with respect to beliefs in general propositions of rejecting all those beliefs which give rise to false predictions. This latter policy is so much part of our pattern of culture that it has been incorporated into the semantics of the language in which we express our general beliefs. What we mean to assert by saying that all swans are white is exactly that proposition [5] which is falsified if any swan is observed not to be white. The behavioural policy of rejecting preparedness-dispositions which yield disappointments is thus the foundation of the way in which falsity is attributed to general empirical statements. Without it our empirical beliefs would be isolated from our preparedness-behaviour.

There are many positive predictive policies used by scientists and discussed by inductive logicians, and they are not easily classifiable as species of one genus. But they all have one feature which they share in common with the unique negative predictive policy: they all have reference to previous experience. The policy corresponding to induction by simple enumeration is to treat any preparedness-disposition as validated, provided that it has been manifested in the past on many occasions and that none of these manifestations have been disappointed. The other predictive policies used—except those based upon authority which I am regarding as derivative—all involve similar provisos: in a more sophisticated policy the proviso may be in terms of the manifestations in the past of preparedness-dispositions other than those covered by the policy. The policy underlying Mill's methods, for example,

[5] To be strictly correct: the logically weakest proposition which....

validates a preparedness-disposition provided that alternative preparedness-dispositions have in the past yielded disappointment. This common feature of all predictive policies used by empirical thinkers corresponds to the inductive logicians' requirement that empirical hypotheses, to be in any way acceptable, must be supported by experience: predictive policies with this feature will therefore be called 'inductive policies'.

The different positive inductive policies correspond to the different inductive methods discussed in books on inductive logic and on scientific methodology: thus there are inductive policies corresponding to induction by simple enumeration, to Mill's methods for eliminating alternative hypotheses, and to the hypothetico-deductive method of subsuming the hypotheses in question under higher-level hypotheses in a scientific system. Each positive policy has its own criterion for validating preparedness-dispositions; or, to speak more exactly, the criterion *is* the policy. The criterion may be a vague one, so that it is uncertain whether or not it validates a particular preparedness-disposition: no defender of induction by simple enumeration has ever been able to say exactly how many instances justify accepting the inductive conclusion. And different criteria may disagree, so that what is validated by the one is not validated by the other. If the preparedness-disposition validated by the one is incompatible with the preparedness-disposition validated by the other, there will be a conflict of policies analogous to a moral conflict of duties. In such cases Aristotle's ἐν τῇ αἰσθήσει ἡ κρίσις ('the decision rests with perception') is as true for scientific as for moral decisions: where inductive policies conflict there is nothing in the last resort but the good sense of the scientist.

To turn now to non-predictive policies. The behaviour-dispositions which they cover are dispositions not covered by predictive policies: they are dispositions called into play by certain circumstances and resulting in courses of action which are not essentially activities of preparedness. Like the predictive policies, these non-predictive policies are to be regarded as validating the behaviour-dispositions they cover: since this validation is a concern of ethics rather than of logic, all non-predictive policies will, for convenience, be called 'moral'. Examples of such moral policies are the policies of fulfilling promises, of repairing injuries done by the agent, of conferring benefits upon those who have benefited the agent—indeed all the policies corresponding to the special obligations which Sir David Ross includes among his '*prima facie* duties'.[6] In all these cases the evaluative criterion applied in the first instance to justify a behaviour-disposition is that the disposition falls under one of these principles. If I happen to remark, 'I shall post this book to Mr. Smith on 28 February', or, 'I shall post this book to Mr. Smith when I have finished reading it' and am asked why I intend to do so, I shall reply, 'Because I promised him I would'; and to give this answer is to justify my intended action as being one which falls under the policy of promise-keeping.

It is interesting to notice that these policies of special obligation, besides covering the behaviour-dispositions which fall under them in a similar way to that in which inductive policies cover beliefs and preparedness-dispositions, have another feature in common with inductive policies, namely, that they all have reference to previous experience. Indeed, policies of special obligation all refer to some particular event or events in the previous experience of the agent. The promise-keeping policy validates the behaviour-dispositions involved in keeping the promise, provided that the agent made the promise. The reparation policy validates the behaviour-dispositions of repairing the injury, provided that the agent did the injury. And so on. Ross calls such duties 'special obligations' because each of them is an obligation not towards all men in general, but towards a special sub-class of men. This sub-class is picked out as consisting of those in a special relationship with the agent, the special relationship having been produced in the past by an action-and-reaction between members of this sub-class and the agent of which the agent is aware in settling his behaviour-dispositions.

[6] W. D. Ross, *The Right and the Good* (1930), chap. ii.

Policies of special obligation then have, like inductive policies, essential reference to known facts about the past. But not all moral policies are of this type. The policies which correspond to Ross's *prima facie* duties of general obligation cannot easily be considered as dependent upon previous experience. It is unplausible to suppose, for example, either that my policy of beneficence is a policy of gratitude for benefits known to have been conferred upon me by humanity at large, or that it arises from an implicit contract between myself and all other men to follow the golden rule in regard to them in consideration of their doing likewise in regard to me. Duties of special obligation, however, have received particular attention from moral philosophers in recent years, for the reason that they do not fit easily into a teleological ethic; and it is therefore noteworthy that they have a resemblance to inductive policies over and above the fact that all these policies, predictive or moral, work in the same way by validating, rationally or morally, the behaviour-dispositions which they cover.

The doctrine here presented is in terms of policies, inductive and moral, validating or invalidating behaviour-dispositions. This way of introducing evaluative concepts will not permit us to say that any particular behaviour-disposition is valid *per se*, but only that it is validated by, or valid in accordance with, some particular policy. The notion of validity is thus essentially relative to the validating policy. Many contemporary philosophers are prepared to stop at this point. The distinction between the world of fact and the world of value—between what will be and what should be—is sufficiently preserved, they say, in the distinction between behaviour-dispositions stating what a man will do under certain circumstances and the policies according to which his behaviour-dispositions should be adjusted. And they may go on to say, with Professor Felix Kaufmann,[7] that to act and to judge rightly means simply to act or to judge in accordance with recognized norms of conduct or of scientific procedure, so that the proposition that

---

[7] *Methodology of the Social Sciences* (1944), chap. ix.

a behaviour-disposition validated by a recognized policy is right or is rational is always an analytic proposition. But even if this were an adequate account of the current use of the words 'right' and 'rational' (and it seems to me a very inadequate account), the question, 'Why should such-and-such a policy be pursued?' remains a significant question, not to be answered by saying merely, 'Because it is a policy'. We have every right to ask for a reason for choosing one policy from among many possible alternatives and for trying to pursue the policy chosen. It is not as if we were not frequently confronted with incompatible policies, as in cases of conflicts of duties, or of inductive methods between which we have to choose, nor that we are not infrequently tempted to avoid regulating our conduct or our beliefs in accordance with the policies which we have chosen. (And most of us are tempted to 'wishful thinking' quite as much as to unprincipled action.) The advice, 'Choose what policies you like and do and think what you like: only don't *call* your actions "right" or your beliefs "rational" unless they accord with the policies you have chosen' is, frankly, not good enough for those of us who have eaten of the forbidden tree. We properly ask for a justification—a second-order justification —of the policies we use to give a first-order justification to our actions and thoughts.

Here I am wholeheartedly with the teleological moralists. The question, 'Why adopt a particular policy?' is a teleological question demanding the statement of an end to the attainment of which the policy is a means. The only other interpretation which I can give to this question is the causal one— 'What causes the adoption of the policy?'—and this does not answer the moral question, though answers to it may be relevant to apportionment of praise or of blame. That the justification of policies lies in reference to the ends which they subserve is the second thesis to be maintained in this lecture.

The objection that has always been felt to teleological systems of ethics—to utilitarianism, whether hedonistic or agathistic—is that it is just not the case that we always evaluate our particular actions by reference to the values of their actual or probable consequences. It is most unplausible to have to justify my obedience to a generally advantageous moral law by saying that the indirect evil effects which would be produced by my bad example if I disobeyed the law would be worse than the direct good effects of the disobedient action. I cannot believe that, except in quite exceptional circumstances, my example would have the demoralizing effects which utilitarians have to attribute to it. These objections, however, do not hold against a view which makes the primary justification for an action that it is in accordance with a moral policy but secondarily justifies that policy by teleological considerations. This point may be elucidated by considering its parallel in the inductive case.

The justification of inductive policies put forward by logicians of the Peircean school is that they are means to the end of making true predictions. Some, like Mr. William Kneale,[8] would say that induction is the only way, or at least the only systematic way, by which we can attempt to attain this end. But there are predictive policies which are not inductive policies; e.g. the policy, attacked by Bacon, of deducing the future from metaphysical premisses, or the policy of trusting a soothsayer's predictions without any evidence of his past success as a prophet. What it is true to say is that no predictive policy which is not an inductive policy has been found to be *reliable* in making predictions. This, however, is a negative remark. The Peircean justification for a particular inductive policy must be that the policy itself is, on the whole, predictively reliable. Different inductive policies differ widely in their reliability: it is for this reason that, while taking over Kneale's useful word 'policy', I have usually put it into the plural.

What is meant by saying of a particular inductive policy that it is predictively reliable? Peirce at one time gave as a criterion of reliability that predictions obtained by following the policy

[8] *Probability and Induction* (1949), 234, 235, 259.

turned out 'for the most part' to be true.[9] As a historic proposition about the predictions given by following any particular inductive policy in the past this is highly doubtful: we have not got enough evidence of the relative number of disappointed and of non-disappointed preparedness-actions that have taken place. But Peirce's criterion is unnecessarily narrow; it is surely a sufficient justification of an inductive policy that it *frequently* gives rise to true predictions. Since no predictive policy which is not an inductive policy does this, there is no way of successfully pursuing our aim of predicting the future except by employing some inductive policy. Much less than half a loaf is a great deal better than no bread.

The rational justification for holding a particular general belief or for having a particular preparedness-disposition is thus given in two stages: firstly, that the belief or the disposition is in accordance with a particular inductive policy; and, secondly, that following this policy frequently leads to true predictions or to preparedness-actions which are not disappointed. The rationality of the belief does not depend upon the belief itself being a means towards the end of predicting truth, but consists in the fact that the inductive policy covering it is, frequently, a means to this end.

Peirce's justification of induction stops at this point—at subserving the end of foretelling the truth or its behavioural counterpart. The moralist may, however, question whether foretelling the truth is an ultimate end, and may ask what is the good of being able to predict the future. This is a perfectly proper question, and one not difficult properly to answer. For those who hold that knowledge is an end in itself, and thus think the question superfluous, will willingly admit that knowledge is also a means, and indeed the only possible means, to almost every other end. Any purposive activity directed towards attaining a goal through a causal chain involving intermediate steps requires the predictive beliefs that one step will

---

[9] *Collected Papers of Charles Sanders Peirce*, vol. ii (1932), 2.649 (1878), 2.693 (1878). In his later life Peirce put forward a different justification of inductive method—that it is self-corrective: see 2.781 (1902), 2.769 (1905).

follow another in this chain and that the goal will follow the penultimate step. Even a goal-directed activity which is not consciously purposive but which proceeds by way of intermediate steps involves preparedness-dispositions to do the next appropriate action when the intermediate goal has been attained. To follow some predictive policy is therefore necessary in order to be able to follow any policy whatever which covers a goal-directed activity. And unless we choose the best predictive policy open to us (and this will be some inductive policy), we shall not pursue our goals as effectively as we might.

It is a platitude that science is equally necessary for the pursuit of good and of evil ends. Inductive policies, for those who do not accept knowledge as an end in itself, may be justified by their service to every end-pursuing moral policy. Since such use of inductive policies is, as mathematicians would say, 'invariant' with respect to all end-pursuing moral policies, this justification does not depend upon a choice of the moral policy to be served by the inductive policies. Similarly, in political philosophy, those who would agree in holding a public policy of liberty, expressed in some such formula as the Four Freedoms of the Atlantic Charter, to be an essential means to the furtherance of most private ends, would defend this policy by asserting its invariance with respect to many other moral policies. The peculiarity of inductive policies is their invariance with respect to every policy which pursues ends indirectly: it is this peculiarity, rather than the virtue of knowledge for its own sake, which gives a relative autonomy to the justification of induction and a relative ethical neutrality to scientific thought.

There is, however, one type of inductive thinking where it is difficult to preserve even this relative autonomy, namely, inductive inference in which the conclusion from the evidence is not a universal hypothesis stating that all B's are C's or that no B's are C's, but a statistical hypothesis stating that a certain proportion between 0 per cent. and 100 per cent. of the B's are C's. Such a statistical law is not proved to be false, in the sense of deductive logic, if future experience yields, and continues to yield, observed proportions of B's that are C's widely different from the proportions asserted by the law. The statistical law that, by and large, the proportion of pennies thrown which fall heads is 50 per cent. is not logically refuted by no heads ever turning up or by no tails ever turning up or by our finding any ratio whatever of heads to tails in any set of throws which we can observe. So the simple negative inductive policy applicable to universal hypotheses—of rejecting those which are contrary to experience—cannot be applied to statistical hypotheses, since, strictly speaking, no such hypothesis is empirically refutable. Instead statistical mathematicians have had to work out sophisticated negative policies all of which depend upon arbitrary factors which have to be chosen by an Aristotelian αἰσθήσις in each case. The negative policy most widely used is that of agreeing to reject a statistical hypothesis if the proportion of B's that are C's in a set of observations differ so widely from the proportion asserted by the hypothesis that the number of possible sets of observations differing at least as widely would, if the hypothesis were true, be less than some small fraction (e.g. 1/20th or 1/100th or 1/1,000th) of the total number of possible sets. The deviation from the asserted proportion which satisfies this condition can be deduced from the hypothesis; if the deviation in a set of observations is greater than this, the policy requires that the hypothesis should be rejected—not because the set of observations are logically incompatible with the truth of the hypothesis, but because, were the hypothesis to be true, it would be very unlikely that a set of observations deviating so widely would have occurred. But what is to fix this degree of unlikelihood? Should it be 1/20th or 1/100th or 1/1,000th? This cannot be decided by considerations falling solely within inductive logic. Imagine the case of a hypothesis which is such that, if it were true, it could be used to develop a treatment for a disease for which no other treatment was known. It would then be justifiable to employ a very small fraction for fixing what the statisticians call the 'size' of the 'critical region', and to reject the hypothesis only if the observations would be very unlikely indeed were the hypothesis to be true. If less were at stake, it might well be preferable to choose a larger critical region, and to reject a hypothesis if the observations would have only a moderate degree of unlikelihood were the hypothesis to be true. Thus the importance of the use to which a statistical hypothesis can be put is highly relevant to the decision as to whether or not the hypothesis is to be rejected on given evidence.[10]

The irruption of ethics into inductive logic is even more striking when there are alternative statistical hypotheses in the field, and we have to select the best of them on the basis of the observed evidence. The general theory of policies for such selection has recently been developed by Professor Abraham Wald,[11] who has shown that a prerequisite for choosing any satisfactory general selection policy is a previous assignment of values to the losses we should sustain should we fail to reject a hypothesis which in fact is false. Without such an assignment there is no good reason for accepting one statistical hypothesis rather than another; but, given such an assignment, there is a policy which has a unique property not depending upon any arbitrary factor, namely, that of selecting among the hypotheses in such a way that we stand to lose least if the selected hypothesis is false. Somewhat surprisingly Wald's result is mathematically equivalent to a theorem which occurs in Professors von Neumann and Morgenstern's Theory of Games;[12] so Wald is able to express his theory metaphorically in terms of the scientist pitting his wits in a game against Nature as opponent. The safest strategy for playing a game is that which reduces to a minimum the maximum of the losses which your opponent can inflict upon you by any method of play open to him: the safest inductive policy for the scientist to

[10] Sinclair Lewis's novel *Martin Arrowsmith* (1925) draws a vivid picture of conflicts between intellectual and moral aims in the practical application of bacteriology.

[11] *Annals of Mathematical Statistics*, x (1939), 299; xviii (1947), 549; xx (1949), 165; *Annals of Mathematics*, xlvi (1945), 265; *Econometrica*, xv (1947), 279; *On the Principles of Statistical Inference* (1942), chap. vi.

[12] John von Neumann and Oskar Morgenstern, *Theory of Games and Economic Behavior* (1944), chap. iii.

adopt is that which minimizes the maximum of the losses which Nature can inflict upon him by behaving in any way whatever. Just as the game player cannot settle his safest strategy without knowing the stakes in the game, so the scientist cannot decide his safest inductive policy without knowing what he stands to gain or lose by the different ways in which Nature may behave. There are, it is true, special simple cases in which the choice of the inductive policy, like that of the strategy of play, does not depend upon the amounts at stake; but even in these special cases the stakes are relevant if we are interested in choosing a policy for selecting hypotheses which, if not exactly true, approximate to the truth. For the amount we should lose by a bad approximation affects the degree of approximateness to the truth with which we shall be satisfied.

Utilitarian moralists have been compelled to bring considerations of probability into ethics in order to avoid the unplausibility of making what a man ought to do depend upon an unknown future. The most plausible form of utilitarianism, therefore, determines the rightness of an action by its probable, and not by its actual, consequences. Scientifically rational beliefs are thus indispensable to moral decisions: we cannot be good, or at least deliberately good, without being wise. The modern principles of statistical inference show that, vice versa, judgements of value are, in the last analysis, inextricably involved in choosing the best way to obtain scientific knowledge: we cannot be wise without making judgements of good and of evil.

The inductive policy of choosing a hypothesis so as to minimize the maximum loss presupposes a method of assigning numbers to gains and losses which raises all the well-known difficulties involved in the notion of a hedonistic or eudaemonistic calculus. One method would be to measure the gains or losses in monetary or other economically measurable terms; and this method is clearly appropriate when the hypothesis in question is that a certain industrial process is turning out goods of a certain standard quality where the firm of manufacturers will suffer a definite monetary loss if the goods are not up to standard. If an economic measurement of gains and losses is used, the pure theory of statistical inference becomes part of pure economics, and its applicability will depend upon the extent to which scientists are prepared to limit themselves to being 'economic men'. It may well be argued, however, that it is a necessary condition for life in a complex community which practises division of labour for most people to approximate to economic men for most of the time. If this be so, inductive policies can be justified as means to maximize economic 'utilities', the economic policy of maximizing utilities being justified by its necessity for social co-operation.

Such social necessity may also be cited as a second-order justification for many of the moral policies which correspond to Ross's *prima facie* obligations. Society as we know it could not exist if we did not speak the truth and fulfil our promises and repair our injuries and refrain from injuring others, or at least unless we accepted the policies of so doing and outweighed our weaknesses of will with legal sanctions.

The perfectly proper question as to why a particular moral or inductive policy should be adopted may therefore in many cases be properly answered by mentioning ends which the adoption of the policy would subserve. Many moral and economic policies subserve social ends directly: inductive policies, to the extent that they are independent of evaluative judgements, subserve the end of predicting the future which itself subserves the end of enabling us to pursue a goal deliberately by indirect means, which itself is of indispensable social utility. But, while I shall have displeased the positivist extremists by proposing any justification whatever for the policies I intend to adopt (except that they will be those current in the 'culture circle' unto which it shall please God to call me), my partial teleology will not have satisfied the absolutists. They will ask what guarantees the value of the ends—social co-operation, knowledge of the laws of Nature, ability to seek a goal by devious means—which I have cited to guarantee my policies. *Quis custodiet custodes ipsos?*

It is tempting to produce an infinitely ascending series of guardians, the integrity of each being guaranteed by the one next higher in the series, and to reply to the demand for a last term in the series with the rejoinder that we ask for no last term in the ascending hierarchy of hypotheses forming a scientific system. We explain the moon's revolution round the earth by subsuming it (together with other phenomena) under Newton's law of gravitation; we explain this law by subsuming it (together with other laws) under Einstein's General Theory of Relativity; we may be able in the future to subsume this (together perhaps with the laws of quantum physics) under some still more general explanation; but we can never produce an ultimate explanation: indeed, it is a nonsense-question to ask for one. So may we not similarly justify pursuit of end A by subsuming it (together with other ends) under a wider end B, justify pursuit of end B by subsuming it (together with other ends) under a still wider end Γ, and so on; but decline to ask for an ultimate end Ω under which all lesser ends may be subsumed? But, alas, there is a logical difference between the two hierarchies: in ascending the scientific hierarchy the propositions become stronger and stronger so that we are saying more and more; in ascending the hierarchy of ends the propositions become weaker and weaker so that we are saying less and less. This arises from the fact that, whereas a lower-level scientific law is a logical consequence of its higher-level explanation, conversely pursuit of a wider end B is a logical consequence of pursuit of a narrower end A (together with the fact that A is subsumed under B, i.e. that all pursuits of A are also pursuits of B). So as we ascend the hierarchy the ends decrease in content and lose all definite outline. This accounts for the peculiar elusiveness that many of us find in concepts which the great moral philosophers have proposed as ultimate ends—Aristotle's $\varepsilon\dot{v}\delta\alpha\iota\mu o\nu\iota\alpha$ or Mill's 'happiness', for example. It is easy to give positive or negative instances of these; but the concepts themselves seem inscrutable—almost as inscrutable as the indefinable 'goodness' of *Principia Ethica*. The reason would seem to be that, in order to justify all lesser goods, they have to be so comprehensive as to lose all cognitive content. An ascending series of ends each of which is a necessary condition for its *predecessors* in the series soon fades into ineluctable obscurity.

Many non-ultimate ends, however, have the opposite property of being necessary conditions for their *successors* in any ascending series of ends which we can imagine. This invariance with respect to further ends has already been remarked upon in several important cases.[13] Thus I find it difficult to conceive of any end to which scientific knowledge is not an essential means. And I cannot easily think of many ends which do not require social co-operation for their attainment. The right line for an empirical moralist to take is surely not to deny that the ends which he pursues require a justification, but to assert boldly that they will stand up to any justification whatsoever.[14] In the past the empiricist has often been cross-examined by a Socrates demanding an ultimate justification for the empiricist's limited aims. Let him instead take on the role of examiner, and demand of his critic whether his own *summum bonum* (whatever it may be) can be sought in any way except by pursuing the modest aims which the empiricist sets before himself. If the answer is in the negative, the empiricist and the absolutist will be in agreement upon the policies which, as moralists, they should advocate, the only difference between them being that the absolutist will justify these common principles by their subservience to an ultimate end, the empiricist by reference to their invariance as means towards any further end. And the empiricist, if he wishes, may perfectly well use traditional teleological language, and speak of pursuing εὐδαιμονία or of pursuing *happiness*, using these abstract nouns not to denote unique but nebulous concepts but, in a way in which both Aristotle

[13] Invariance is an essential characteristic of Stevenson's 'focal aims' (*Ethics and Language*, 179, 189, 203, 329). I have not used Stevenson's term because he introduces it in the context of a conflation of means with ends to which I cannot altogether subscribe.

[14] Even G. E. Moore, for all his insistence that the question of the goodness of means is secondary to that of the goodness of the ends subserved, is willing to admit that 'rules [which] can be recommended as a means to that which is itself only a necessary condition for the existence of any great good can be defended independently of correct views upon the primary ethical question of what is good in itself' (*Principia Ethica* (1903), 158).

and Mill seem frequently to have used them, as collective names for the Kingdom of all final Ends.

In this Kingdom are many mansions. It is more reasonable to seek to enter this Kingdom by the only known modes of entry than to postpone the attempt until assured as to which, if any, of the mansions is the ultimate end of the quest.

IFS AND CANS

BY J. L. AUSTIN

Are *cans* constitutionally iffy? Whenever, that is, we say that we can do something, or could do something, or could have done something, is there an *if* in the offing—suppressed, it may be, but due nevertheless to appear when we set out our sentence in full or when we give an explanation of its meaning?

Again, if and when there *is* an *if*-clause appended to a main clause which contains a *can* or *could* or *could have*, what sort of an *if* is it? What is the meaning of the *if*, or what is the effect or the point of combining this *if*-clause with the main clause?

These are large questions, to which philosophers, among them some whom I most respect, have given small answers: and it is two such answers, given recently by English philosophers, that I propose to consider. Both, I believe, are mistaken, yet something is to be learned from examining them. In philosophy, there are many mistakes that it is no disgrace to have made: to make a first-water, ground-floor mistake, so far from being easy, takes one (*one*) form of philosophical genius.[1]

Many of you will have read a short but justly admired book written by Professor G. E. Moore of Cambridge, which is called simply *Ethics*. In it, there is a point where Moore, who is engaged in discussing Right and Wrong, says that if we are to discuss whether any act that has been done was right or wrong then we are bound to discuss what the person concerned *could have* done instead of what he did in fact do. And this, he thinks, may lead to an entanglement in the problem, so-called, of Free Will: because, though few would deny, at least expressly, that a man could have done something other than what he did actually do *if he had chosen*, many people would

[1] Plato, Descartes, and Leibniz all had this form of genius, besides of course others.

deny that he *could* (absolutely) have done any such other thing. Hence Moore is led to ask whether it is ever true, and if so in what sense, that a man could have done something other than what he did actually do. And it is with his answer to this question, not with its bearings upon the meanings of *right* and *wrong* or upon the problem of Free Will, that we are concerned.

With his usual shrewdness Moore begins by insisting that there is at least *one* proper sense in which we can say that a man can do something he doesn't do or could have done something he didn't do—even though there may perhaps be *other* senses of *can* and *could have* in which we cannot say such things. This sense he illustrates by the sentence 'I could have walked a mile in 20 minutes this morning, but I certainly could not have run two miles in 5 minutes': we are to take it that in fact the speaker did not do either of the two things mentioned, but this in no way hinders us from drawing the very common and necessary distinction between undone acts that we could have done and undone acts that we could not have done. So it is certain that, at least in *some* sense, we often could have done things that we did not actually do.

Why then, Moore goes on to ask, should anyone try to deny this? And he replies that people do so (we may call them 'determinists') because they hold that everything that happens has a *cause* which precedes it, which is to say that once the cause has occurred the thing itself is *bound* to occur and *nothing* else *could* ever have happened instead.

However, on examining further the 20-minute-mile example, Moore argues that there is much reason to think that 'could have' in such cases simply means 'could have *if* I had chosen', or, as perhaps we had better say in order to avoid a possible complication (these are Moore's words), simply means '*should* have if I had chosen'. And if this *is* all it means, then there is after all no conflict between our conviction that we often could have, in this sense, done things that we did not actually do and the determinist's theory: for he certainly holds himself that I often, and perhaps even always, should have done something different from what I did do *if I had chosen* to do that different thing, since my choosing differently would constitute a change in the causal antecedents of my subsequent act, which would therefore, on his theory, naturally itself be different. If, therefore, the determinist nevertheless asserts that in *some* sense of 'could have' I could *not* ever have done anything different from what I did actually do, this must simply be a second sense[2] of 'could have' different from that which it has in the 20-minute-mile example.

In the remainder of his chapter, Moore argues that quite possibly his first sense of 'could have', in which it simply means 'could or should have if I had chosen', is all we need to satisfy our hankerings after Free Will, or at least is so if conjoined in some way with yet a third sense of 'could have' in which sense 'I could have done something different' means 'I might, for all anyone could know for certain beforehand, have done something different'. This third kind of 'could have' might, I think, be held to be a vulgarism, 'could' being used incorrectly for 'might': but in any case we shall not be concerned with it here.

In the upshot, then, Moore leaves us with only one important sense in which it can be said that I could have done something that I did not do: he is not convinced that any other sense is necessary, nor has he any clear idea what such another sense would be: and he is convinced that, on his interpretation of 'could have', even the determinist can, and indeed must, say that I could very often have done things I did not do. To summarize his suggestions (he does not put them forward with complete conviction) once again:

1. 'Could have' simply means 'could have if I had chosen'.
2. For 'could have if I had chosen' we may substitute 'should have if I had chosen'.
3. The *if* clauses in these expressions state the causal conditions upon which it would have followed that I could or should have done the thing different from what I did actually do.

[2] About which Moore has no more to tell us.

Moore does not state this third point expressly himself: but it seems clear, in view of the connexions he alleges between his interpretation of 'could have' and the determinist theory, that he did believe it, presumably taking it as obvious.

There are then three questions to be asked:

1. Does 'could have if I had chosen' mean the same, in general or ever, as 'should have if I had chosen?'
2. In either of these expressions, is the *if* the *if* of causal condition?
3. In sentences having *can* or *could have* as main verb, are we required or entitled always to supply an *if*-clause, and in particular the clause 'if I had chosen'?

It appears to me that the answer in each case is No.

1. Anyone, surely, would admit that in general *could* is very different indeed from *should* or *would*.[3] What a man *could* do is not at all the same as what he *would* do: perhaps he could shoot you if you were within range, but that is not in the least to say that he would. And it seems clear to me, in our present example, that 'I could have run a mile if I had chosen' and 'I should have run a mile if I had chosen' mean quite different things, though unfortunately it is not so clear exactly what either of them, especially the latter, does mean. 'I should have run a mile in 20 minutes this morning if I had chosen' seems to me an unusual, not to say queer, specimen of English: but if I had to interpret it, I should take it to mean the same as 'If I had chosen to run a mile in 20 minutes this morning, I should (jolly well) have done so', that is, it would be an assertion of my strength of character, in that I put my decisions into execution (an assertion which is, however, more naturally made, as I have now made it, with the *if*-clause preceding the main clause). I should certainly not myself understand it to mean that if I had made a certain choice my making that choice would have

---

[3] Since Moore has couched his example in the first person, he uses 'should' in the apodosis: but of course in the third person, everyone would use 'would'. For brevity, I shall in what follows generally use 'should' to do duty for both persons.

caused me to do something. But in whichever of these ways we understand it, it is quite different from 'I *could* have walked a mile in 20 minutes this morning if I had chosen', which surely says something rather about my opportunities or powers. Moore, unfortunately, does not explain why he thinks we are entitled to make this all-important transition from 'could' to 'should', beyond saying that by doing so we 'avoid a possible complication'. Later I shall make some suggestions which may in part explain why he was tempted to make the transition: but nothing can justify it.

2. Moore, as I pointed out above, did not discuss what sort of *if* it is that we have in 'I can if I choose' or in 'I could have if I had chosen' or in 'I should have if I had chosen'. Generally, philosophers, as also grammarians, have a favourite, if somewhat blurred and diffuse, idea of an *if*-clause as a 'conditional' clause: putting our example schematically as 'If p, then q', then it will be said that q follows from p, typically either in the sense that p *entails* q or in the sense that p is a *cause* of q, though other important variations are possible. And it seems to be on these lines that Moore is thinking of the *if* in 'I can if I choose'. But now, it is characteristic of this general sort of *if*, that from 'If p then q' we *can* draw the inference 'If not q, then not p', whereas we can *not* infer either 'Whether or not p, then q' or 'q' simpliciter. For example, from 'If I run, I pant' we *can* infer 'If I do not pant, I do not run' (or, as we should rather say, 'If I am not panting, I am not running'), whereas we can *not* infer either 'I pant, whether I run or not' or 'I pant' (at least in the sense of 'I am panting'). If, to avoid these troubles with the English tenses, which are unfortunately prevalent but are not allowed to matter, we put the example in the past tense, then from 'If I ran, I panted' it *does* follow that 'If I did not pant, I did not run', but it does *not* follow either that 'I panted whether or not I ran' or that 'I panted' period. These possibilities and impossibilities of inference are typical of the *if* of causal condition: but they are precisely reversed in the case of 'I can if I choose' or 'I could have if I had chosen'. For from these we should not draw the curious inferences that 'If I

cannot, I do not choose to' or that 'If I could not have, I had not chosen to' (or 'did not choose to'), whatever these sentences may be supposed to mean. But on the contrary, from 'I can if I choose' we certainly should infer that 'I can, whether I choose to or not' and indeed that 'I can' period: and from 'I could have if I had chosen' we should similarly infer that 'I could have, whether I chose to or not' and that anyway 'I could have' period. So that, whatever this *if* means, it is evidently not the *if* of causal condition.

This becomes even clearer when we observe that it is quite common *elsewhere* to find an ordinary causal conditional *if* in connexion with a *can*, and that then there is no doubt about it, as for example in the sentence 'I can squeeze through if I am thin enough', which *does* imply that 'If I cannot squeeze through I am not thin enough', and of course does *not* imply that 'I can squeeze through'. 'I can if I choose' is precisely different from this.

Nor does *can* have to be a very special and peculiar verb for *if*s which are not causal conditional to be found in connexion with it: all kinds of *if*s are found with all kinds of verbs. Consider for example the *if* in 'There are biscuits on the sideboard if you want them', where the verb is the highly ordinary *are*, but the *if* is more like that in 'I can if I choose' than that in 'I panted if I ran': for we can certainly infer from it that 'There are biscuits on the sideboard whether you want them or not' and that anyway 'There are biscuits on the sideboard', whereas it would be folly to infer that 'If there are no biscuits on the sideboard you do not want them', or to understand the meaning to be that you have only to want biscuits to cause them to be on the sideboard.

The *if*, then, in 'I can if I choose' is not the causal conditional *if*. What of the *if* in 'I shall if I choose'? At first glance, we see that this is quite different (one more reason for refusing to substitute *shall* for *can* or *should have* for *could have*). For from 'I shall if I choose' we clearly cannot infer that 'I shall whether I choose to or not' or simply that 'I shall'. But on the other hand, can we infer, either, that 'If I shan't I don't choose to'?

(Or should it be rather 'If I don't I don't choose to'?) I think not, as we shall see: but even if some such inference can be drawn, it would still be patently wrong to conclude that the meaning of 'I shall if I choose' is that my choosing to do the thing is sufficient to cause me inevitably to do it or has as a consequence that I shall do it, which, unless I am mistaken, is what Moore was supposing it to mean. This may be seen if we compare 'I shall ruin him if I choose' with 'I shall ruin him if I am extravagant'. The latter sentence does indeed obviously state what would be the consequence of the fulfilment of a condition specified in the *if*-clause—but then, the first sentence has clearly different characteristics from the second. In the first, it makes good sense in general to stress the 'shall', but in the second it does not.[4] This is a symptom of the fact that in the first sentence 'I shall' is the present of that mysterious old verb *shall*, whereas in the second 'shall' is simply being used as an auxiliary, without any meaning of its own, to form the future indicative of 'ruin'.

I expect you will be more than ready at this point to hear something a little more positive about the meanings of these curious expressions 'I can if I choose' and 'I shall if I choose'. Let us take the former first, and concentrate upon the *if*. The dictionary tells us that the words from which our *if* is descended expressed, or even meant, 'doubt' or 'hesitation' or 'condition' or 'stipulation'. Of these, 'condition' has been given a prodigious innings by grammarians, lexicographers, and philosophers alike: it is time for 'doubt' and 'hesitation' to be remembered, and these do indeed seem to be the notions present in 'I can if I choose'. We could give, on different occasions and in different contexts, many different interpretations of this sentence, which is of a somewhat primitive and *loose-jointed* type. Here are some:

I can, quaere do I choose to?
I can, but do I choose to?

[4] In general, though of course in some contexts it does: e.g. 'I may very easily ruin him, and I *shall* if I am extravagant', where 'shall' is stressed to point the contrast with 'may'.

I can, but perhaps I don't choose to
I can, but then I should have to choose to, and what about *that*?
I can, but would it really be reasonable to choose to?
I can, but whether I choose to is another question
I can, I have only to choose to
I can, in case I (should) choose to,
and so on.

These interpretations are not, of course, all the same: which it is that we mean will usually be clear from the context (otherwise we should prefer another expression), but sometimes it can be brought out by stress, on the 'if' or the 'choose' for example. What is common to them all is simply that the *assertion*, positive and complete, that 'I can', is linked to the *raising of the question* whether I choose to, which may be relevant in a variety of ways.[5]

*If*s of the kind I have been trying to describe are common enough, for example the *if* in our example 'There are biscuits on the sideboard if you want them'. I don't know whether you want biscuits or not, but in case you do, I point out that there are some on the sideboard. It is tempting, I know, to 'expand' our sentence here to this: 'There are biscuits on the sideboard *which you can* (*or may*) *take* if you want them': but this, legitimate or not, will not make much difference, for we are still left with 'can (or may) if you want', which is (here) just like 'can if you choose' or 'can if you like', so that the *if* is still the *if* of doubt or hesitation, not the *if* of condition.[6]

I will mention two further points, very briefly, about 'I can if I choose', important but not so relevant to our discussion here. Sometimes the *can* will be the *can*, and the choice the

---

[5] If there were space, we should consider other germane expressions: e.g. 'I can do it or not as I choose', 'I can do whichever I choose' (*quidlibet*). In particular, 'I can whether I choose to or not' means 'I can, but whether I choose to or not is an open question': it does *not* mean 'I can on condition that I choose and likewise on condition that I don't', which is absurd.

[6] An account on these lines should probably be given also of an excellent example given to me by Mr. P. T. Geach: 'I paid you back yesterday, if you remember.' This is much the same as 'I paid you back yesterday, don't you remember?' It does not mean that your now remembering that I did so is a condition, causal or other, of my having paid you back yesterday.

choice, of legal or other *right*, at other times these words will refer to practicability or feasibility: consequently, we should sometimes interpret our sentence in some such way as 'I am entitled to do it (if I choose)', and at other times in some such way as 'I am capable of doing it (if I choose)'. We, of course, are concerned with interpretations of this second kind. It would be nice if we always said 'I *may* if I choose' when we wished to refer to our rights, as perhaps our nannies once told us to: but the interlocking histories of *can* and *may* are far too chequered for there to be any such rule in practice.[7] The second point is that *choose* is an important word in its own right, and needs careful interpretation: 'I can if I like' is not the same, although the 'can' and the 'if' may be the same in both, as 'I can if I choose'. Choice is always between alternatives, that is between several courses to be weighed in the same scale against each other, the one to be *preferred*. 'You can vote whichever way you choose' is different from 'You can vote whichever way you like'.

And now for something about 'I *shall* if I choose'—what sort of *if* have we here? The point to notice is, that 'I shall' is not an assertion of *fact* but an expression of *intention*, verging towards the giving of some variety of undertaking: and the *if*, consequently, is the *if* not of condition but of *stipulation*. In sentences like:

I shall | marry him if I choose
I intend | to marry him if I choose
I promise | to marry him if he will have me

the *if*-clause is a part of the object phrase governed by the initial verb ('shall', 'intend', 'promise'), if this is an allowable way of putting it: or again, the *if* qualifies the *content* of the undertaking given, or of the intention announced, it does *not* qualify the giving of the undertaking. Why, we may ask, is it

[7] Formerly I believed that the meaning of 'I can if I choose' was something like 'I can, I have the choice', and that the point of the *if*-clause was to make clear that the 'can' in the main clause was the 'can' of right. This account, however, does not do justice to the role of the 'if', and also unduly restricts in general the meaning of 'choice'.

perverse to draw from 'I intend to marry him if I choose' the inference 'If I do not intend to marry him I do not choose to'? Because 'I intend to marry him if I choose' is not like 'I panted if I ran' in this important respect: 'I panted if I ran' does not assert anything 'categorically' about me—it does not assert that I did pant, and hence it is far from surprising to infer something beginning 'If I did not pant': but 'I intend to marry him if I choose' (and the same goes for 'I shall marry him if I choose') *is* a 'categorical' expression of intention, and hence it is paradoxical to make an inference leading off with 'If I do *not* intend'.

3. Our third question was as to when we are entitled or required to supply *if*-clauses with *can* or *could have* as main verb.

Here there is one thing to be clear about at the start. There are *two* quite distinct and incompatible views that may be put forward concerning *if*s and *can*s, which are fatally easy to confuse with each other. One view is that wherever we have *can* or *could have* as our main verb, an *if*-clause must always be understood or supplied, if it is not actually present, in order to complete the sense of the sentence. The other view is that the meaning of 'can' or 'could have' can be more clearly reproduced by *some other verb* (notably 'shall' or 'should have') with an *if*-clause appended to *it*. The first view is that an *if* is required to *complete* a *can*-sentence: the second view is that an *if* is required in the *analysis* of a *can*-sentence. The suggestion of Moore that 'could have' means 'could have if I had chosen' is a suggestion of the first kind: but the suggestion also made by Moore that it means 'should have if I had chosen' is a suggestion of the second kind. It may be because it is so easy (apparently) to confuse these two kinds of theory that Moore was tempted to talk as though 'should have' could mean the same as 'could have'.

Now we are concerned at this moment solely with the *first* sort of view, namely that *can*-sentences are not complete without an *if*-clause. And if we think, as Moore was for the most part thinking, about 'could have' (rather than 'can'), it is easy to see why it may be tempting to allege that it always requires an *if*-clause with it. For it is natural to construe 'could have' as a past subjunctive or 'conditional', which is practically as much as to say that it needs a *conditional* clause with it. And of course it is quite true that 'could have' *may* be, and very often is, a past conditional: but it is *also* true that 'could have' may be and often is the *past (definite) indicative* of the verb *can*. Sometimes 'I could have' is equivalent to the Latin 'Potui' and means 'I *was* in a position to': sometimes it is equivalent to the Latin 'Potuissem' and means 'I *should have been* in a position to'. Exactly similar is the double role of 'could', which is sometimes a conditional meaning 'should be able to', but also sometimes a past indicative (indefinite) meaning 'was able to': no one can doubt this if he considers such contrasted examples as 'I could do it 20 years ago' and 'I could do it if I had a thingummy'. It is not so much that 'could' or 'could have' is ambiguous, as rather that two parts of the verb *can* take the same shape.

Once it is realized that 'could have' can be a past indicative, the general temptation to supply *if*-clauses with it vanishes: at least there is no more temptation to supply them with 'could have' than with 'can'. If we ask how a Roman would have said 'I could have ruined you this morning (although I didn't)', it is clear that he would have used 'potui', and that his sentence is complete without any conditional clause. But more than this, if he had wished to add 'if I had chosen', and however he had expressed that in Latin, he would still not have changed his 'potui' to 'potuissem': but this is precisely what he *would* have done if he had been tacking on some other, more 'normal' kind of *if*-clause, such as 'if I had had one more vote'.[8]

That is to say, the 'could have' in 'could have if I had chosen'

---

[8] If the *if*-clause is 'if I had chosen', then I *was* able, *was* actually in a position, to ruin you: hence 'potui'. But if the *if*-clause expresses a genuine *unfulfilled condition*, then plainly I was *not* actually in a position to ruin you, hence not 'potui' but 'potuissem'. My colleague Mr. R. M. Nisbet has pointed out to me the interesting discussion of this point in S. A. Handford, *The Latin Subjunctive*, pp. 130 ff. It is interesting that although this author well appreciates the Latin usage, he still takes it for granted that in English the 'could have' is universally subjunctive or conditional.

is a past indicative, *not* a past conditional, despite the fact that there is what would, I suppose, be called a 'conditional' clause, that is an *if*-clause, with it. And this is, of course, why we can make the inferences that, as we saw, we can make from 'I could have if I had chosen', notably the inference to 'I could have' absolutely. Hence we see how mistaken Moore was in contrasting 'I could have if I had chosen' with the 'absolute' sense of 'I could have': we might almost go so far as to say that the addition of the 'conditional' clause 'if I had chosen' makes it certain that (in Moore's language) the sense of 'could have' is the absolute sense, or as I should prefer to put it, that the mood of 'could have' is indicative.

It might at this point be worth considering in general whether it makes sense to suppose that a language could contain any verb such as *can* has been argued or implied to be, namely one that can never occur without an *if*-clause appended to it. At least if the *if* is the normal 'conditional' *if* this would seem very difficult. For let the verb in question be *to X*: then we shall never say simply 'I X', but always 'I X if I Y': but then also, according to the accepted rules, if it is true that 'I X if I Y', and *also* true (which it must surely sometimes be) that 'I do, in fact, Y', it must surely follow that 'I X', simpliciter, without any *if* about it any longer. Perhaps this was the 'possible complication' that led Moore to switch from the suggestion that 'I could have' (in one sense) has always to be *expanded* to 'I could have if' to the suggestion that it has always to be *analysed* as 'I should have if': for of course the argument I have just given does not suffice to show that there could not be some verb which has always to be *analysed* as something containing a conditional *if*-clause: suggestions that this is in fact the case with some verbs are common in philosophy, and I do not propose to argue this point, though I think that doubt might well be felt about it. The only sort of 'verb' I can think of that might always demand a conditional clause with it is an 'auxiliary' verb, if there is one, which is used solely to form subjunctive or conditional moods (whatever exactly they may be) of other verbs: but however this may be, it is quite clear that *can*, and I should be prepared also to add *shall* and *will* and *may*, are not in this position.

To summarize, then, what has been here said in reply to Moore's suggestions in his book:

(*a*) 'I could have if I had chosen' does not mean the same as 'I should have if I had chosen'.
(*b*) In neither of these expressions is the *if* clause a 'normal conditional' clause, connecting antecedent to consequent as cause to effect.
(*c*) To argue that *can* always requires an *if*-clause with it to complete the sense is totally different from arguing that *can*-sentences are always to be analysed into sentences containing *if*-clauses.
(*d*) Neither *can* nor any other verb always requires a conditional *if*-clause after it: even 'could have', when a past indicative, does not require such a clause: and in 'I could have if I had chosen' the verb is in fact a past indicative, not a past subjunctive or conditional.

Even, however, if all these contentions are true so far, we must recognize that it may nevertheless still be the case that *can*, *could*, and *could have*, even when used as indicatives, are to be analysed as meaning *shall*, *should*, and *should have*, used as auxiliaries of tense or mood with another verb (i.e. so as to make that other verb into a future or subjunctive), followed by a conditional *if*-clause. There is some plausibility,[9] for example,

---

[9] Plausibility, but no more. Consider the case where I miss a very short putt and kick myself because I could have holed it. It is not that I should have holed it if I had tried: I did try, and missed. It is not that I should have holed it if conditions had been different: that might of course be so, but I am talking about conditions as they precisely were, and asserting that I could have holed it. There's the rub. Nor does 'I can hole it this time' mean that I shall hole it this time if I try or if anything else: for I may try and miss, and yet not be convinced that I couldn't have done it; indeed, further experiments may confirm my belief that I could have done it that time although I didn't.

But if I tried my hardest, say, and missed, surely there *must* have been *something* that caused me to fail, that made me unable to succeed? So that I *could not* have holed it. Well, a modern belief in science, in there being an explanation of everything, may make us assent to this argument. But such a belief is not in line with the traditional beliefs enshrined in the word *can*: according to *them*, a human

in the suggestion that 'I can do X' means 'I shall succeed in doing X, if I try' and 'I could have done X' means 'I should have succeeded in doing X, if I had tried'.

It is indeed odd that Moore should have plumped so simply, in giving his account whether of the necessary supplementation or of the analysis of 'could have', for the one particular *if*-clause 'if I had chosen', which happens to be particularly exposed to the above objections, without even mentioning the possibility of invoking other *if*-clauses, at least in some cases. Perhaps the reason was that *choose* (a word itself much in need of discussion) presented itself as well fitted to bridge the gulf between determinists and free-willers, which *try* might not so readily do. But as a matter of fact Moore does himself at one point give an analysis of 'I could have done X' which is different in an interesting way from his usual version, although confusible with it. At a crucial point in his argument, he chooses for his example 'The ship could have gone faster', and the suggestion is made that this is equivalent to 'The ship *would* have gone faster *if her officers had chosen*'. This may well seem plausible, but so far from being in line, as Moore apparently thinks, with his general analysis, it differs from it in two important respects:

(*a*) the subject of the *if*-clause ('her officers') is different from the subject of the main clause ('the ship'), the subject of the original sentence;

(*b*) the verb in the *if*-clause following 'chosen' is different from the verb in the main clause, the verb in the original sentence. We do not readily observe this because of the ellipsis after 'chosen': but plainly the verb must be, not 'to go faster', but 'to make her go faster' or, e.g., 'to open the throttle'.

These two features are dictated by the fact that a ship is inanimate. We do not wish seriously to ascribe free will to inanimate objects, and the 'could' of the original sentence is perhaps only

---

ability or power or capacity is inherently liable not to produce success, on occasion, and that for no reason (or are bad luck and bad form sometimes reasons?).

justifiable (as opposed to 'might') because it is readily realized that some person's free will is in question

If we follow up the lines of this new type of analysis, we should have to examine the relations between 'I could have won' and 'I could, or should, have won if I had chosen to lob' and 'I could, or should, have won if he had chosen to lob'. I will do no more here than point out that the difference between 'could' and 'should' remains as before, and that the sense of 'I could have won', if it really is one, in which it means something of the sort 'I should have won if he had chosen to lob' or 'to let me win' (the parallel to the ship example), is of little importance—the 'if' here is of course the conditional *if*.

It is time now to turn to a second discussion of *if*s and *can*s. Quite recently my colleague Mr. Nowell-Smith, in another little book called *Ethics*, also reaches a point in his argument at which he has to examine the sentence 'He could have acted otherwise', that is, could have done something that he did not in fact do. His reason for doing so is that, unless we can truly say this of people, we might find ourselves unable to blame people for things, and this would be generally regretted. This reason is not unrelated to Moore's reason for embarking on his earlier discussion, and Nowell-Smith's views show some resemblances to Moore's: perhaps this is because Nowell-Smith, like Moore at the time he wrote his book, is willing, if not anxious, to come to terms with determinism.

Nowell-Smith begins his discussion by saying (p. 274) that ' "could have" is a modal phrase, and modal phrases are not normally used to make categorical statements'. I am not myself at all sure what exactly a 'modal phrase' is, so I cannot discuss this assertion: but I do not think this matters, because he proceeds to give us two other examples of modal phrases, viz. 'might have' and 'would have',[10] and to tell us first what they are not (which I omit) and then what they are:

'Would have' and 'might have' are clearly suppressed hypotheticals, incomplete without an 'if . . .' or an 'if . . . not . . .'. No-

[10] Also perhaps 'may have', for he discusses 'It *might* have rained last Thursday' in terms that seem really do apply to 'It *may* have rained last Thursday'.

body would say 'Jones would have won the championship' unless (*a*) he believed that Jones did not win and (*b*) he was prepared to add 'if he had entered' or 'if he had not sprained his ankle' or some such clause.

Here (*a*) is actually incorrect—we can say 'Jones would (still) have won the championship, (even) if Hagen had entered'—but this does not concern us. (*b*), however, seems to be fairly correct, at least as far as concerns 'would have' (in the case of 'might have' it might well be doubted[11]). So we have it that, when Nowell-Smith says that 'would have' is a 'suppressed hypothetical' he means that it requires the addition of an *if*-clause to complete the sense. And he goes on to say that 'could have' sentences also (though not so obviously) 'express hypotheticals', if not always at least in important cases, such as notably those where we say someone could have done something he didn't actually do: in these cases 'could have' . . . is equivalent to 'would have . . . if. . . .'.

It will be clear at once that Nowell-Smith, like Moore, is not distinguishing between the contention that 'could have' *requires supplementation by* an *if*-clause and the quite different contention that *its analysis contains* an *if*-clause.[12] On the whole it seems

---

[11] I refrain here from questioning it in the case of 'would have'. Yet 'would' is agreed to be often a past indicative of the old verb *will*, requiring no *if*-clause: and I think myself that in, say, 'X would have hanged him, but Y was against it' 'would have' is likewise a past indicative—indeed it is from this sort of example that we can see how the past tenses of *will* have come to be used as auxiliaries of mood for forming the conditionals of other verbs.

To state what seem to be some grammatical facts (omitting all reference to the use of the words concerned in expressing wishes):

Could have is sometimes a past indicative, sometimes a past subjunctive of the verb *can*. When it is the main verb and is a subjunctive, it does require a conditional clause with it. *Can* and its parts are *not* used as auxiliaries of tense or mood to form tenses or moods of other verbs.

Would have, whether or not it is used as a past indicative or subjunctive of the verb *will*, is now commonly used (*should have* in the first person) as an auxiliary for forming the past subjunctive of other verbs: hence if it is the main verb it does in general require a conditional clause with it.

[12] It is true that he uses two different expressions: 'would have' *is* a (suppressed) hypothetical, while 'could have' sentences *express* hypotheticals. But it does not look as if any distinction is intended, and if it is, the protracted initial

plain that it is the second (analysis) view that he wishes to argue for: but the argument he produces is that 'could have' is (in important cases) like 'would have', the point about which is that it needs an *if*-clause to complete it—as though this, which is an argument in favour of the *first* view, told in favour of the second view. But it cannot possibly do so: and in any event *could have* is liable, as we have already seen, to be in important cases a past indicative, so that the contention that it is like *would have* in requiring a conditional *if*-clause is unfounded.

Nevertheless, it must be allowed that Nowell-Smith may still be right in urging that 'could have' *means* 'would have if' and that, as he eventually adds, 'can' means 'will if'. What has he to say in support of this?

He propounds two examples for discussion, which I think do not differ greatly, so I shall quote only the first. Here it is:

He could have read *Emma* in bed last night, though he actually read *Persuasion*; but he could not have read *Werther*, because he does not know German.

This is evidently of the same kind as Moore's 20-minute-mile example. The first thing that Nowell-Smith urges is that such a 'could have' statement is not a categorical, or a 'straightforward' categorical, statement. And his argument in favour of this view is derived from the way in which he should establish its truth or falsity. No inspection of what the man actually did will, he says, verify directly that he could have done something else (here, read *Emma*) which he didn't do: rather, we should, to establish this, have to show

(*a*) that he has performed tasks of similar difficulty sufficiently often to preclude the possibility of a fluke, and (*b*) that nothing prevented him on this occasion. For example, we should have to establish that there was a copy of *Emma* in the house.

---

analogy between 'could have' and 'would have' seems irrelevant and misleading. Moreover, discussing the (unimportant) case of 'It could have been a Morris', he writes that 'it would be absurd to ask under what conditions it *could or would have* been a Morris' (my italics): this seems to show an indifference to the distinction that I am insisting on.

To refute it, on the other hand, we should have to show either 'that some necessary condition was absent' (there was no copy of *Emma*)' or 'that the capacity was absent'. That is, let us say, we have to show on the one hand that he had both the ability and the opportunity to read *Emma*, or on the other hand that he lacked either the ability or the opportunity.

Nowell-Smith seems, at least at first, to be less interested in the matter of opportunity: for he says that we can establish 'directly', i.e. by considering what the facts at the time actually were, at least that he did *not* have the opportunity, that is, that something did prevent him, and he does not seem daunted by the obviously greater difficulty of establishing, in order to establish that he *could* have done it, the general negative that *there was nothing* to prevent him. At any rate, it is at first upon our manner of establishing that he had (or had not) the *ability* to do this thing that he did not do that Nowell-Smith fastens in order to support his assertion that the 'could have' statement is not categorical. That the man had the *ability* to read *Emma* can *not*, he says, be established 'directly', i.e. by observing what happened on that past occasion, but only by considering what prowess he has displayed in the face of similar tasks in the past on other occasions, or displays now when put to the test: the argument that we have perforce to use is an 'inductive' one (and, he adds, none the worse for that).

Now let us pass all this, at least for the sake of argument.[13] What interests us is to discover why Nowell-Smith thinks that these considerations show that 'He had the ability to read *Emma*' is not a categorical statement. I confess I fail to follow the argument:

> The very fact that evidence for or against 'could have' statements must be drawn from occasions other than that to which they refer is

---

[13] Yet I think it is not hard to see that we cannot establish 'directly', at least in many cases, that something 'prevented' him: he was drugged or dazzled, which prevented him from reading, which establishes that he could not have read—but how do we know that being drugged or dazzled 'prevents' people from reading? Surely on 'inductive' evidence? And, in short, to be prevented is to be rendered unable.

enough to show that 'He could have acted otherwise' is not a straightforward categorical statement.

But do we really know what is meant by a 'straightforward categorical statement'? Certainly it is not the case that statements made on the strength of inductive evidence are in general not categorical—for example, the statement that the next mule born will prove sterile: this seems categorical enough. Perhaps this example should be ruled out as not in point, on the ground that here there *will some day* be 'direct' evidence relevant to the assertion, even if it is not available at the moment. Could the same, I wonder, be said of the inductive conclusion 'All mules are sterile'? Or is that not categorical? I know that this has been interpreted by some philosophers to mean 'If anything is a mule then it is sterile', but I see no reason to support that curious interpretation.

The situation becomes still more puzzling when we remember that Nowell-Smith is about to generalize his theory, and to assert, not merely that 'could have' means 'would have . . . if', but also that 'can' means 'shall or will . . . if'. Suppose then that I assert 'I can here and now lift my finger', and translate this as 'I shall lift my finger if . . .': then surely this will be 'directly' verified if the conditions are satisfied and I do proceed to lift the finger? If this is correct, and if the theory is indeed a general one, then there seems to be no point in insisting on the non-availability of 'direct' evidence, which is only a feature of certain cases. Incidentally, it is not in fact the case that to say 'He could have done it' is always used in a way to imply that he did not in fact do it: we make a list of the suspects in a murder case, all of whom we think could have done it and one of whom we think did do it. True, this is not Nowell-Smith's case: but unless we are prepared to assert that the 'could have' in his case differs in meaning from that in the murder case, and so to rule out the latter as irrelevant, we are in danger of having to admit that even 'could have' sentences can be 'directly' verified in favourable cases. For study of the facts of that past occasion can prove to us that he did it, and hence that our original 'He could have' was correct.[14]

However, to proceed. Whether or not we should describe our conclusion here as 'categorical' it seems that it should still be a conclusion of the form 'he *could* have done so and so', and not in the least a conclusion concerning what he *would* have done. We are interested, remember, in his abilities: we want to know whether he could have read *Emma* yesterday: we ascertain that he did read it the day before yesterday, and that he does read it today: we conclude that he could have read it yesterday. But it does not appear that this says anything about what he *would* have done yesterday or in what circumstances: certainly, we are now convinced, he *could* have read it yesterday, but *would* he have, considering that he had read it only the day before? Moreover, supposing the view is that our conclusion is not of the 'could have' but of the 'would have if' form, nothing has yet been said to establish this, nor to tell us what follows the 'if'. To establish that he would have read it yesterday if . . ., we shall need evidence not merely as to his abilities and opportunities, but also as to his character, motives, and so on.

It may indeed be thought, and it seems that Nowell-Smith does at least partly think this, that what follows the 'if' should be suppliable from the consideration that to say he could have, in the full sense, is to say not merely that he had the ability, which is what we have hitherto concentrated on, but also that he had the *opportunity*. For to establish *this*, do we not have to establish that certain *conditions* were satisfied, as for instance that there was a copy of *Emma* available? Very well. But here there is surely a confusion: we allow that, in saying that he could have, I do assert or imply that certain *conditions*, those of opportunity, *were satisfied*: but this is totally different from

---

[14] There are, I should myself think, good reasons for not speaking of 'I can lift my finger' as being directly verified when I proceed to lift it, and likewise for not speaking of 'He could have done it' as being directly verified by the discovery that he did do it. But on Nowell-Smith's account I think that these would count as direct verifications.

allowing that, in saying that he could have, I *assert something conditional*. It is, certainly, entirely possible to assert something conditional such as 'he could have read *Emma* yesterday if there had been a copy available', *could* being then of course a subjunctive: but to say this sort of thing is precisely not to say the sort of thing that we say when we say 'He could have acted otherwise', where 'could have' is an indicative—implying, as we now do, that there was no copy available, we imply that *pro tanto* he could *not* have acted otherwise. And the same will be true if we try saying 'He would have read *Emma* yesterday if there had been a copy available': this too certainly implies that he could not in fact have read it, and so cannot by any means be what we mean by saying that he could have read it.

In the concluding paragraph of his discussion, Nowell-Smith does finally undertake to give us his analysis not merely of 'could have', but also of 'can' (which he says means 'will if'). And this last feature is very much to be welcomed, because if an analysis is being consciously given of 'can' at least we shall at length be clear of confusions connected with the idea that 'could have' is necessarily a subjunctive.[15]

The argument of the last paragraph runs as follows. It is 'logically odd' to say something of this kind (I am slightly emending Nowell-Smith's formula, but only in ways that are favourable to it and demanded by his own argument):

Smith has the ability to run a mile, has the opportunity to run a mile, has a preponderant motive for running a mile, but does not in fact do so.

From this it follows directly, says Nowell-Smith, that 'can' means 'will if', that is, I suppose, that 'Smith can run a mile' *means* 'If Smith has the opportunity to run a mile and a preponderant motive for running it, he will run it'.

[15] It must, however, be pointed out once again that if we are to discuss the assertion that somebody *can* (now) do something, the previous arguments that our assertions are not categorical because they are based on induction and cannot be verified directly, whether they were good or not, must now be abandoned: because of course it *is* possible to verify this 'directly' by the method Nowell-Smith has specified in another connexion earlier, viz. by getting the man to try and seeing him succeed.

It seems, however, plain that nothing of the kind follows. This may be seen first by setting the argument out formally. Nowell-Smith's premiss is of the form

Not (p and q and r and not -s)

that is

Logically odd (ability + opportunity + motive + non-action).

Now from this we can indeed infer

$p \supset ((q$ and $r) \supset s)$,

that is that

If he has the ability, then, if he has the opportunity and the motive, he will do it.

But we can*not infer* the converse

$((q$ and $r) \supset s) \supset p$,

or in other words that

If, when he has the opportunity and the motive, he does it, he has the ability to do it.

(I do not say this last is not something to which we should, when so put into English, assent, only that it does not follow from Nowell-Smith's premiss: of course it follows merely from the premiss that he does it, that he has the ability to do it, according to ordinary English.) But unless this second, converse implication *does* follow, we cannot, according to the usual formal principles, infer that p is *equivalent* to, nor therefore that it means the same as, $(q$ and $r) \supset s$, or in words that ability *means* that opportunity plus motive leads to action.

To put the same point non-formally. From the fact that, if three things are true together a fourth must also be true, we cannot argue that one of the three things *simply means* that if the other two are true the fourth will be true. If we could argue indeed in this way, then we should establish, from Nowell-Smith's premiss, not merely that

'He has the ability to do X' simply means that 'If he has the opportunity and the motive to do X, he will do X'

but also equally that

'He has the opportunity to do X' *simply means* that 'If he has the ability and the motive to do X, he will do X'

and likewise that

'He has a preponderant motive to do X' *simply means* that 'If he has the ability and the opportunity to do X, he will do X'.

For clearly we can perform the same operations on *q* and *r* as on *p*, since the three all occupy parallel positions in the premiss. But these are fantastic suggestions. Put shortly, Nowell-Smith is pointing out in his premiss that if a man both can and wants to (more than he wants to do anything else), he will: but from this it does not follow that 'he can' *simply means* that 'if he wants to he will'. Nowell-Smith is struggling to effect a transition from *can* to *will* which presents difficulties as great as those of the transition from *could* to *would*: he puts up his show of effecting it by importing the additional, and here irrelevant, concept of motive, which needless to say is in general very intimately connected with the question of what 'he will' do.

When, in conclusion, Nowell-Smith finally sets out his analysis of 'Smith could have read *Emma* last night', it is this:

He would have read it, if there had been a copy, if he had not been struck blind, &c., &c., and if he had wanted to read it more than he had wanted to read (this should be 'do') anything else.

But so far from this being what we mean by saying he could have read it, it actually implies that he could *not* have read it, for more than adequate reasons: it implies that he was blind at the time, and so on. Here we see that Nowell-Smith actually does make the confusion I referred to above between a statement which implies or asserts that certain conditions *were* fulfilled and a conditional statement, i.e. a statement about what would have happened if those conditions had been fulfilled. This is unfortunately a confusion of a general kind that is not uncommon: I need only mention the classic instance of Keynes, who confused asserting on evidence h that p is probable with asserting that on evidence h p is probable, both of which can be ambiguously expressed by 'asserting that p is probable on evidence h', but only the former of which asserts that p is (really) probable. Here similarly there is a confusion between asserting on the supposition (or premiss) that he had a copy that he could/would have read it, and asserting that on the supposition that he had a copy he could/would have read it, both of which can be ambiguously expressed by 'asserting that he could/would have read it on the supposition that he had a copy', but only the former of which asserts that he (actually) could have read it.

To some extent, then, we learn from studying Nowell-Smith's arguments lessons similar to those that we learned in the case of Moore. But some are new, as for instance that many assertions about what a man *would have* done or *will do* depend, in critical cases, upon premisses about his *motives* as well as, or rather than, about his abilities or opportunities: hence these assertions cannot be what assertions about his abilities *mean*.[16]

On one point I may perhaps elaborate a little further. It has been maintained that *sometimes* when we say 'He could have done X' this is a conditional: it requires completion by an *if*-clause, typically 'if he had had the opportunity', and so does *not* require us, if we are to establish its truth, to establish that he did in fact have the opportunity. Sometimes on the other hand it is a past indicative, implying that he did have the opportunity: in which case we do, to establish its truth, have to establish that certain conditions were satisfied, but the assertion is *not* to be described as a conditional assertion.

[16] Yet here it must be pointed out once more that it has not been shown that *all* assertions about what he would have done are so dependent, so that this particular argument against the analysis of 'could have' as 'would have if' is not conclusive: in particular, it does not dispose of the possible suggestion that 'could have' means 'would have if he had *tried*', for here considerations of motive may be irrelevant.

Now while I have no wish to retract this account in general or in all cases, I doubt whether it is the whole story. Consider the case where what we wish to assert is that somebody had the opportunity to do something but lacked the ability—'He could have smashed that lob, if he had been any good at the smash': here the *if*-clause, which may of course be suppressed and understood, relates not to opportunity but to ability. Now although we might describe the whole sentence as 'conditional', it nevertheless manages to assert, by means of its main clause, something 'categorical' enough, viz. that he did have a certain opportunity. And in the same way Nowell-Smith's 'He could have read *Emma*, if he had had a copy', does seem to assert 'categorically' that he had a certain ability, although he lacked the opportunity to exercise it. Looking at it in this way, there is a temptation to say that 'could have' has, besides its 'all-in' *sense* several more *restricted senses*: this would be brought out if we said 'He could have smashed it, *only* he is no good at the smash' or 'He could have read *Emma but* he had no copy', where, we should say, 'could have' is being used in the restricted senses of opportunity or of ability[17] only, and is a past indicative, not a past conditional.

This view might be reinforced by considering examples with the simple 'can' itself. We are tempted to say that 'He can' sometimes means just that he has the ability, with *nothing said* about opportunity, sometimes *just* that he has the chance, with nothing said about ability, sometimes, however, that he really actually *fully can* here and now, having both ability and opportunity. Now nobody, I think, would be tempted to say that 'can', where it means one of the two lesser things, e.g. 'has the opportunity', i.e. 'can in the full sense if he has the ability', is grammatically a subjunctive or conditional. Perhaps, then, it was not correct to describe 'He could have', either, as always a conditional where it asserts ability or opportunity only, with

---

[17] I talk here and throughout of 'ability' and 'opportunity' only: but I realize that other abstract nouns like 'capacity', 'skill', and even 'right' are equally involved. All these terms need listing and elucidating before we really get to grips with 'can'.

nothing said about the other, or even where the other is denied to have existed.

The verb *can* is a peculiar one. Let us compare it for a moment with another peculiar verb, *know*, with which it shares some grammatical peculiarities, such as lack of a continuous present tense. When I say that somebody *knows* what the thing in my hand is, I may mean merely that he has the ability to identify it given the opportunity, or that he has the opportunity to identify it if he has the ability, or that he has both. What do we say about *know* here? Certainly we are not prone to invoke the idea of a conditional, but rather that of different senses, or perhaps the still obscure idea of the dispositional. I must be content here merely to say that I do not think that the old armoury of terms, such as 'mood' and 'sense', is altogether adequate for handling such awkward cases. The only point of which I feel certain is that such verbs as *can* and *know* have each an all-in, paradigm use, around which cluster and from which divagate, little by little and along different paths, a whole series of other uses, for many of which, though perhaps not for all, a synonymous expression ('opportunity', 'realize', and so on) can be found.

It is not unusual for an audience at a lecture to include some who prefer things to be important, and to them now, in case there are any such present, there is owed a peroration. Why, in short, does all this matter? First, then, it needs no emphasizing that both *if* and *can* are highly prevalent and protean words, perplexing both grammatically and philosophically: it is not merely worth while, but essential, in these studies to discover the facts about *if*s and *can*s, and to remove the confusions they engender. In philosophy it is *can* in particular that we seem so often to uncover, just when we had thought some problem settled, grinning residually up at us like the frog at the bottom of the beer mug. Furthermore and secondly, we have not here been dissecting these two words in general or completely, but in a special connexion which perhaps no one will hold trivial. It has been alleged by very serious philosophers (not only the two I have mentioned) that the things we ordinarily say about what we can do and could have done may actually be consistent with determinism. It is hard to evade all attempt to decide whether this allegation is true—hard even for those who, like myself, are inclined to think that determinism itself is still a name for nothing clear, that has been argued for only incoherently. At least I should like to claim that the arguments considered tonight fail to show that it *is* true, and indeed in failing go some way to show that it is *not*. Determinism, whatever it may be, may yet be the case, but at least it appears not consistent with what we ordinarily say and presumably think. And finally there is a third point. Reflecting on the arguments in this lecture, we may well ask ourselves whether they might not be as well assigned to grammar as to philosophy: and this, I think, is a salutary question to end on. There are constant references in contemporary philosophy, which notoriously is much concerned with language, to a 'logical grammar' and a 'logical syntax' as though these were things distinct from ordinary grammarian's grammar and syntax: and certainly they do seem, whatever exactly they may be, different from traditional grammar. But grammar today is itself in a state of flux; for fifty years or more it has been questioned on all hands and counts whether what Dionysius Thrax once thought was the truth about Greek is the truth and the whole truth about all language and all languages. Do we know, then, that there will prove to be any ultimate boundary between 'logical grammar' and a revised and enlarged *Grammar*? In the history of human inquiry, philosophy has the place of the initial central sun, seminal and tumultuous: from time to time it throws off some portion of itself to take station as a science, a planet, cool and well regulated, progressing steadily towards a distant final state. This happened long ago at the birth of mathematics, and again at the birth of physics: only in the last century we have witnessed the same process once again, slow and at the time almost imperceptible, in the birth of the science of mathematical logic, through the joint labours of philosophers and mathematicians. Is it not possible that the next century may see the birth, through the joint labours of philosophers, grammarians, and numerous other students of language, of a true and comprehensive *science of language*? Then we shall have rid ourselves of one more part of philosophy (there will still be plenty left) in the only way we ever can get rid of philosophy, by kicking it upstairs.

THE PHILOSOPHY OF LANGUAGE IN REVOLUTIONARY FRANCE

BY H. B. ACTON

I

In 1793 the Convention dissolved the existing academies of science and learning as the first stage in a plan for their reorganization. The plan was not completed until 1795, when the Institut National des Sciences et Arts was founded. This was divided into three main 'classes' devoted respectively to the natural sciences, the moral and political sciences, and the fine arts, among which were included literature and grammar. The second class, that of the moral and political sciences, was divided into six sections, as follows: 'the analysis of sensations and ideas'; ethics; social science; political economy; history; geography.

Our concern, in this lecture, is with the section on the analysis of sensations and ideas. It is apparent from its name that its creators had a definite point of view about the nature of philosophical inquiry. We can get a preliminary idea of this if we briefly consider some views of the two most distinguished philosophers who were members of it at the beginning, Volney and Cabanis. Volney, a deist, was author of *Les Ruines* (1791), in which he had argued that whenever people perceive things as they are, they agree about them, and that disagreement is a sign that things are not being perceived as they are. From this he inferred that disagreement and social disunity arise when men insist on making pronouncements about matters which cannot be verified in sense experience. He therefore concluded that 'a line of demarcation should be drawn between what is verifiable and what is not verifiable, and an insuperable barrier set up between the world of fantasy and the world of reality; that is to say, that theological and religious opinions should be withdrawn from the social sphere'. If this were done, he believed, the old erroneous religions would be replaced by 'the religion of evidence and of truth'.[1] Cabanis, who had been the friend and physician of Mirabeau, belonged to the circle which met for philosophical discussion at the house at Auteuil to which Madame Helvétius had retired after the death of her husband. Cabanis is said to have interrupted a deistic effusion delivered by Bernadin de St. Pierre at the Institute with the words: 'I swear that there is no God, and I ask that his name be not uttered within these walls.'[2] Cabanis contributed a long series of essays to the early meetings of the section on the analysis of sensations and ideas, under the title of *Les Rapports du physique et du moral de l'homme*. This work is much concerned with the physiological conditions of sensation, and some sentences in it became, in a modified form, one of the catchphrases of nineteenth-century materialism. The passage I have in mind occurs in the first of the essays where he says 'that the brain in a manner digests impressions: that it organically produces the secretion of thought',[3] a passage which in the popular materialism of the nineteenth century was rendered picturesque and absolute in the phrase: 'The brain secretes thought as the liver secretes bile.'

The members of the Institute had rooms on the premises and were expected to possess both a walking-out uniform (*habit de ville*) and a ceremonial dress (*un costume d'apparat pour les grandes cérémonies*). There were also, however, non-resident associate members, some of whom were very active in the proceedings. Among them was Destutt de Tracy, who was soon regarded as the most considerable philosopher in the section for the analysis of sensations and ideas. On the 2nd Floréal of the Year IV, de Tracy began the reading of an essay entitled *Mémoire sur la faculté de pensée*. In it he made a comparison between the

[1] *Œuvres* (Paris, 1821), i. 244 and 245.
[2] E. Joyau, *La Philosophie en France pendant la Révolution* (Paris, 1893), p. 176.
[3] *Mémoires de l'Institut National des Sciences et Arts. Sciences morales et politiques*, i (Paris, thermidor, an VI), 148.

history of astronomy and the history of the subject which he and his listeners were there to promote. Locke, he said, was the Copernicus of this new science, since he discovered the true explanation of the phenomena with which it was concerned. But if Locke was its Copernicus, then Condillac was its Kepler, for just as Kepler, by means of his laws of planetary motion, had shown how the various parts of the solar system are related, so Condillac had discovered 'the true connection of ideas', and had shown that 'language is as necessary for thought itself as for giving expression to it'. It was unfortunate, de Tracy went on, that for this science which Locke had founded and Condillac had elaborated, no suitable name had been invented. The word 'metaphysics' was not acceptable, because it had hitherto been applied to the science of the natures of things, and of souls, intelligences, and origins. Metaphysics is ordinarily distinguished from physics, yet Locke had rightly said that the knowledge of human faculties and powers should form an important part of physics. Indeed, 'metaphysics', de Tracy maintains, is a thoroughly discredited word, so that to use it for the analysis of sensations and ideas would be like continuing to use the word 'astrology' for the science of the heavenly bodies. Condillac had suggested the word 'psychology', but there is no science of the soul, and to introduce this word would give the impression 'that you are occupied with vague enquiries into first causes, whereas the aim of all your exertions is the knowledge of effects and of their practical consequences'. De Tracy therefore proposed that the word 'ideology' should be coined to stand for this branch of knowledge. The word 'idea' had originally meant 'perception by means of sight', but had now come to be used for the perceptions of any of the senses, and for experience and thought generally. Those attending the meetings of the section were analysts and physiologists, and de Tracy regretted that there were no grammarians there as well, 'for the formation of ideas is very closely linked with the formation of words, as we shall see later. Every science is reducible to a well made language; and to make progress in a science is nothing but improving its language, whether by changing its words or by rendering its meanings precise.'[4]

At that meeting of the Institut National, within the walls where Bernadin de St. Pierre was to be shouted down for pronouncing the name of God, a new and most volatile word was thus introduced into the vocabulary of the learned world. Later on, of course, this word 'ideology' was to serve the purpose of stigmatizing religion as a form of fantasy. In what follows, however, we shall not be concerned with these later phases of the word's history, but with the new science it was originally intended to designate. This new science, we have seen, was thought to have been founded by Locke and developed by Condillac. What Condillac was supposed to have added to Locke's foundations was the idea that language was necessary for thinking itself as well as for expressing or communicating thoughts. From the proposition that language is necessary for thinking there followed the proposition that the development of the sciences depends on the development of language. This is the account of the matter given by Destutt de Tracy, and we shall therefore begin by examining those opinions of Condillac to which he was referring.

In the Introduction to his first book, *Essai sur l'origine des connoissances humaines* (1746), Condillac remarked that Locke in his *Essay* had started by assuming that once ideas were received by the senses, they could be repeated, put together, taken apart, and recomposed at will. But as Locke proceeded with his book he had come to see that at any rate some of the things which the mind is supposed to do with ideas might not be done without the use of words. In the passage in the *Essay* to which Condillac refers, Locke says that when he started to write his book he had not the least thought that any consideration of words was at all necessary in it. But when, having passed over the original and composition of our ideas, I began to examine the extent and certainty of our knowledge, I found it had so near a connexion with words, that, unless their force and manner of signification was first well observed, there could be very little said clearly and pertinently concerning

[4] *Mémoires de l'Institut National*, i. 318, 323–4, 326.

knowledge; which being conversant about truth, had constantly to do with propositions. And though it terminated in things, yet it was for the most part so much by the intervention of words, that they seemed scarce separable from our general knowledge (iii, chap. ix, § 21).

Condillac, by going over the whole argument again with this consideration in mind, showed that 'the way of ideas' required the development of a philosophy of signs and of language.[5]

According to Condillac, knowledge would be impossible without breaking up or decomposing, analysing, and sorting out what is presented to the senses. If someone were taken at night into a castle which overlooked an extensive landscape, and if, in the morning, a window were opened and immediately closed again, the visitor would *see* the whole landscape, that is to say it would affect his sense of sight, but he would not be able to *observe* it or to describe it to others. If he is to get *knowledge* of the landscape, the window must be kept open long enough for him to attend first to one part and then to another. What is simultaneously presented to the sense of sight must be successively attended to and thus *decomposed* into its elements. Sight is only transformed into knowledge and observation when the parts that have been distinguished from one another are recomposed so as to be apprehended in the relations they actually have with one another. Condillac uses the word 'analysis' for this decomposition and recomposition, and it is his view that it is by means of analysis that human knowledge is gained and advanced. This method, he holds, is natural to mankind, and is used, for example, by the mechanic and the dressmaker as well as by the mathematician and philosopher. Correct analysis leads to survival, incorrect analysis to misfortune and death. Thus analysis is taught to mankind by nature herself.[6]

---

[5] This was also the view of Horne Tooke who in ΕΠΕΑ ΠΤΕΡΟΕΝΤΑ *or The Diversions of Purley* (1786) wrote that Locke's *Essay* is really 'a *Grammatical* Essay, or a Treatise on *Words*, or on *Language* (chap. 2).

[6] *La Logique: ou les premiers développemens de l'art de penser* (1780), *Œuvres* (ed. G. LeRoy, 1947–51), ii, esp. 374–8 and 393 ff. As the account of Condillac which follows is taken from this work, I shall give no further references.

Analysis, Condillac goes on, is only possible with the use of signs and hence by means of language. Although none of our ideas are innate, there is, according to Condillac, a sense in which our language is, since we naturally and spontaneously express ourselves by means of cries and gestures. We do not start by *intending* to communicate our feelings to other men, but the natural signs by which we express them are seen and heard in any case. A man who is thwarted by the removal of some object which satisfies his needs shows this by noises and movements, and other men come to learn what these exertions of his mean, and even to sympathize with him and to bring him help. The natural signs which are spontaneously given by one man are spontaneously decomposed by others, for with time the prominent elements in them and in the accompanying circumstances will be distinguished and observed. Once the natural language of other men is understood, it becomes possible for individuals to make gestures and cries *with the intention* of making themselves understood. In this way conventional and arbitrary signs may be formed, and an important step has been taken towards the development of language as we know it.

But if language is to be taken any further, signs must be applied not only to particular occurrences, but must be extended, by analogy, to occurrences *like* those they were first used for. In nature there is nothing that is not particular, but generality is essential if there is to be speech, knowledge, and reasoning. A child who is taught that 'tree' is the name for a tree which has been shown to him, will not ask for the name of another, similar tree which he meets with later, but will use the same word for that as well, since it is easier to do this than to seek another name. Just as he first expresses his feelings and desires without intending to do so, he first generalizes without any intention either. His generalizations take the form they do because his system of names is linked with the system of his needs. There are no genera and species in nature, but general words have been used in the course of distinguishing what satisfies human desires from what frustrates them. By means of a system of general names we are enabled to recall to memory and to locate things and circumstances that are useful to us. Where our system of species and genera is not definite, we make it definite if our needs and desires require us to do so. There is no point, for example, in asking whether this particular growth is *really* a shrub or *really* a tree. The proper question to ask is whether it is more convenient to classify it one way rather than the other.

The view so far described may be summarized as follows. There could be no knowledge without analysis. Analysis would be impossible without the use of signs and hence of language. The natural language of signs and gestures would not, on its own, enable analysis to be carried very far. It grows, however, by natural stages, into a language in which conventional or arbitrary signs are *intentionally* employed. The signs that are at first applied to a particular thing become general names as the result of inertia, analogy, which is to some extent a species of inertia, and convenience. They are first devised and used because they help men to satisfy their needs. Hence the natural method of analysis and the language which simple but successful men make use of in their mundane affairs are reliable models to copy and elaborate. But those who divorce language from experience, or claim to have methods of inquiry superior to those of practical men, can only fall into prejudice and error.

From these propositions about the nature of analysis and of language Condillac draws an important conclusion about the nature of science. A language, he holds, is essentially an analytic method, and the art of reasoning consists in establishing a well-made language. In the course of sorting out the confusion of our original impressions, we come to notice likenesses and differences and, by means of general names, to classify the things that are of importance to us. As our investigations proceed, new classes are discovered and new names given to them by analogy with the names for the classes already familiar to us. 'Analysis', he says, 'makes us form the habit of seeking for the first meaning of a word in its first use, and all the others by analogy.' According to Condillac, therefore, 'the whole art of reasoning is reduced to the art of speaking well', and as languages are analytic methods, successful sciences are well made languages. Condillac was greatly impressed by algebra, which he calls 'the language of mathematics'. He held that all scientific problems could be solved by the same methods, and that mathematics was the model to be aspired to. '... *equations, propositions, judgements*', he says, 'are at bottom the same thing, and hence one reasons in the same way in all the sciences'. If the answers for which we are seeking were not implicit in the questions we ask, we should never find them. Since the classifications enshrined in the vocabulary of a language have been made as a result of and with a view to human convenience, analysis may be compared with a set of levers which enable mankind to treat the phenomena of nature as if they were the result of human art.

The idea that a science is a well made language was enthusiastically adopted by Lavoisier. The notes from which his *Traité élémentaire de chimie* (1789) was put together still exist, and include passages copied out from Condillac's *Logic*.[7] In the Preface to the *Treatise* itself, and in the earlier *Méthode de nomenclature chimique* (1787, in collaboration with Guyton de Morveau), Lavoisier quotes and summarizes Condillac's arguments. A child is rapidly taught by nature, since loss and pain are the penalties of failure. The theoretical inquirer, however, has no such constant spur, but is inclined to let his imagination run freely, and to stick to inadequate views because of his personal pride in them. Furthermore, if chemistry is his sphere of inquiry, he is introduced to a nomenclature handed on from the alchemists and expressing their unfounded prejudices.

A well made language [Lavoisier writes] adapted to the natural and successive order of ideas will bring in its train a necessary and immediate revolution in the method of teaching, and will not allow teachers of chemistry to deviate from the course of nature; either they must reject the nomenclature or they must irresistibly follow

[7] M. Daumas, *Lavoisier, théoricien et expérimentateur* (Paris, 1955), p. 99. Lavoisier's views on the nomenclature of chemistry are described by D. McKie in *Antoine Lavoisier* (London, 1952), chap. 22.

the course marked out by it. The logic of the sciences is thus essentially dependent on their language.[8]

Such a language, of course, must be based on what is revealed by observation and experiment, but in its turn it will open the way to further inquiry. 'By correcting their language', Condillac had said, philosophers 'have reasoned better'.[9] Lavoisier then goes on to show how the names for chemical compounds should be based on the names of the elements from which they are formed. So too, he distinguished bases, acids, and metals, and invented such terms as phosphoric acid, sulphuric acid, and carbonic acid, in order to indicate, in the name, the composition of the substance. It should be noticed that in Lavoisier's writings the word 'decomposition' means the breaking down of a compound into its elements, or into parts for which no further method of decomposition is known, as in part I of the *Traité élémentaire de chimie*, which is headed 'Of the Formation and Decomposition of Aeriform Fluids'. The decomposition which, according to Condillac, is a necessary feature of thought, is not a real separation of physical elements, but rather a metaphorical sort of distinction or separation, the objects of which he says are ideas, reasonings, and systems.[10]

II

We have now sketched in the background to Destutt de Tracy's lectures at the Institut National. The section on the analysis of sensations and ideas, we now see, was founded by men who believed that Locke's empiricism, along with Condillac's elaboration of it into a philosophy of language, was the base from which further philosophical advances would be made. Now one method by which the section encouraged discussion of the problems it considered important was by

[8] *Méthode de nomenclature chimique* (Paris, 1787), p. 12.
[9] Quoted by Lavoisier, *Elements of Chemistry* (English translation, 3rd edn., Edinburgh, 1796), p. xxxvi.
[10] Condillac, *Dictionnaire des synonymes*, art. 'Décomposer', *Œuvres* (Le Roy), iii. 179.

sponsoring prizes for the best essays submitted on topics chosen by its members. The second and third of these competitions are fairly well known, since they elicited contributions by Maine de Biran, viz. his *Influence de l'habitude sur la faculté de pensée*, which gained him the prize, and his *Mémoire sur la décomposition de la pensée*, which would have gained him the prize if the Class of Moral and Political Sciences had not been abolished before it could be awarded. The first of these competitions, however, is less well known, but the topic set for discussion, the work which gained the prize, and some other essays on the same subject are, it seems to me, of sufficient philosophical interest to merit our attention for a while.

The subject set, then, for the prize essay in the Year V of the Republic was 'to determine the influence of signs on the faculty of thought'. In proposing this subject the Institute set out the following five specific questions in elucidation of the general theme.

1. Is it really the case that sensations can only be transformed into ideas by means of signs? Or, what comes to the same thing, do our earliest ideas essentially depend on the help of signs?

2. Would the art of thought be perfect if the art of signs were brought to perfection?

3. In those sciences where there is general agreement as to what is true, is this the result of the perfection of the signs used in them?

4. In those branches of knowledge which are a constant source of disputes, is not this division of views a necessary result of the inexactitude of the signs employed?

5. Is there any means of correcting signs that are badly made, and of rendering all sciences equally susceptible of demonstration?[11]

In the event the prize was awarded to Joseph Degérando.[12] An essay by Pierre Prévost,[13] Professor of Philosophy at Geneva, was judged second in merit, and a contribution by

---

[11] *Mémoires de l'Institut National des Sciences et Arts. Sciences morales et politiques*, i, pp. i–ii.
[12] Ibid. ii. 2. The surname is often printed as 'de Gérando.
[13] *Des signes envisagés relativement à leur influence sur la formation des idées* (Paris, an VIII).

P.-F. Lancelin was considered worthy of commendation.[14] It should also be mentioned that Maine de Biran started to write an entry for this competition, but did not complete it. His notes survive, and as they make a contribution to the subject, they will be referred to as occasion demands. But we shall chiefly consider Degérando's answers to these questions in the form they took in his *Des signes et de l'art de penser, considérés dans leurs rapports mutuels*, a work in four large volumes which was published in the Year VIII.

Degérando, the author of the book we are now to consider, was a Catholic from Lyons who had fought with the inhabitants of that city against the troops of the Convention in 1793, and thereupon fled to Switzerland. He returned after the amnesty and later supported Camille Jordan's attempts to get autonomy for the Church. As a result Degérando was among those who fled the country in Fructidor of the Year V. This time he went to Germany, and got to know some of the leading German writers. There are no indications of Catholic philosophy in his book which, in my opinion, is a very good example of the philosophical work of the Idéologues, as well as a good, if lengthy, piece of philosophical thinking on its own account. It was Degérando's view that Condillac and his most faithful expositors had 'gone beyond (*traversé*) the truth, a fault which is very common in philosophy'.[15] It will be convenient to consider the answers he gave to the five questions posed by the Institute, and compare some of them with what Maine de Biran had written but had not published.

The first question was whether our earliest ideas essentially depend on the use of signs. For this question to have any point, there must clearly be an initial distinction between sensations, which, according to the empiricist view we are examining, are the source of all knowledge, and the ideas which arise from

---

[14] *Introduction à l'analyse des sciences, ou de la génération, des fondements, et des instruments de nos connaissances* (Paris, an IX–an XI). This book is briefly discussed by Picavet, *Les Idéologues* (Paris, 1891), pp. 424–33. It was much admired by Stendhal. See V. Del Litto, *La Vie intellectuelle de Stendhal* (Paris, 1959), pp. 47–50, 122–4, 142–5.

[15] Degérando, *Des signes et de l'art de penser* (Paris, an VIII), p. xx.

them and are the knowledge to which the sensations give rise. Thus the questioners were in effect asking whether it is possible to pass beyond mere sensation without the help of signs of some sort. They were assuming Condillac's general account of decomposition and analysis, and in particular his belief that they required the use of signs. I do not find that Condillac's views on this matter are very clearly set out, but Cabanis, in his *Rapports du physique et du moral de l'homme*, had maintained that 'we only distinguish sensations from one another by attaching to them signs which represent and characterise them; we only compare them in so far as we both represent and characterise by means of signs either their connections or their differences'. He even goes as far as to say that in the absence of signs there might not be any genuine sensations at all, for signs are necessary in order to 'stabilize' (*fixer*) them.[16] But why, we naturally ask, should not this distinguishing and stabilizing take place by means of an act of attention? To admit this, however, would have been to admit some agency of the self distinct from passive sensation; Locke's 'reflection', instead of being analysed into signs, as Condillac had suggested, might then have been reinstated as a primary activity of the soul. Hence it was considered important to account for mental activity in terms of signs, and signs in terms of association. Now Degérando, as I understand him, rejects this view on various grounds. In the first place he argues that the passage from sensation to perception is inconceivable apart from attention in the sense of an activity of the mind. In saying this, of course, he accepts the distinction made by Condillac between sensation and observation, but holds that the attention which differentiates the two cannot be the exclusive prominence of one element in sensation as Condillac had argued, but is an act by which the mind 'fixes itself' (*se fixe*) by relation to an object in order to perceive it (i. 10). According to Cabanis 'fixing' (or 'stabilizing' as I translated it earlier) required a sign for its accomplishment. According to Degérando, it is the mind which, in attending, does the 'fixing', and needs no sign in order to do so. Whereas

[16] *Mémoires de l'Institut*, i. 87–88.

Cabanis seems to have thought of the decomposition of a given complex of sensations in terms of labelling or signposting—as when someone sticks a flag in a map in order to mark some place on it or come back to it—Degérando seems to have thought of it in terms of what we do when we focus our eyes. When we fix our attention on part of a landscape there is, on his view, an activity of attending to one part rather than another to which the movement of the eyes is subordinated. This it is which makes perception different from sensation, and this it is which makes possible the genesis and use of signs themselves. Hence the use of signs, far from being the analysis of what mental activity really is, in fact presupposes mental activity in an irreducible sense. Maine de Biran, in the notes to which I have referred, makes a similar point when he speaks of 'our active power' (*puissance motrice*) which 'recalls the word and awakens the idea', and is thus necessary if there are to be words at all.[17]

It should not be supposed that Degérando, in making these criticisms of Condillac's and Cabanis's linguistic extremism, rejected their thesis that signs are of very great importance in that developing analysis which thought consists of. Indeed, he elaborated and improved Condillac's theory of signs in ways that might have been fruitful had the philosophy of the Idéologues succeeded in getting a longer hearing. For example, he argues that an important difference between prelinguistic and linguistic signs is that the former *excite* ideas in us but retain our attention on themselves, as with the pain that arouses images of what had relieved it in the past, whereas the latter *conduct* or *lead* our attention away from themselves to their meanings, as with the words on a page. Thus even *demonstrative* signs (*signes indicateurs*), although they engage our attention, lead it away from themselves to the object that is being indicated. Demonstratives or indicators are themselves imperfect, however, since they require their objects to be present, and hence presuppose others which signify what is absent: '... in language and perception they are nothing but simple

[17] *Œuvres* (ed. Pierre Tisserand) (Paris, 1920 ff.), i. 280.

auxiliaries: their function is to complete, to specify the effect of other signs' (i. 202). This, I suggest, is a great improvement on Condillac's assumption (he can hardly be said to have had a view on the matter) that demonstratives are natural signs, part of 'the language of nature', by which a child, for example, 'shows with a gesture the object which it needs'.[18] Again, Degérando distinguishes between the signs we have for complex ideas of sensible things, such as the words 'dog' or 'house', and the signs we have for complex ideas 'of the second order', as he puts it, such as 'nation' or 'constitution'. We can hardly be said to have 'ideas' of this second sort at all, since nations and constitutions cannot be pictured, so that in such cases we have to make do with the words themselves. They retain their meaning despite the absence of imagery by virtue of the fact that by means of them 'we enjoy the power of recalling all their primitive elements. . . . With signs of the second order we possess like the merchant with his till, sums which for the moment are out of view but which we can take account of and enumerate in detail whenever we consider it advisable' (i. 200–1). Degérando also compares these signs with paper money that can be cashed (i. 199), and says that they 'do not show us objects, but only the road that must be followed to discover them' (i. 199).

We have seen that Condillac regarded the theory of signs as a means of showing how thinking arises naturally from the circumstances in which men with sense organs find themselves. His account of attention as a prominence of one part, or a lack of prominence of other parts of the original sense manifold, is clearly designed to dispense with acts or activities of the mind. Experience and thought were to arise by natural means out of the association of sensations and images. His aim would today be called 'reductionist'. That is, he set out to show that reasoning, judgement, thought generally, are identical with, or nothing but, sensation. This he expressed in his famous phrase that thought is 'transformed sensation'. The transformation here meant is not magical but symbolical or logical. Although

[18] *Cours d'études*, ii, *Grammaire* (*Œuvres*, ed. Le Roy), i. 428.

de Tracy criticized Condillac on many points, he too, in his *Éléments de l'idéologie* (1801), took the same course when he said 'penser c'est sentir', which I translate 'to think is to have sensations'. Now the discussion whether a distinct activity is required in order to distinguish observation (or perception, as Degérando called it) from sensation, is about this very issue. If observation or perception cannot be reduced to sensation, then it could hardly be maintained that judgement and reasoning can. But there emerged, in the course of the arguments we are describing, another, more effective objection to Condillac's reductionism. This objection is stated very clearly by Degérando in a book published in 1804, *Histoire comparée des systèmes de philosophie relativement aux principes des connaissances humaines.*

Those who put forward the view that all the operations of the human mind are reducible to sensation [wrote Degérando] are either bestowing a single collective name on phenomena of very different kinds, and hence differ from the general run of philosophers by their idiosyncratic mode of expression, or else they suppose that these phenomena are really identical with one another, and thus they lose sight of essential differences (iii. 499).

Elsewhere in the same book he writes of Condillac that 'confining all the operations of the mind under the general heading of "transformed sensation", he believes himself to have given the facts a simplicity which he has introduced only into the terms' (i. 346). This objection to Condillac, he says, was first made by Pierre Prévost in 1800 in his entry for the prize that was awarded to Degérando, and was later made again by Maine de Biran, in his *Influence de l'habitude sur la faculté de pensée*. Maine de Biran's formulation calls for no comment, but Prévost's takes the matter a stage further. Condillac, he says, extends the use of the word 'language' when he says that language is necessary for 'fixing' an object for separate attention (*Des Signes*, p. 26). Prévost also generalized the criticism still more widely.

I ask [he writes] whether those philosophers who, like Boscowich, for example, endeavour to assimilate impulse to attraction, have not committed a sort of violence against our common conceptions; and whether, after a lot of argumentation, they do not leave us where they found us. Monads are another example of this, all the more striking because they are the result of the most extensive generalisation that thought can conceive (*Des Signes*, p. 56).

Let us now turn to the second and third questions set by the Institute. The second is in effect the question whether the way to perfect the sciences is to perfect their language, and the third is whether the success of the successful sciences is due to the adequacy of the language used in them. It will be convenient to start with the third, since an affirmative answer to it would provide a ground for giving an affirmative answer to the second. If, on the other hand, the success of the successful sciences is not wholly or mainly due to the adequacy of their language, this would be a reason for holding that perfecting the language of the sciences is not the only way to bring them to perfection.

Degérando's answer to the third question is that improvements in the language of a science are consequences of the advances made rather than their ground. 'The nomenclature of a science', he writes, 'is related to the science itself as monuments are related to history; it preserves what is, but can neither predict what is not yet, nor explain the future' (iii. 199). The advance of a science, he argues, is to a considerable degree a matter of chance, and is hence beyond the possibility of prediction, although the more advanced a science is, the less the part played in it by accidental discoveries (iii. 75). Degérando was aware that the claims made on behalf of Condillac's linguistic theory of science gained support from the example of chemistry. He argued, however, that chemistry is rather a special case, since the elements requiring names are relatively few, and of comparable type one with another. He contrasts this state of affairs with that obtaining in anatomy and physiology, where the named objects differ widely in type, as do bones and flesh, nerves and liquids, muscles and arteries. There are great differences of type in the functions too, as between seeing and digesting. Degérando does not think that all these different features could be brought into the kind of single linguistic scheme which chemists at that time were constructing (iii. 213 ff.). It is interesting to notice that he saw clearly the way in which the language of chemistry would have to develop. He observed that if the language established by Lavoisier and his associates was to be taken further, simple, self-explanatory names like 'sulphuric acid' would prove inadequate, and names for highly complex substances would have to be found, and would then become a sort of formulae (iii. 204). He mentions the possibility of using letters for the basic elements and building them into 'a set of algebraical formulae', as had been done by von Humboldt in his studies of 'galvanism' (iii. 319-20). Lavoisier had not taken this step, and the possibility indicated by Degérando was realized by Berzelius in 1813.

Having concluded that the success of the successful sciences is not mainly due to the adequacy of the language used in them, Degérando had no strong ground for supposing that the way to perfect human knowledge is to perfect human language or to construct an ideal language. In putting this as their second question, the Institute undoubtedly had in mind the numerous schemes for a universal and fault-free language, known in France as 'Pasigraphie' and in England sometimes as 'Pantigraphia', for by the end of the eighteenth century Condillac's linguisticism had encouraged the revival of projects similar to those of Wilkins and Leibniz. According to Degérando, the whole idea of constructing such a language is a 'chimaera' (ii. 224), since it is impossible for one generation to anticipate the observations and experiences of future generations.[19] Like Locke, he also emphasizes the extent to which the languages of different peoples depend upon the level and nature of their civilization. Among different peoples there

[19] Destutt de Tracy had used the same expression in the *Mémoires de l'Institut*, i. 416: 'la langue parfaite est sans doute une chimère.' He discusses the matter in some detail in *Mémoires de l'Institut* (iii, an IX), pp. 535 ff., e.g. 'Je crois une langue universelle dans le même cas que le mouvement perpétuel.' See especially p. 458.

are words for different 'bundles of ideas', because their circumstances and their customs give rise to different nomenclatures (i. 215). The words for 'bundles of ideas' relating to sensible objects may well be similar or function in similar ways among different peoples, but where institutions and interests vary widely, the languages must vary widely also. Maine de Biran discusses this topic in the unpublished notes to which I have referred. He quotes Locke to the effect that Augustus himself could not have changed by any law or decree the meaning of a single Latin word, and paints a picture of the difficulties that would beset anyone who tried to do so. In effect, such a man would have to control not only the wills of everyone, but also their intelligences, since the will to obey his linguistic decrees might not be accompanied by the ability to carry them out.[20] In this context Maine de Biran calls attention to the *emotive* force of ethical terms, and remarks that this is a feature of meaning which must vary even within a single society since, for example, the word 'theft' cannot evoke similar feelings in a property-owner and a pauper.[21]

We now come to the fourth question posed by the Institute, the question whether the constant and unresolved disputes characteristic of certain sciences are the result of the inexactitude of the terms used in them. Degérando does not deny, of course, that inexact language has been a source of confusion and hence of intellectual stalemate, but he thinks it important to mention other sources as well, such as differences of temperament, circumstance, prejudice, and interest (iii, chap. ix). Competing prejudices will never produce agreement, but when the truth is sought, competing views will help to locate it. 'If we were wise', he writes, 'diversity of opinion would be related to the progress of truth as the division of labour is related to the prosperity of society; we should find in the exertions of others a supplement to our own weakness' (iii. 331). These comments, of course, apply to the experimental

[20] Maine de Biran, *Œuvres*, i. 248 ff. Cf. Destutt de Tracy, *Mémoires de l'Institut*, i. 415–16.
[21] Ibid., p. 266.

sciences, but there are two further observations which may be intended to apply to metaphysics as well. Degérando agreed with Condillac's view that metaphysicians like Spinoza believed themselves to be making reports on the nature of things when in fact they were developing the consequences of their own definitions. But, unlike Condillac, he considered the possibility that philosophers sometimes want to *change* the meanings of words. 'How many systems of philosophy', he writes, 'have owed their apparent novelty to their authors' art of changing the language of their predecessors, and how many years have often had to pass in order to reinstate them in their true position, by recognising the artifice on which they were based' (i. 258). One wishes that Degérando had had more to say about this interesting idea.[22] He also points out that not all cases where a word is used by the disputants in different senses are *verbal* disputes. 'For their diversity of meaning', he says, 'is often the consequence and not the cause of the difference of opinions....' He gives as an example of this the different meanings attached to the word 'virtue' by the Stoics and Epicureans respectively. The dispute between these two philosophical schools was not a confusion based on their different uses of the word. On the contrary, they used the word differently because of the different ends of life which they each recommended (iii. 343–4).

The fifth question was whether the system of signs could be so improved that all sciences would be equally susceptible of demonstration. And in the first place it should be pointed out that Condillac's views on the matter—which the Institute had in mind in putting the question—are not easy to reconcile with one another, for on the one hand he had emphasized the importance of sense experience and criticized Spinoza and Leibniz for confusing tautologies with information, and yet on the other hand he had said that '*equations, propositions, judgements* are at bottom the same thing, and hence one reasons in the same way in all the sciences'. The sentence I have just quoted

---

[22] An idea worked out, in complete independence of Degérando, of course, by Professor Lazerowitz in his *The Structure of Metaphysics* (London, 1955).

comes from his *Logic*, his last published work, but in his *La Langue des calculs*, published posthumously in 1798 while the competitors for the prize were at work on their entries, this point of view is stated even more strongly.[23] Degérando, as de Tracy had done before him, put forward two main objections to this view. In the first place, in language reminiscent of Hume, he distinguished between 'truths of fact, which consist in the relation of our ideas to things', and 'abstract truths, which consist only in the relations of our ideas to one another' (i. xxxi–xxxii). Condillac's view that all sciences must be equally susceptible to demonstration neglects, according to Degérando, this important distinction, and, by implying that all sciences are abstract sciences, goes against the empiricism which Condillac had endeavoured to establish (ii. 121). In the second place, Degérando argued that the ideas of algebra, which he takes to be ideas of quantity, are built up by performing the same operation on units all of which are of the same kind. But such a simple and uniform procedure is not to be found outside mathematics. In other branches of knowledge our language relates to what Locke had called 'mixed modes', that is, complex ideas built up from ideas of different kinds in different relations to one another. (The reference to Locke is to the *Essay*, ii, chap. xxxii, § 1.) Degérando's view is that with such heterogeneous materials the reasoning of the non-mathematical sciences can never achieve the certainty of

[23] J. Joseph Garat, a philosopher-politician and member of the Institute, in the course of a speech commending the new edition of Condillac's works to the Legislative Body, said that it had been Condillac's merit 'de donner à la langue de la morale et des lois la certitude de la géométrie' (*Discours . . . par le citoyen Garat en offrant les œuvres de Condillac à la séance du 3 fructidor, an 6*). Maine de Biran (*Œuvres*, i. 290–1) asked what would be gained if moral truths were proved with the same evidence as geometrical truths, and answered: 'One more abstract truth would have been established, which would have had no more influence on human conduct than mathematical truths of the same sort.' Degérando discusses this topic (*Des Signes*, iv. 293 ff.), and argues that there are few demonstrable moral truths (those few concern the relationships of individual men to one another in a state of nature), and that most moral truths, being about mixed modes, such as ambition and the like, are not susceptible of demonstration. He is using 'moral' in a wider sense, of course, but writes of the *mania* of trying to demonstrate everything (iv. 277).

calculation (i. 290 ff.). A calculus is a simple language, but not the form of all language.

III

It is now time that we made some comments. From what has been said it is pretty clear that a number of the views about the philosophy of language which have been prominent in the twentieth century were discussed by the Idéologues and then allowed to slip into oblivion. That thinking is essentially talking, that a language is a calculus, and that philosophical problems are pseudo-problems that can be exposed and dispersed by means of linguistic reform, were ideas held and discussed then as now. Condillac and the Idéologues, however, used a terminology based on Locke's *Essay* as they understood it, with a threefold division into sensations, ideas, and words, and with 'idea' sometimes meaning 'image' and sometimes meaning 'meaning'. A philosophical examination of their views, therefore, would take us into the tedious and dubious business of disentangling their terminology and relating it to our own. We can avoid this, and conform to the requirements laid down for the Dawes Hicks Lecture, by concentrating on what can be discussed in their own terms, and this is what I propose to do.

It is worthy of some notice that the prize was awarded to a Catholic *émigré* by a learned body composed mainly of republican deists and atheists. The competitors, it is true, presented their entries under pseudonyms, but any idea that the judges felt themselves deceived is dispelled by the fact that Degérando was himself made a member of the Institute, in spite of his antirevolutionary connexions. He did not, to begin with, find it easy to strike the right note. The four volumes into which he later on expanded his prize essay were described as 'a hotchpotch' (*un fatras*) by the philosophers who made the award, and de Tracy advised Maine de Biran not to spoil his own work by a similar discursiveness. Degérando saw his own situation very clearly. 'I am', he said, 'in a pretty awkward position between the batteries of the philosophers of Auteuil on the one side, and those of the enemies of reason on the other.'[24] Nevertheless, the philosophy of language was at this time discussed in a spirit largely free from party predilections, as when the writings of a proscribed priest, the Abbé Sicard, were respectfully reviewed in the republican press.[25] A more detailed account than I have been able to give here of Degérando's work on signs would show that he was investigating a subject which is to a large degree independent of creeds and parties. We have already given examples of this, in his denial of the view that demonstrative symbols are natural signs capable of having meaning independently of other types of sign, and his distinction between stimulus-signs (*signes excitateurs*), which just arouse or excite ideas, and conductor-signs (*signes conducteurs*) which have the function (essential for language) of directing attention away from themselves to their meanings.

Nevertheless, the discussion was not wholly on the grammatico-philosophical level. Maine de Biran, in the unpublished notes to which we have more than once referred, called (his own) attention to some social implications of the views of Helvétius and of Condillac. Condillac's views about language, he wrote, like Helvétius's views about knowledge in general, assumed a natural equality between men that is not compatible with the facts. He paraphrases Condillac in the following disapproving terms:

... the genius creates nothing and discovers nothing; to begin with he crawls, and then he moves along more quickly, guided by the analogy of signs which cannot deceive him if he has learned to make them well; the consequence is that since everyone has the power of analysing well, everyone can reach the same degree of knowledge, so that inequality of understanding does not come from nature, but is the result of departing from her original course, of neglecting to

[24] Maine de Biran, *Œuvres* (ed. Tisserand), vi. 140–2, and 144.

[25] P.-L. Roederer, *Opuscules* (Paris, an IX), i. 285 and 395–8. 'Sicard, en mettant pour ainsi dire en peinture l'opération des abstractions a plus fait que Locke par ses belles discussions pour la destruction de ces erreurs qui ne sont pas innocentes, car elles sont un obstacle à tout perfectionnement de la logique et de la raison humaine' (p. 397).

analyse, of abandoning oneself to confused conceptions, and of setting up a faulty linguistic usage.[26]

This is an accurate though jaundiced summary of Condillac's view. Indeed, Condillac believed that ordinary men who confine their curiosity to what serves their own needs, make use of the true method which philosophers, in order to distinguish themselves from the vulgar, have abused and abandoned. Dressmakers 'know how to analyse as well as philosophers'. Condillac, like Bacon, believed that the correct method of inquiry would serve for 'a levelling of wits'. Linguistic empiricism, as expounded by Condillac, is the epistemology of egalitarianism. Maine de Biran's objection is that no amount of analytic or linguistic skill can lead to those discoveries which consist in looking at the facts in a totally new light, or in noticing connexions and analogies which have hitherto been overlooked. I quote his statement of this.

> The strength with which, in an indivisable instant, the mind simultaneously conceives a host of things, all this seems to me quite independent of the artifice of signs, and it is just in this instantaneous forming of thoughts and of thoughts of a certain order, rather than in their analytic development, that the preeminence of certain minds consists.

It should be mentioned, in this connexion, that Prévost, in his entry for the prize, pointed out that in so far as thinking is regarded as the working out of a calculus, it is something that can be done very effectively by machines, as Pascal and Leibniz had shown in the previous century (*Des Signes*, p. 14). According to Maine de Biran, if thinking is calculating, then the genius becomes redundant. According to Prévost, if thinking is calculating, it is men who can be dispensed with.

The Idéologues we have been considering had no confidence in the projects for a universal and perfect language. They were agreed that if there were to be such a thing at all, it would have to be imposed by a linguistic dictator. But they also believed that a linguistic dictator would be unable to impose it anyway. Maine de Biran, it will be remembered, quoted Locke on

[26] Maine de Biran, *Œuvres* (Tisserand), i. 302 ff.

the linguistic impotence of Augustus. Locke's own argument is curious. He said that the significance of words is 'perfectly arbitrary', so that every man can annex what words he likes to what ideas he wishes. Hence, whatever Augustus may have decreed, each individual could thwart his will by annexing the word to a different idea from the idea he is commanded to annex it to. Locke was thus an extreme linguistic individualist. He states this view in almost political terms: '. . . every man hath so inviolable a liberty to make words stand for what he pleases, that no one hath the power to make others have the same ideas in their minds that he has, when they use the same words that he does' (*Essay*, iii, chap. ii, § 8). According to Locke, therefore, each man can escape linguistic tyranny into his own private language, where words are made by *him* to stand for *his* ideas. As we have seen, the Idéologues believed that words were applied to things by being used for the ideas or thoughts of the things. Nevertheless, de Biran and de Tracy explained the impossibility of linguistic dictatorship without recourse to Locke's theory of linguistic natural rights. Their common point of view is that languages are *inherently* imperfect. Destutt de Tracy, who states the argument at some length,[27] maintains that a sign is only immune from misunderstanding or misuse at the moment when it is first invented and then only by the inventor himself. From that moment onwards the user cannot be sure that he 'collects under this sign exactly the same collection of ideas that he did the first time'. The possibility of differences in meaning, therefore, is all the greater when the same word is used by different people, who themselves learnt it from different people at different times and have different types of experience and expectation. The main point is, therefore, not that individuals can at will disobey the commands of the linguistic dictator, but that the command itself is bound to be differently interpreted in the course of transmission. It is not a matter of natural right, but of natural incompetence.

In conclusion, I must say a word or two about the great in-

[27] *Mémoires de l'Institut National*, i. 410 ff. and iii. 535 ff.

fluence of Locke upon the French philosophers whose work I have been discussing. Condillac constantly refers to him in respectful terms, and undoubtedly owed a lot to him. But in endeavouring to introduce order and economy into Locke's sprawling asymmetry Condillac substituted, in spite of himself, a system for a method. Destutt de Tracy, Degérando, Prévost, and Maine de Biran were also close students of Locke, and their work shows how fruitful his method could be. But in their different ways they went back from Condillac's Palladian Locke to the more Gothic original. Furthermore, they had some knowledge of Berkeley, Hume, Hartley, and Reid, and drew upon it with skill and discretion to supplement what they had learnt from Locke. It will be fitting, therefore, to end this lecture by quoting Degérando's comment on the British philosophers of the century. 'The English School', he writes,

has in general a calm, pacific and reserved character, although from time to time it is too dry and too torpid; above all things it respects the findings of common sense; it has a high regard for practical results, and has an attachment for those of its members who write books on moral philosophy.[28]

[28] *Histoire comparée*, iii. 105.

ON THE SOURCES OF KNOWLEDGE AND OF IGNORANCE

BY KARL R. POPPER

It follows, therefore, that truth manifests itself...
BENEDICTUS DE SPINOZA

Every man carries about him a touchstone... to distinguish... truth from appearances.
JOHN LOCKE

... it is impossible for us to *think* of any thing, which we have not antecedently *felt*, either by our external or internal senses.
DAVID HUME

The title of this lecture is likely, I fear, to offend some critical ears. For although 'Sources of Knowledge' is in order, and 'Sources of Error' would have been in order too, the phrase 'Sources of Ignorance' is another matter. 'Ignorance is something negative: it is the absence of knowledge. But how on earth can the absence of anything have sources?'[1] This question was put to me by a friend when I confided to him the title I had chosen for this lecture. I was a little shaken by this for I had been, I confess, quite pleased with the title. Hard

---

[1] Descartes and Spinoza went even further, and asserted that not only ignorance but also error is 'something negative'—a '*privation*' of knowledge and even of the proper use of our freedom. (See Descartes' *Principles*, part I, 33–42, and the Third and Fourth *Meditations*; also Spinoza's *Ethics*, part II, *propos.* 35 and *schol.*; his 21st letter, para 3 f., *Editio Tertia*, J. van Vloten and J. P. N. Land, 1914 = 34th letter, para 7 f., ed. C. H. Bruder, 1844; and his *Principles of Descartes' Philosophy*, part I, *propos.* 15 and *schol.*) Nevertheless, Spinoza speaks (e.g. *Ethics*, part II, *propos.* 41) also of the 'cause' of falsity (or error). Aristotle, on the other hand, (*Met.* 1052a 1) seems to say that only total ignorance is quite negative (like blindness; cp. *Cat.* 12a 26–13a 35) and that even 'privation' (*sterēsis*; *Met.* 1046a 30–35) may have something like a cause if a thing suffers privation (not by nature but) by violence.

Annual Philosophical Lecture read before the British Academy on 20 *January* 1960. *First published in the* Proceedings of the British Academy, **46**, 1960. Most of the footnotes, of p. 179, and pp. 192 f. as well as paragraph (9) on p. 210 have been newly added in the present revised version.

pressed for a reply I found myself improvising a rationalization, and explaining to my friend that the curious linguistic effect of the title was actually intended. I told him that I hoped to direct attention, through the phrasing of this title, to a number of historically important although unrecorded philosophical doctrines and among them (apart from the important theory that *truth is manifest*) especially to the *conspiracy theory of ignorance* which interprets ignorance not as a mere lack of knowledge but as the work of some mischievous power, the source of impure and evil influences which pervert and poison our minds and instil in us the habit of resistance to knowledge.

I am not quite sure whether this explanation allayed my friend's misgivings, but it did silence him. Your case is different since you are silenced by the rules of the present transactions. So I can only hope that I have allayed your misgivings sufficiently, for the time being, to allow me to begin my story at the other end—with the sources of knowledge rather than with the sources of ignorance. However, I shall presently come back to the sources of ignorance, and also to the conspiracy theory of these sources.

I

The problem which I wish to examine afresh in this lecture, and which I hope not only to examine but to solve, may perhaps be described as an aspect of the old quarrel between the British and the Continental schools of philosophy—the quarrel between the classical empiricism of Bacon, Locke, Berkeley, Hume, and Mill, and the classical rationalism or intellectualism of Descartes, Spinoza, and Leibniz. In this quarrel the British school insisted that the ultimate source of all knowledge was observation, while the Continental school insisted that it was the intellectual intuition of clear and distinct ideas.

Most of these issues are still very much alive. Not only has empiricism, still the ruling doctrine in England, conquered the United States, but it is now widely accepted even on the European Continent as the true theory of *scientific* knowledge.

Cartesian intellectualism, alas, has been only too often distorted into one or another of the various forms of modern irrationalism.

I shall try to show in this lecture that the differences between classical empiricism and rationalism are much smaller than their similarities, and that both are mistaken. I hold that they are mistaken although I am myself both an empiricist and a rationalist of sorts. But I believe that, though observation and reason have each an important role to play, these roles hardly resemble those which their classical defenders attributed to them. More especially, I shall try to show that neither observation nor reason can be described as a source of knowledge, in the sense in which they have been claimed to be sources of knowledge down to the present day.

II

Our problem belongs to the theory of knowledge, or to epistemology, reputed to be the most abstract and remote and altogether irrelevant region of pure philosophy. For example Hume, one of the greatest thinkers in the field, predicted that owing to the remoteness and abstractness and practical irrelevance of some of his results none of his readers would believe in them for more than an hour.

Kant's attitude was different. He thought that the problem 'What can I know?' was one of the three most important questions a man could ask. Bertrand Russell, in spite of being closer to Hume in philosophic temperament, seems to side in this matter with Kant. And I think Russell is right when he attributes to epistemology practical consequences for science, ethics, and even politics. For he says that epistemological relativism, or the idea that there is no such thing as objective truth, and epistemological pragmatism, or the idea that truth is the same as usefulness, are closely linked with authoritarian and totalitarian ideas.[2]

Russell's views are of course disputed. Some recent philosophers have developed a doctrine of the essential impotence

[2] See Bertrand Russell, *Let the People Think*, 1941, pp. 77 ff.

and practical irrelevance of all genuine philosophy, and thus, one can assume, of epistemology. Philosophy, they say, cannot by its very nature have any significant consequences, and so it can influence neither science nor politics. But I think that ideas are dangerous and powerful things, and that even philosophers have sometimes produced ideas. Indeed, I have no doubt that this new doctrine of the impotence of all philosophy is amply refuted by the facts.

The situation is really very simple. The belief of a liberal—the belief in the possibility of a rule of law, of equal justice, of fundamental rights, and a free society—can easily survive the recognition that judges are not omniscient and may make mistakes about facts and that, in practice, absolute justice is hardly ever realized in any particular legal case. But the belief in the possibility of a rule of law, of justice and of freedom, can hardly survive the acceptance of an epistemology which teaches that there are no objective facts; not merely in this particular case, but also in any other case; and that the judge cannot have made a factual mistake because he can no more be wrong about the facts than he can be right.

III

The great movement of liberation which started in the Renaissance and led through the many vicissitudes of the reformation and the religious and revolutionary wars to the free societies in which the English-speaking peoples are privileged to live, this movement was inspired throughout by an unparalleled epistemological optimism: by a most optimistic view of man's power to discern truth and to acquire knowledge.

At the heart of this new optimistic view of the possibility of knowledge lies the doctrine that *truth is manifest*. Truth may perhaps be veiled. But it may reveal itself.[3] And if it does not

---

[3] See my mottoes: Spinoza, *Of God, Man, and Human Happiness*, ch. 15. (Parallel passages are: *Ethics*, II, *scholium* to *propos*. 43: 'Indeed, as light manifests itself and darkness, so with truth: it is its own standard, and that of falsity.' Also: *De intell. emend.*, 35, 36; 76th letter, end of para. 5, *Editio Tertia*, van Vloten and Land, 1914 = 74th letter, para. 7, ed. Bruder, 1844: '*est enim verum index sui et falsi.*') Locke, *The Conduct of the Understanding*, section 3. (Cp. also *Romans*, i. 19.)

reveal itself, it may be revealed by us. Removing the veil may not be easy. But once the naked truth stands revealed before our eyes, we have the power to see it, to distinguish it from falsehood, and to know that it *is* truth.

The birth of modern science and modern technology was inspired by this optimistic epistemology whose main spokesmen were Bacon and Descartes. They taught that there was no need for any man to appeal to authority in matters of truth because each man carried the sources of knowledge in himself; either in his power of sense perception which he may use for the careful observation of nature, or in his power of intellectual intuition which he may use to distinguish truth from falsehood by refusing to accept any idea which is not clearly and distinctly perceived by the intellect.

Man can know: thus he can be free. This is the formula which explains the link between epistemological optimism and the ideas of liberalism.

This link is paralleled by the opposite link. Disbelief in the power of human reason, in man's power to discern the truth, is almost invariably linked with distrust of man. Thus epistemological pessimism is linked, historically, with a doctrine of human depravity, and it tends to lead to the demand for the establishment of powerful traditions and the entrenchment of a powerful authority which would save man from his folly and his wickedness. (There is a striking sketch of this theory of authoritarianism, and a picture of the burden carried by those in authority, in the story of *The Grand Inquisitor* in Dostoievsky's *The Brothers Karamazov*.)

The contrast between epistemological pessimism and optimism may be said to be fundamentally the same as that between epistemological traditionalism and rationalism. (I am using the latter term in its wider sense in which it is opposed to irrationalism, and in which it covers not only Cartesian intellectualism but Lockean empiricism also.) For we can interpret traditionalism as the belief that, owing to the absence of an objective and discernible truth, we are faced with the choice between accepting the authority of tradition, and chaos; while rationalism has, of course, always claimed the right of reason and of empirical science to criticize, and to reject, any tradition, and any authority, as being based on sheer unreason or prejudice or accident.

IV

It is a disturbing fact that even an abstract study like pure epistemology is not as pure as one might think (and as Aristotle believed) but that its ideas may, to a large extent, be motivated and unconsciously inspired by political hopes and by Utopian dreams. This should be a warning to the epistemologist. What can he do about it? As an epistemologist I have only one interest—to find out the truth about the problems of epistemology, whether or not this truth fits in with my political ideas. But am I not liable to be influenced, unconsciously, by my political hopes and beliefs?

It so happens that I am not only an empiricist and a rationalist of sorts but also a liberal (in the English sense of this term); but just because I am a liberal, I feel that few things are more important for a liberal than to submit the various theories of liberalism to a searching critical examination.

While I was engaged in a critical examination of this kind I discovered the part played by certain epistemological theories in the development of liberal ideas; and especially by the various forms of epistemological optimism.[4] And I found that, as an epistemologist, I had to reject these epistemological theories as untenable. This experience of mine may illustrate the point that our dreams and our hopes need not necessarily control our results, and that, in searching for the truth, it may be our best plan to start by criticizing our most cherished beliefs. This may seem to some a perverse plan. But it will not seem so to those who want to find the truth and are not afraid of it.

[4] See chapter 17 of my *Conjectures and Refutations*.

V

In examining the optimistic epistemology inherent in certain ideas of liberalism, I found a cluster of doctrines which, although often accepted implicitly, have not, to my knowledge, been explicitly discussed or even noticed by philosophers or historians. The most fundamental of them is one which I have already mentioned—the doctrine that truth is manifest. The strangest of them is the conspiracy theory of ignorance, which is a curious outgrowth from the doctrine of manifest truth.

By the doctrine that truth is manifest I mean, you will recall, the optimistic view that truth, if put before us naked, is always recognizable as truth. Thus truth, if it does not reveal itself, has only to be unveiled, or dis-covered. Once this is done, there is no need for further argument. We have been given eyes to see the truth, and the 'natural light' of reason to see it by.

This doctrine is at the heart of the teaching of both Descartes and Bacon. Descartes based his optimistic epistemology on the important theory of the *veracitas dei*. What we clearly and distinctly see to be true must indeed be true; for otherwise God would be deceiving us. Thus the truthfulness of God must make truth manifest.

In Bacon we have a similar doctrine. It might be described as the doctrine of the *veracitas naturae*, the truthfulness of Nature. Nature is an open book. He who reads it with a pure mind cannot misread it. Only if his mind is poisoned by prejudice can he fall into error.

This last remark shows that the doctrine that truth is manifest creates the need to explain falsehood. Knowledge, the possession of truth, need not be explained. But how can we ever fall into error if truth is manifest? The answer is: through our own sinful refusal to see the manifest truth; or because our minds harbour prejudices inculcated by education and tradition, or other evil influences which have perverted our originally pure and innocent minds. Ignorance may be the work of powers conspiring to keep us in ignorance, to poison our minds by filling them with falsehood, and to blind our eyes so that they cannot see the manifest truth. Such prejudices and such powers, then, are sources of our ignorance.

The conspiracy theory of ignorance is fairly well known in its Marxian form as the conspiracy of a capitalist press that perverts and suppresses truth and fills the workers' minds with false ideologies. Prominent among these, of course, are the doctrines of religion. It is surprising to find how unoriginal this Marxist theory is. The wicked and fraudulent priest who keeps the people in ignorance was a stock figure of the eighteenth century and, I am afraid, one of the inspirations of liberalism. It can be traced back to the protestant belief in the conspiracy of the Roman Church, and also to the beliefs of those dissenters who held similar views about the Established Church. (Elsewhere I have traced the prehistory of this belief back to Plato's uncle Critias; see chapter 8, section ii, of my *Open Society*.)

This curious belief in a conspiracy is the almost inevitable consequence of the optimistic belief that truth, and therefore goodness, must prevail if only truth is given a fair chance. 'Let her and falsehood grapple; who ever knew Truth put to the worse, in a free and open encounter?' (*Areopagitica*. Compare the French proverb: *La vérité triomphe toujours*.) So when Milton's Truth was put to the worse, the necessary inference was that the encounter had not been free and open: if the manifest truth does not prevail, it must have been maliciously suppressed. One can see that an attitude of tolerance which is based upon an optimistic faith in the victory of truth may easily be shaken.[5] For it is liable to turn into a conspiracy theory which would be hard to reconcile with an attitude of tolerance.

I do not assert that there was never a grain of truth in this conspiracy theory. But in the main it was a myth, just as the theory of manifest truth from which it grew was a myth.

For the simple truth is that truth is often hard to come by, and that once found it may easily be lost again. Erroneous beliefs may have an astonishing power to survive, for thousands of years, in defiance of experience, with or without the aid of

[5] Cp. J. W. N. Watkins on Milton in *The Listener*, 22 January 1959.

any conspiracy. The history of science and especially of medicine could furnish us with a number of good examples. One example is, indeed, the general conspiracy theory itself. I mean the erroneous view that whenever something evil happens it must be due to the evil will of an evil power. Various forms of this view have survived down to our own day.

Thus the optimistic epistemology of Bacon and of Descartes cannot be true. Yet perhaps the strangest thing in this story is that this false epistemology was the major inspiration of an intellectual and moral revolution without parallel in history. It encouraged men to think for themselves. It gave them hope that through knowledge they might free themselves and others from servitude and misery. It made modern science possible. It became the basis of the fight against censorship and the suppression of free thought. It became the basis of the nonconformist conscience, of individualism, and of a new sense of man's dignity; of a demand for universal education, and of a new dream of a free society. It made men feel responsible for themselves and for others, and eager to improve not only their own condition but also that of their fellow men. It is a case of a bad idea inspiring many good ones.

VI

This false epistemology, however, has also led to disastrous consequences. The theory that truth is manifest—that it is there for everyone to see, if only he wants to see it—this theory is the basis of almost every kind of fanaticism. For only the most depraved wickedness can refuse to see the manifest truth: only those who have every reason to fear truth can deny it, and conspire to suppress it.

Yet the theory that truth is manifest not only breeds fanatics —men possessed by the conviction that all those who do not see the manifest truth must be possessed by the devil—but it may also lead, though perhaps less directly than does a pessimistic epistemology, to authoritarianism. This is so, simply, because truth is not manifest, as a rule. The allegedly manifest truth is therefore in constant need, not only of interpretation and affirmation, but also of re-interpretation and re-affirmation. An authority is required to pronounce upon, and lay down, almost from day to day, what is to be the manifest truth, and it may learn to do so arbitrarily and cynically. And many disappointed epistemologists will turn away from their own former optimism and erect a resplendent authoritarian theory on the basis of a pessimistic epistemology. It seems to me that the greatest epistemologist of all, Plato, exemplifies this tragic development.

VII

Plato plays a decisive part in the pre-history of Descartes' doctrine of the *veracitas dei*—the doctrine that our intellectual intuition does not deceive us because God is truthful and will not deceive us; or in other words, the doctrine that our intellect is a source of knowledge because God is a source of knowledge. This doctrine has a long history which can easily be traced back at least to Homer and Hesiod.

To us, the habit of referring to one's sources would seem natural in a scholar or an historian, and it is perhaps a little surprising to find that this habit stems from the poets; but it does. The Greek poets refer to the sources of their knowledge. These sources are divine. They are the Muses. '... the Greek bards', Gilbert Murray observes, 'always owe, not only what we should call their inspiration, but their actual knowledge of facts to the Muses. The Muses "are present and know all things" ... Hesiod ... always explains that he is dependent on the Muses for his knowledge. Other sources of knowledge are indeed recognized. ... But most often he consults the Muses. ... So does Homer for such subjects as the Catalogue of the Greek army.'[6]

As this quotation shows, the poets were in the habit of claiming not only divine sources of inspiration, but also divine sources of knowledge—divine guarantors of the truth of their stories.

Precisely the same two claims were raised by the philosophers Heraclitus and Parmenides. Heraclitus, it seems, sees himself

[6] See Gilbert Murray, *The Rise of the Greek Epic*, 3rd edn., 1924, p. 96.

ON SOURCES OF KNOWLEDGE AND IGNORANCE 179

as a prophet who 'talks with raving mouth, ... possessed by the god'—by Zeus, the source of all wisdom.[7] And Parmenides, one could almost say, forms the missing link between Homer or Hesiod on the one side and Descartes on the other. His guiding star and inspiration is the goddess Dikē, described by Heraclitus[8] as the guardian of truth. Parmenides describes her as the guardian and keeper of the keys of truth, and as the source of all his knowledge.[9] But Parmenides and Descartes

---

[7] See DK (DK = Diels-Kranz, *Fragmente der Vorsokratiker*, 10th edn., 1960) Heraclitus B 92 and 32; cp. also 93, 41, 64, and 50.

[8] DK, Heraclitus B 28 (see also B 94 and cp. DK Orpheus B 14 and Plato's *Laws* 716A).

[9] The '*goddess*' of Parmenides (DK, B 1, line 22) was identified by Sextus, *Adv. math.* vii, 113, with the goddess Dikē (of lines 14 to 17), in an otherwise admittedly dubious interpretation. It seems to me that the text strongly suggests this identification. The widely accepted view (cp. W. K. C. Guthrie, *A History of Greek Philosophy*, ii, 1965, p. 10; L. Tarán, *Parmenides*, 1965, p. 31) that Parmenides leaves his goddess 'unnamed' seems to me without foundation, though it has been supported by subtle arguments. Yet most of these arguments (especially Tarán's) make it incomprehensible why Dikē (and perhaps even Anankē in B 8, 30) was not left 'nameless' also. My own positive arguments for identifying the 'goddess' with Dikē are two: (1) The whole balance of B 1, down to line 23, and especially 11 to 22, suggests the identification, as the following details show: Dikē (though on the other view she would be no more than a turnkey) is introduced elaborately, in keeping with the whole passage; she is the main person acting from line 14 down to line 20 (*arērote*); also, the sentence does not seem to stop here—not indeed until the end of line 21, just before the 'goddess' comes in. Moreover, between line 20 and the end of line 21 no more is said than: 'Straight on the road through the gates did the maidens steady the horses.' This in no way implies that Parmenides' journey (elaborately described up to this point) continues any further; rather I find here a strong suggestion that, upon passing through the gates (where he must encounter Dikē), his journey ends. And how can we believe that the highest authority and main speaker of the poem enters not only unnamed, but without any introduction or any further ado—even without one epithet? And why should the maidens have to introduce Parmenides to Dikē (and 'appease' her) who, on the view here combatted, is the inferior person, but not to the superior one? (2) If we believe (as I do) with Guthrie, op. cit., ii, p. 32 (see also pp. 23 f., and Tarán, op. cit., pp. 5 and 61 f.) that there is ('cumulative') 'evidence that Parmenides, in his criticism of earlier thought, had Heraclitus especially in mind', then the role played by Dikē in the *logos* of Heraclitus (see the preceding note) would make it understandable why Parmenides in his *antilogia* cites her now as his authority for his own *logos*. (Incidentally, there seems to me no difficulty in assuming that in the important passage B 8, line 14, Dikē is speaking about herself, but great difficulty in assuming that the 'goddess' speaks in these terms about her own turnkey or gate keeper.)

have more in common than the doctrine of divine veracity. For example, Parmenides is told by his divine guarantor of truth that in order to distinguish between truth and falsehood, he must rely upon the intellect alone, to the exclusion of the senses of sight, hearing, and taste.[10] And even the principle of his physical theory which he, like Descartes, founds upon his intellectualist theory of knowledge, is the same as that adopted by Descartes: it is the impossibility of a void, the necessary fullness of the world.

In Plato's *Ion* a sharp distinction is made between divine inspiration—the divine frenzy of the poet—and the divine sources or origins of true knowledge. (The topic is further developed in the *Phaedrus*, especially from 259E on; and in 275B-C Plato even insists, as Harold Cherniss pointed out to me, on the distinction between questions of origin and of truth.) Plato grants that the poets are inspired, but he denies to them any divine authority for their alleged knowledge of facts. Nevertheless, the doctrine of the divine source of our knowledge plays a decisive part in Plato's famous theory of *anamnēsis* which in some measure grants to each man the possession of divine sources of knowledge. (The knowledge considered in this theory is knowledge of the *essence or nature* of a thing rather than of a particular historical fact.) According to Plato's *Meno* (81B-D) there is nothing which our immortal soul does not know, prior to our birth. For as all natures are kindred and akin, our soul must be akin to all natures. Accordingly it knows them all: it knows all things.[11] In being born we forget; but we may recover our memory and our knowledge, though only partially: only if we see the truth again shall we recognize it. All knowledge is therefore re-cognition—recalling or remembering the essence or true nature that we once knew.[12]

[10] See note 33 and text, below. Compare also DK, Heraclitus B 54, 123; 88 and 126 contain hints that *unobservable* changes may yield observable opposites.

[11] For the relation between *kinship* and *knowledge* (cp. Russell's 'knowledge by acquaintance') see also *Phaedo*, 79D; *Republic*, 611D; and *Laws*, 899D.

[12] Cp. *Phaedo* 72E ff.; 75E; 76A-B. Like all great epistomological theories, the theory of *anamnēsis* (or of 'innate ideas') has influenced religion and literature. Bryan Magee has drawn my attention to Wordsworth's 'Ode: Intimations of Immortality from Recollections of Early Childhood'.

This theory implies that our soul is in a divine state of omniscience as long as it dwells, and participates, in a divine world of ideas or essences or natures, prior to being born. The birth of a man is his fall from grace; it is his fall from a natural or divine state of knowledge; and it is thus the origin and cause of his ignorance. (Here may be the seed of the idea that ignorance is sin or at least related to sin.)

It is clear that there is a close link between this theory of *anamnēsis* and the doctrine of the divine origin or source of our knowledge. At the same time, there is also a close link between the theory of *anamnēsis* and the doctrine of manifest truth: if, even in our depraved state of forgetfulness, we see the truth, we cannot but recognize it as the truth. So, as the result of *anamnēsis*, truth is restored to the status of that which is not forgotten and thus not concealed (*alēthēs*): it is that which is manifest.

Socrates demonstrates this in a beautiful passage of the *Meno* by helping an uneducated young slave to 'recall' the proof of a special case of the theorem of Pythagoras. Here indeed is an optimistic epistemology, and the root of Cartesianism. It seems that, in the *Meno*, Plato was conscious of the highly optimistic character of his theory; for he describes it as a doctrine which makes men eager to learn, to search, and to discover.

Yet disappointment must have come to Plato; for in the *Republic* (and also in the *Phaedrus*) we find the beginnings of a pessimistic epistemology. In the famous story of the prisoners in the cave (514 ff.) he shows that the world of our experience is only a shadow, a reflection, of the real world. And he shows that even if one of the prisoners should escape from the cave and face the real world, he would have nearly insuperable difficulties in seeing and understanding it—to say nothing of his difficulties in trying to make those understand who stayed behind. The difficulties in the way of an understanding of the real world are all but superhuman, and only the very few, if anybody at all, can attain to the divine state of understanding the real world—the divine state of true knowledge, of *epistēmē*.

This is a pessimistic theory with regard to almost all men, though not with regard to all. (For it teaches that truth may be attained by a few—the elect. With regard to these it is, one might say, more wildly optimistic than even the doctrine that truth is manifest.) The authoritarian and traditionalist consequences of this pessimistic theory are fully elaborated in the *Laws*.

Thus we find in Plato the first transition from an optimistic to a pessimistic epistemology. Each of these forms the basis of one of two diametrically opposed philosophies of the state and of society: on the one hand an anti-traditionalist, anti-authoritarian, revolutionary and Utopian rationalism of the Cartesian kind, and on the other hand an authoritarian traditionalism.

This development may well be connected with the fact that the idea of an epistemological fall of man can be interpreted not only in the sense of the optimistic doctrine of *anamnēsis*, but also in a pessimistic sense.

In this latter interpretation, the fall of man condemns all mortals—or almost all—to ignorance. I think one can discern in the story of the cave (and perhaps also in the story of the fall of the city, when the Muses and their divine teaching are neglected[13]) an echo of an interesting older form of this idea. I have in mind Parmenides' doctrine that the opinions of mortals are delusions, and the result of a misguided choice—a misguided convention. (This may stem from Xenophanes' doctrine that all human knowledge is guesswork, and that his own theories are, at best, merely *similar to the truth*.[14]) The misguided convention is a linguistic one: it consists in giving *names* to what is non-existing. The idea of an epistemological fall of man can perhaps be found, as Karl Reinhardt suggested,

---

[13] See *Republic* 546D.

[14] Xenophanes' fragment here alluded to is DK, B 35:

These things are, we conjecture, like the truth.

For the idea of *truthlikeness*—of a doctrine that partly corresponds to the facts (and so may '*seem like the real*' or '*pass for the real*', as Parmenides has it here)—see my *Conjectures and Refutations*, especially pp. 236 f., where *verisimilitude* is contrasted with *probability*, and *Addendum* 6.

in those words of the goddess that mark the transition from the way of truth to the way of delusive opinion.[15]

> But you also shall learn how it was that delusive opinion,
> Destined to pass for the truth, was forcing its way through all things. . . .
> Now of this world thus arranged to seem wholly like truth I shall tell you;
> Then you will be nevermore overawed by the notions of mortals.

Thus though the fall affects all men, the truth may be revealed to the elect by an act of grace—even the truth about the unreal world of the delusions and opinions, the conventional notions and decisions, of mortal men: the unreal world of appearance that was destined to be accepted, and to be approved of, as real.[16]

The revelation received by Parmenides, and his conviction that a few may reach certainty about both the unchanging world of eternal reality and the unreal and changing world of verisimilitude and deception, were two of the main inspirations of Plato's philosophy. It was a theme to which he was for ever returning, oscillating between hope, despair, and resignation.

VIII

Yet what interests us here is Plato's optimistic epistemology, the theory of *anamnēsis* in the *Meno*. It contains, I believe, not only the germs of Descartes' intellectualism, but also the germs of Aristotle's and especially of Bacon's theories of induction.

---

[15] For the *naming* of what is non-existing (non-existing opposites) cp. DK, Parmenides B 9, with B 8 : 53: 'for they decided to give names . . .'. Concerning the transition to the way of delusive opinion (*doxa*), see Karl Reinhardt, *Parmenides*, 2nd ed., p. 26; see also pp. 5–11 for the text of Parmenides, DK, B 1 : 31–32, which are the first two lines here quoted. My third line is Parmenides, DK, B 8 : 60, cp. Xenophanes, B 35. My fourth line is Parmenides, DK, B 8 : 61.

[16] It is interesting to contrast this pessimistic view of the necessity of error (or of *almost* necessary error) with the optimism of Descartes, or of Spinoza who, in his 76th letter (paragraph 5), scorns those 'who dream of an impure spirit inspiring us with false ideas which are similar to true ones (*veris similes*)'; see also ch. 10, section xiv, and *Addendum* 6, of my *Conjectures and Refutations*.

For Meno's slave is helped by Socrates' judicious questions to remember or recapture the forgotten knowledge which his soul possessed in its pre-natal state of omniscience. It is, I believe, this famous Socratic method, called in the *Theaetetus* the art of midwifery or *maieutic*, to which Aristotle alluded when he said that Socrates was the inventor of the method of induction.[17]

Aristotle, and also Bacon, I wish to suggest, meant by 'induction' not so much the inferring of universal laws from particular observed instances as a method by which we are guided to the point whence we can intuit, or perceive, the essence or the true nature of a thing.[18] But this, as we have seen, is precisely the aim of Socrates' *maieutic*: its aim is to help or lead us to *anamnēsis*; and *anamnēsis* is the power of seeing the true nature or essence of a thing, the nature or essence with which we were acquainted before birth, before our fall from grace. Thus the aims of the two, *maieutic* and induction, are the same. (Incidentally, Aristotle taught that the result of an induction—the intuition of the essence—was to be expressed by a definition of that essence.)

Now let us look more closely at the two procedures. The *maieutic* art of Socrates consists, essentially, in asking questions designed to destroy prejudices; false beliefs which are often traditional or fashionable beliefs; false answers, given in the spirit of ignorant cocksureness. Socrates himself does not

[17] *Metaphysics*, 1078b 17–33; see also 987b 1.

[18] Aristotle meant by 'induction' (*epagōgē*) at least two different things which he sometimes links together. One is a method by which we are 'led to intuit the general principle' (*An. Pr.*, 67a 22 f., on *anamnēsis* in the *Meno*; *An. Post.*, 71a 7, 81a 38 ff., 100b 4 f.). The other (*Topics*, 105a 13, 156a 4, 157a 34; *An. Post.*, 78a 35, 81b 5 ff.) is a method of *adducing* (particular) *evidence*—*positive* evidence rather than *critical* evidence or counter examples. The first method seems to me the older one, and the one which can be better connected with Socrates and his *maieutic* method of criticism and counter examples. The second method seems to originate in the attempt to systematize induction logically or, as Aristotle (*An. Pr.*, 68b 15 ff.) puts it, to construct a valid 'syllogism which springs out of induction'; this, to be valid, must of course be a syllogism of perfect or complete induction (complete enumeration of instances); and ordinary induction in the sense of the second method here mentioned is just a weakened (and invalid) form of this valid syllogism. (See also my *Open Society*, note 33 to ch. 11.)

pretend to know. His attitude is described by Aristotle in the words, 'Socrates raised questions but gave no answers; for he confessed that he did not know.'[19] Thus Socrates' *maieutic* is not an art that aims at teaching any belief, but one that aims at purging or cleansing[20] the soul of its false beliefs, its seeming knowledge, its prejudices. It achieves this by teaching us to doubt our own convictions.

Fundamentally the same procedure is part of Bacon's induction.

IX

The framework of Bacon's theory of induction is this. He distinguishes in the *Novum Organum* between a true method and a false method. His name for the true method, '*interpretatio naturae*', is ordinarily translated by the phrase 'interpretation of nature', and his name for the false method, '*anticipatio mentis*', by 'anticipation of the mind'. Obvious as these translations may seem, they are misleading. What Bacon means by '*interpretatio naturae*' is, I suggest, the reading of, or better still, *the spelling out of, the book of Nature.*[21]

The term 'interpretation' has in modern English a decidedly subjectivistic or relativistic tinge. When we speak of Rudolf Serkin's interpretation of the *Emperor Concerto*, we imply that there are different interpretations, but that this one is Serkin's. We do not of course wish to imply that Serkin's is not the best, the truest, the nearest to Beethoven's intentions. But although we may be unable to imagine that there is a better one, by using the term 'interpretation' we imply that there are other interpretations or readings, leaving the question open whether some of these other readings may, or may not, be equally true.

---

[19] See Aristotle, *Sophist. El.*, 183b 7; cp. Plato's *Theaetetus*, 150C–D, 157C, 161B.

[20] Cp. the allusion to the rite called *amphidromia*—a purification ceremony after the birth of a child (which sometimes ended in the purge or exposure of the child) alluded to in *Theaetetus* 160E.

[21] Galileo, in a famous passage of his *Il saggiatore*, section 6, of which Mario Bunge has kindly reminded me, speaks of 'that great book which lies before our eyes—I mean the universe'; cp. also Descartes' *Discourse*, section 1.

I have here used the word 'reading' as a synonym for 'interpretation', not only because the two meanings are so similar but also because 'reading' and 'to read' have suffered a modification analogous to that of 'interpretation' and 'to interpret'; except that in the case of 'reading' both meanings are still in full use. In the phrase 'I have read John's letter', we have the ordinary, non-subjectivist meaning. But 'I read this passage of John's letter quite differently' or perhaps 'My reading of this passage is very different' may illustrate a later, a subjectivistic or relativistic, meaning of the word 'reading'.

I assert that the meaning of 'interpret' (though not in the sense of 'translate') has changed in exactly the same way, except that the original meaning—perhaps 'reading aloud for those who cannot read themselves'—has been virtually lost. Today even the phrase 'the judge must interpret the law' means that he has a certain latitude in interpreting it; while in Bacon's time it would have meant that the judge had the duty to read the law as it stood, and to expound it and to apply it in the one and only right way. *Interpretatio juris* (or *legis*) means either this or else the expounding of the law to the layman.[22] It leaves the legal interpreter no latitude; at any rate no more than would be allowed to a sworn interpreter translating a legal document.

Thus the translation 'the interpretation of nature' is misleading; it should be replaced by something like 'the (true) reading of nature'; analogous to 'the (true) reading of the law'. And I suggest that 'reading the book of Nature as it is' or better still 'spelling out the book of Nature' is what Bacon meant. The point is that the phrase should suggest the avoidance of all interpreting in the modern sense, and that it should *not* contain, more especially, any suggestion of an attempt to interpret what is manifest in nature in the light of non-manifest causes, or of hypotheses; for all this would be an *anticipatio mentis*, in Bacon's sense. (It is a mistake, I think, to ascribe to Bacon the teaching that hypotheses—or conjectures—may result from his method of induction; for Baconian induction

---

[22] Cp. T. Manley, *The Interpreter: ... Obscure Words and Terms used in the Lawes of this Realm*, 1672.

results in *certain or established* knowledge rather than in conjecture.)

As to the meaning of '*anticipatio mentis*' we have only to quote Locke: 'men give themselves up to the first anticipations of their minds'.[23] This is, practically, a translation from Bacon; and it makes it amply clear that '*anticipatio*' means 'prejudice' or even 'superstition'. We can also refer to the phrase '*anticipatio deorum*' which means harbouring naïve or primitive or superstitious views about the gods. But to make matters still more obvious: 'prejudice'[24] derives from a legal term, and according to the *Oxford English Dictionary* it was Bacon who introduced the verb 'to prejudge' into the English language, in the sense of 'to judge adversely in advance'—that is, in violation of the judge's duty.

Thus Bacon's two methods are (1) 'the spelling out of the open book of Nature', leading to knowledge or *epistēmē*, and (2) 'the prejudice of the mind that wrongly prejudges, and perhaps misjudges, Nature', leading to *doxa*, or mere guesswork, and to the misreading of the book of Nature. This latter method, rejected by Bacon, is in fact a method of interpretation, in the modern sense of the word. It is the *method of conjecture or hypothesis* (a method of which, incidentally, I happen to be a convinced advocate).

How can we prepare ourselves to read the book of Nature properly or truly? Bacon's answer is: by purging our minds of all anticipations or conjectures or guesses or prejudices.[25] There are various things to be done in order so to purge our minds. We have to get rid of all sorts of 'idols', or generally held false beliefs; for these distort our observations.[26] But we have also, like Socrates, to look out for all sorts of counter instances by which to destroy our prejudices concerning the kind of thing whose true essence or nature we wish to ascertain. Like Socrates, we must, by purifying our intellects, prepare our

[23] John Locke, *The Conduct of the Understanding*, section 26.
[24] Cp. also Descartes, *Principles*, I, 50.
[25] Cp. Bacon's *Novum Organum*, I, 68, and the end of 69.
[26] Op. cit., I, 97.

souls to face the eternal light of essences or natures:[27] our impure prejudices must be exorcised by the invocation of counter instances.[28]

Only after our souls have been cleansed in this way may we begin the work of spelling out diligently the open book of Nature, the manifest truth.

In view of all this I suggest that the Baconian (as well as the Aristotelian) *method of induction* is the same, fundamentally, as Socratic *maieutic*; that is to say, the preparation of the mind by cleansing it of prejudices, in order to enable it to recognize the manifest truth, or to read the open book of Nature.

Descartes' *method of systematic doubt* is also fundamentally the same: it is a method of destroying all false prejudices of the mind, in order to arrive at the unshakable basis of self-evident truth.

We can now see more clearly how, in this optimistic epistemology, the state of knowledge is the natural or the pure state of man, the state of the innocent eye which can see the truth, while the state of ignorance has its source in the injury suffered by the innocent eye in man's fall from grace; an injury which can be partially healed by a course of purification. And we can see more clearly why this epistemology, not only in Descartes' but also in Bacon's form, remains essentially a religious doctrine in which the source of all knowledge is divine authority.

One might say that, encouraged by the divine 'essences' or divine 'natures' of Plato, and by the traditional Greek opposition between the truthfulness of nature and the deceitfulness of man-made convention, Bacon substitutes, in his epistemology, 'Nature' for 'God'.[29] This may be the reason why we have to purify ourselves before we may approach the goddess *Natura*: when we have purified our minds, even our sometimes unreliable senses (held by Plato to be hopelessly impure) will be

[27] Cp. St. Augustine, *De Civitate Dei*, VIII, 3.

[28] Cp. *Novum Organum*, II, 16 ff.

[29] Hegel and Marx went one step further and substituted the goddess History (or Historical Necessity) for Nature. Cp. my *Conjectures and Refutations*, section xii of chapter 16.

pure. The sources of knowledge must be kept pure, because any impurity may become a source of ignorance.

X

In spite of the religious character of their epistemologies, Bacon's and Descartes' attacks upon prejudice, and upon traditional beliefs which we carelessly or recklessly harbour, are in tendency clearly anti-authoritarian and anti-traditionalist. For they require us to shed all beliefs except those whose truth we have perceived ourselves. Thus their attacks were intended to be attacks upon authority and tradition: they were part of the war against authority which it was the fashion of the time to wage, the war against the authority of Aristotle and the tradition of the schools. Men do not need such authorities if they can perceive the truth themselves.

But I do not think that Bacon and Descartes succeeded in freeing their epistemologies from authority; not so much because they appealed to religious authority—to Nature or to God—but for an even deeper reason.

In spite of their individualistic tendencies, they did not dare to appeal to our critical judgement—to your judgement, or to mine; perhaps because they felt that this might lead to subjectivism and to arbitrariness. Yet whatever the reason may have been, they certainly were unable to give up thinking in terms of authority, much as they wanted to do so. They could only replace one authority—that of Aristotle and the Bible—by another. Each of them appealed to a new authority; the one to *the authority of the senses*, and the other to *the authority of the intellect*.

This means that they failed to solve the great problem: How can we admit that our knowledge is a human—an all too human—affair, without at the same time implying that it is all individual whim and arbitrariness?

Yet this problem had been seen and solved long before; first, it appears, by Xenophanes, and then by Democritus, and by Socrates (the Socrates of the *Apology* rather than of the *Meno*). The solution lies in the realization that all of us may and often do err, singly and collectively, but that this very idea of error and human fallibility involves another one: the idea of *objective truth*: the standard which we may fall short of. Thus the doctrine of fallibility should not be regarded as part of a pessimistic epistemology. This doctrine implies that we may seek for truth, for objective truth, though more often than not we may miss it by a wide margin. And it implies that if we respect truth, we must search for it by persistently searching for our errors: by indefatigable rational criticism, and self-criticism.

Erasmus of Rotterdam attempted to revive this Socratic doctrine—the important though unobtrusive doctrine, 'Know thyself, and thus admit to thyself how little thou knowest!'. Yet this doctrine was swept away by the belief that truth is manifest, and by the new self-assurance exemplified and taught in different ways by Luther and Calvin, by Bacon and Descartes.

It is important to realize, in this connexion, the difference between Cartesian doubt and the doubt of Socrates, or Erasmus, or Montaigne. While Socrates doubts human knowledge or wisdom, and remains firm in his rejection of any pretension to knowledge or wisdom, Descartes doubts everything —but only to end up with the possession of *absolutely certain* knowledge; for he finds that his universal doubt would lead him to doubt the truthfulness of God, which is absurd. Having proved that universal doubt is absurd, he concludes that we *can* know securely, that we *can* be wise, if only we distinguish conscientiously, in the natural light of reason, between clear and distinct ideas whose source is God, and all other ideas whose source is our own impure imagination. Cartesian doubt, we see, is merely a *maieutic* instrument for establishing a criterion of truth and, with it, a way to secure knowledge and wisdom. Yet for the Socrates of the *Apology*, wisdom consisted in the awareness of our limitations; in knowing how little we know, every one of us.

It was this doctrine of an essential human fallibility which Nicolas of Cusa and Erasmus of Rotterdam (who refers to Socrates) revived; and it was this 'humanist' doctrine (in contradistinction to the optimistic doctrine on which Milton relied, the doctrine that truth will prevail) which Nicolas and Erasmus, Montaigne and Locke and Voltaire, followed by John Stuart Mill and Bertrand Russell, made the basis of the doctrine of tolerance. 'What is tolerance?' asks Voltaire in his *Philosophical Dictionary*; and he answers: 'It is a necessary consequence of our humanity. We are all fallible, and prone to error; let us then pardon each other's folly. This is the first principle of natural right.' (More recently the doctrine of fallibility has been made the basis of a theory of political freedom; that is, freedom from coercion.[30])

XI

Bacon and Descartes set up observation and reason as new authorities, and they set them up within each individual man. But in doing so they split man into two parts, into a higher part which has authority with respect to truth—Bacon's observations, Descartes' intellect—and a lower part. It is this lower part which constitutes our ordinary selves, the old Adam in us. For it is always 'we ourselves' who are alone responsible for error, if truth is manifest. It is we, with *our* prejudices, *our* negligence, *our* pigheadedness, who are to blame; it is we ourselves who are the sources of our ignorance.

Thus we are split into a human part, we ourselves, the part which is the source of our fallible opinions (*doxa*), of our errors, and of our ignorance; and a super-human part, such as the senses or the intellect, the part which is the source of real knowledge (*epistēmē*), and which has an almost divine authority over us.

But this will not do. For we know that Descartes' physics, admirable as it was in many ways, was mistaken; yet it was based only upon ideas which, he thought, were clear and distinct, and which therefore should have been true. And as to the authority of the senses as sources of knowledge, the fact that the senses were not reliable seems to have been known to

[30] See F. A. von Hayek, *The Constitution of Liberty*, 1960, especially pp. 22 and 29.

Xenophanes[31] and to Heraclitus[32]; at any rate, with Parmenides it became one of the foundations of Eleatic thought. According to Parmenides, reliance on the senses is one of the two main sources of ignorance or delusion (the other is conventional language—the misguided convention of giving names to the non-existent; see section VII above). For he teaches that whatever is contained in our much-erring sense organs will appear in the form of a 'thought' to the erring intellect of mortal men:[33]

[31] See DK Xenophanes B 18 and 34 (quoted below in section XV); it is important that Xenophanes teaches that the knowledge of mortal men is only guesswork, *doxa*, and so prepares for the contempt shown by Heraclitus and Parmenides for the opinion of ordinary mortal men—a contempt which may have provoked Protagoras to turn the tables upon them.

[32] See for anti-sensualist or pro-intellectualist allusions in Heraclitus for example DK, Heraclitus B 46 and 54 (also B 8 and 51); 123 (also B 8 and 56), all discussed in *Conjectures and Refutations*. In addition see B 107, 'eyes and ears are false witnesses . . .' (false witnesses are also alluded to in B 28; cp. also 101a which in view of B 19 probably means only: 'eyewitnesses are better than hearsay'). See also B 41: 'wisdom is knowing the *thought* [that is, the *logos*: see *pantōn kata ton logon* in B 1] that steers everything through everything'.

[33] Cp. DK, Parmenides, B 16. The passage is translated and commented upon in the second edition of my *Conjectures and Refutations*, pp. 164 f. Crucial for my translation (which, like almost all translations, is an interpretation) are two points: (1) '*poluplanktos*' means here 'much-erring' rather than 'wandering' (Kirk and Raven) or 'changing' (Tarán, op. cit.) or 'straying' (Guthrie, op.cit.). My arguments are (*a*) the accepted general tendency of Parmenides; (*b*) that '*plakton noon*' in B 6:6 means 'erring thought' (or 'erring mind': Guthrie, p. 21; not 'wandering', as in Tarán, or Kirk and Raven); (*c*) that '*plattontai*' (Diels-Kranz = *plazontai*) in B 6:5 also means 'err (helplessly)', or 'stray' and not merely 'wander'; it is 'typically used for an intellectual error' (Tarán, p. 63); (*d*) that '*peplanēmenoi*' in B 8:54 means (Tarán, op. cit., p. 86) 'they have gone astray', in a sense which again (cp. Tarán, op. cit., p. 63) clearly indicates an intellectual error: 'they decided to name two forms whose unity is not necessary—in which they erred' (or 'were mistaken'). (2) '*melea*' (*poluplanktōn meleōn*) means here '*sense organs*', rather than 'limbs' or (Tarán) 'body'. Guthrie (op. cit., p. 67) says 'body, for which no collective word was yet in common use'. But (*a*) '*demas*' was in use in Homer, Xenophanes, B 14:2; B 15:5; B 23:2; '*demas*' in Parmenides B 8:55 has perhaps a different meaning; (*b*) *sōma* was in use in Hesiod and Pindar, and in the following Presocratics: Orpheus B 3 = Plato, *Cratylus* 400c; Xenophanes B 15:4 (perhaps not decisive because the 'body' is here not necessarily living); Epicharmus B 26. Moreover, (*c*) there is little doubt that for 'sense organs' no collective word was yet in common use. Here it is most interesting to find that Empedocles tries hard to find an acceptable description for sense organs in B 2:1: 'For narrow are the openings of the sense organs [*palamai*, lit. hands,

ON SOURCES OF KNOWLEDGE AND IGNORANCE 193

What at each time the much-erring sense organs mix themselves up with
That occurs as a thought to mankind. For these two are the same thing:
That which thinks and the mixture which makes up the sense organs' nature.
What this mixture contains becomes thought, in each man and all.

This anti-sensualist theory of knowledge prevailed in the Eleatic and Platonic schools. It was criticized, though mildly, by Empedocles[34] but (according to Plato) strongly attacked by Protagoras who, if Plato is right,[35] intended by his famous proposition 'Man is the measure of all things' to turn the tables upon Parmenides: as we are mortal men we are constrained to accept what Parmenides had contemptuously described as delusive opinion and as mere appearance.[36]

---

instruments for gripping] which like soft mounds are distributed over the limbs [*guia*]; and much of poor significance is bursting upon them, dulling their attention.' (That Empedocles complains here about the 'narrow senses' is confirmed not only by B 3:9 ff., but also by Cicero, *Acad. post.* I, 12:44, where he speaks of Empedocles and '*angustos sensus*'; cp. DK, Anaxagoras, A 95.) That the '*palamai*' are sense organs comes out very clearly in B 3:9, in which they are specified as eyes, ears, the tongue, and the other *limbs* (= *guia*). Now since '*guia*' and '*melea*' (*kata melea* = limb by limb) are synonyms, we have here a strong argument for the thesis that '*melea*' in Parmenides B 16 means indeed 'sense organs' like '*guia*' in Empedocles B 3:13.

I may add that '*pleon*' in line 4 of Parmenides B 16 which I have here translated by 'contains' (for metrical reasons) should more literally be translated by 'is full of'; see Tarán, op. cit., p. 169, who seems to be right when he connects it with B 9:3.

[34] This mild criticism is contained in DK Empedocles, B 3 : 9 to 13. Empedocles admits (B 2) that the senses are bad, but seems to say there that by using them all for mutual corroboration, together with all other sources of knowledge, we might get somewhere. (The passage seems to allude to Parmenides B 7 : 4 and 5.)

[35] Cp. Plato, *Theaetetus*, 152A–B and E, and later passages.

[36] If we assume that Democritus was under the influence of both Parmenides and Protagoras, then the famous dialogue between the Intellect and the Senses DK Democritus B 125 may be described as a summing up of these two influences: the Intellect says: 'Sweet: by convention; bitter: by convention; cold: by convention; colour: by convention. In truth, there are only atoms and the void.' The Senses reply: 'Poor Intellect! You who are taking your evidence from us are trying to overthrow us? Our overthrow will be your downfall.' A later and quite Parmenidean summing up is to be found in C. Bovillus (1470–1533), *De intellectu*: 'Nothing is in the senses that was not previously in the intellect. Nothing is in

It is strange that the criticism of the authority of the senses which is one of the oldest of philosophical traditions (though it was not accepted by either Epicurus or the Stoics) has been almost ignored by modern empiricists, including phenomenalists and positivists; yet it is ignored in most of the problems posed by positivists and phenomenalists, and in the solutions they offer. The reason is this: they believe that it is not our senses that err, but that it is always 'we ourselves' who err in *our interpretation* of what is 'given' to us by our senses. Our senses tell the truth, but we may err, for example, when we try to put into *language—conventional, man-made, imperfect language*—what they tell us. It is our linguistic description which is faulty because it may be tinged with prejudice.

(So our man-made, conventional, language was at fault—almost exactly as Parmenides had said, long ago. But more recently it was discovered that our language too was 'given' to us, in an important sense: that it embodied the wisdom and experience of countless generations, and that it should not be blamed if we misused it. So language too became a truthful authority that could never deceive us. If we fall into temptation and use language in vain, then it is we who are to blame for the trouble that ensues. For Language is a jealous God Who will not hold him guiltless that taketh His words in vain, but will throw him into darkness and confusion.[37])

By blaming *us*, and our language (or misuse of Language), it is possible to uphold the divine authority of the senses (and even of Language). But it is possible only at the cost of widening the gap between this authority and ourselves: between the pure sources from which we can obtain an authoritative knowledge of the truthful goddess Nature, and our impure and guilty selves: between God and man. As indicated before, this idea of the truthfulness of Nature which, I believe, can be discerned in Bacon, derives from the Greeks; for it is part of the

---

the intellect that was not previously in the senses. The first is true for angels [= the way of truth], the second for humans [= the way of delusion].' The second is, of course, a formulation to be found in St. Thomas.

[37] This paragraph alludes to the changes from the early to the late Wittgenstein.

classical opposition between *nature* and human *convention* which, according to Plato, is due to Pindar; which may be discerned in Parmenides; and which is identified by him, and by some Sophists (for example, by Hippias), and partly also by Plato himself, with the opposition between divine truth and human error, or even falsehood. After Bacon, and under his influence, the idea that nature is divine and truthful, and that all error or falsehood is due to the deceitfulness of our own human conventions, continued to play a major role not only in the history of philosophy, of science, and of politics, but also in that of the visual arts. This may be seen, for example, from Constable's most interesting theories on nature, veracity, prejudice, and convention, quoted in E. H. Gombrich's *Art and Illusion*.[38] It has also played a role in the history of literature, and even in that of music.

XII

Can the strange view that the truth of a statement may be decided upon by inquiring into its sources—that is to say its *origin*—be explained as due to some logical mistake which might be cleared up? Or can we do no better than explain it in terms of religious beliefs, or in psychological terms—referring perhaps to parental authority? I believe that it is indeed possible to discern here a logical mistake which is connected with the close analogy between the *meaning* of our words, or terms, or concepts, and the *truth* of our statements or propositions. (See the table on the next page.)

It is easy to see that the meaning of our words does have some connexion with their history or their origin. A word is, logically considered, a conventional sign; psychologically considered, it is a sign whose meaning is established by usage or custom or association. Logically considered, its meaning was indeed established by an initial decision—something like a primary definition or convention, a kind of original social contract; and psychologically considered, its meaning was

[38] See E. H. Gombrich, *Art and Illusion*, new edn. 1962, especially pp. 29 and 321 f.

established when we originally learned to use it, when we first formed our linguistic habits and associations. Thus there is a point in the complaint of the schoolboy about the unnecessary artificiality of French in which 'pain' means bread, while English, he feels, is so much more natural and straightforward in calling pain 'pain' and bread 'bread'. He may understand

---

IDEAS
that is

| DESIGNATIONS *or* TERMS *or* CONCEPTS | STATEMENTS *or* JUDGEMENTS *or* PROPOSITIONS |

may be formulated in

| WORDS | ASSERTIONS |

which may be

| MEANINGFUL | TRUE |

and their

| MEANING | TRUTH |

may be reduced, by way of

| DEFINITIONS | DERIVATIONS |

to that of

| UNDEFINED CONCEPTS | PRIMITIVE PROPOSITIONS |

the attempt, incidentally, to establish rather than to reduce their

| MEANING | TRUTH |

by these means leads to an infinite regress

---

the conventionality of the usage perfectly well, but he gives expression to the feeling that there is no reason why the original conventions—original for him—should not be binding. So his mistake may consist merely in forgetting that there can be several equally binding original conventions. But who has not made, implicitly, the same mistake? Most of us have caught ourselves in a feeling of surprise when we find that in France even little children speak French fluently. Of course, we smile about our own naïvety; but we do not smile about the policeman who discovers that *the real name* of the man called 'Samuel Jones' was 'John Smith'—though here is, no doubt, a last vestige of the magical belief that we gain power over a man or a god or a spirit by gaining knowledge of his *real* name: by pronouncing it, we can summon or cite him.

Thus there is indeed a familiar as well as a logically defensible sense in which the 'true' or 'proper' meaning of a term is its original meaning; so that if we understand it, we do so because we learned it correctly—from a true authority, from one who knew the language. This shows that the problem of the meaning of a word is indeed linked to the problem of the authoritative source, or the origin, of our usage.

It is different with the problem of the truth of a statement of fact, a proposition. For anybody can make a factual mistake—even in matters on which he should be an authority, such as his own age or the colour of a thing which he has just this moment clearly and distinctly perceived. And as to origins, a statement may easily have been false when it was first made, and first properly understood. A word, on the other hand, must have had a proper meaning as soon as it was ever understood.

If we thus reflect upon the difference between the ways in which the meaning of words and the truth of statements is related to their origins, we are hardly tempted to think that the question of origin can have much bearing on the question of knowledge or of truth. There is, however, a deep analogy between meaning and truth; and there is a philosophical view —I have called it 'essentialism'—which tries to link meaning and truth so closely that the temptation to treat them in the same way becomes almost irresistible.

In order to explain this briefly, we may once more contemplate the table on the preceding page, noting the relation between its two sides.

How are the two sides of this table connected? If we look at the left side of the table, we find there the word *'Definitions'*. But a definition is a kind of *statement* or *judgement* or *proposition*, and therefore one of those things which stand on the right side of our table. (This fact, incidentally, does not spoil the symmetry of the table, for derivations are also things that transcend the kind of things—statements, etc.—which stand on the side where the word 'derivation' occurs: just as a definition is formulated by a special kind of *sequence of words* rather than by a word, so a derivation is formulated by a special kind of *sequence of statements* rather than by a statement.) The fact that definitions, which occur on the left side of our table, are nevertheless statements suggests that somehow they may form a link between the left and the right side of the table.

That they do this is, indeed, part of that philosophic doctrine to which I have given the name 'essentialism'. According to essentialism (especially Aristotle's version of it) a definition is a statement of the inherent essence or nature of a thing. At the same time, it states the meaning of a word—of the name that designates the essence. (For example, Descartes, and also Kant, held that the word 'body' designates something that is, essentially, *extended*.)

Moreover, Aristotle and all other essentialists held that *definitions are 'principles'*; that is to say, they yield primitive propositions (example: 'All bodies are extended') which cannot be derived from other propositions, and which form the basis, or are part of the basis, of every demonstration. They thus form the basis of every science.[39] It should be noted that this particular tenet, though an important part of the essentialist creed, is free of any reference to 'essences'. This explains why it was accepted by some nominalistic opponents of essentialism such as Hobbes or, say, Schlick.[40]

I think we have now the means at our disposal by which we can explain the logic of the view that questions of origin may decide questions of factual truth. For if origins can determine the *true meaning* of a term or word, then they can determine the *true definition* of an important idea, and therefore some at least of the basic 'principles' which are descriptions of the essences

[39] See my *Open Society*, especially notes 27 to 33 to ch. 11.
[40] See M. Schlick, *Erkenntnislehre*, 2nd edn., 1925, p. 62.

or natures of things and which underlie our demonstrations and consequently our scientific knowledge. *So it will then appear that there are authoritative sources of our knowledge.*

Yet we must realize that essentialism is mistaken in suggesting that definitions can add to our *knowledge of facts* (although *qua* decisions about conventions they may be influenced by our knowledge of facts, and although they create instruments which may in their turn influence the formation of our theories and thereby the evolution of our knowledge of facts). Once we see that definitions never give any factual knowledge about 'nature', or about 'the nature of things', we also see the break in the logical link between the problem of origin and that of factual truth which some essentialist philosophers tried to forge.

XIII

I will now leave all these largely historical reflections aside, and turn to the problems themselves, and to their solution.

This part of my lecture might be described as an attack on *empiricism*, as formulated for example in the following classical statement of Hume's: 'If I ask you why you believe any particular matter of fact . . ., you must tell me some reason; and this reason will be some other fact, connected with it. But as you cannot proceed after this manner, *in infinitum*, you must at last terminate in some fact, which is present to your memory or senses; or must allow that your belief is entirely without foundation.'[41]

The problem of the validity of empiricism may be roughly put as follows: is observation the ultimate source of our knowledge of nature? And if not, what are the sources of our knowledge?

These questions remain, whatever I may have said about Bacon, and even if I should have managed to make those parts of his philosophy on which I have commented somewhat unattractive for Baconians and for other empiricists.

[41] See David Hume, *An Enquiry concerning Human Understanding*, Section v, Part I; Selby-Bigge, p. 46; see also my motto, taken from Section vii, Part I; p. 62.

The problem of the sources of our knowledge has recently been restated as follows. If we make an assertion, we must justify it; but this means that we must be able to answer the following questions.

How do you know? What are the sources of your assertion?

This, the empiricist holds, amounts in its turn to the question,

What observations (or memories of observations) *led you to your assertion?*

I find this string of questions quite unsatisfactory.[42]

First of all, most of our assertions are not based upon observations, but upon all kinds of other sources. 'I read it in *The Times*' or perhaps 'I read it in the *Encyclopaedia Britannica*' is a more likely and a more definite answer to the question 'How do you know?' than 'I have observed it' or 'I know it from an observation I made last year'.

'But', the empiricist will reply, 'how do you think that *The Times* or the *Encyclopaedia Britannica* got their information? Surely, if you only carry on your inquiry long enough, you will end up with *reports of the observations of eyewitnesses* (sometimes called "protocol sentences" or—by yourself—"basic statements"). Admittedly', the empiricist will continue, 'books are largely made from other books. Admittedly, a historian, for example, will work from documents. But ultimately, in the last analysis, these other books, or these documents, must have been based upon observations. Otherwise they would have to be described as poetry, or invention, or lies, but not as testimony. It is in this sense that we empiricists assert that observation must be the ultimate source of our knowledge.'

Here we have the empiricist's case, as it is still put by some of my positivist friends.

I shall try to show that this case is as little valid as Bacon's; that the answer to the question of the sources of knowledge goes against the empiricist; and, finally, that this whole question of ultimate sources—sources to which one may

[42] The string of questions is suggested by Carnap's formulation of what he takes to be the central problem of epistemology; cp. *Logical Foundations of Probability*, 1950, p. 189.

appeal, as one might to a higher court or a higher authority—must be rejected as based upon a mistake.

First I want to show that if you actually went on questioning *The Times* and its correspondents about the sources of their knowledge, you would in fact never arrive at all those observations by eyewitnesses in the existence of which the empiricist believes. You would find, rather, that with every single step you take, the need for further steps increases in snowball-like fashion.

Take as an example the sort of assertion for which reasonable people might simply accept as sufficient the answer 'I read it in *The Times*'; let us say the assertion, 'The Prime Minister has decided to return to London several days ahead of schedule.' Now assume for a moment that somebody doubts this assertion, or feels the need to investigate its truth. What shall he do? If he has a friend in the Prime Minister's office, the simplest and most direct way would be to ring him up; and if this friend corroborates the message, then that is that.

In other words, the investigator will, if possible, try to check, or to examine, *the asserted fact itself*, rather than trace the source of the information. But according to the empiricist theory, the assertion 'I have read it in *The Times*' is merely a first step in a justification procedure consisting in tracing the ultimate source. What is the next step?

There are at least two next steps. One would be to reflect that 'I have read it in *The Times*' is also an assertion, and that we might ask 'What is the source of your knowledge that you read it in *The Times* and not, say, in a paper looking very similar to *The Times*?' The other is to ask *The Times* for the sources of its knowledge. The answer to the first question may be 'But we have only *The Times* on order and we always get it in the morning' which gives rise to a host of further questions about sources which we shall not pursue. The second question may elicit from the editor of *The Times* the answer: 'We had a telephone call from the Prime Minister's Office.' Now according to the empiricist procedure, we should at this stage ask next: 'Who is the gentleman who received the telephone call?'

and then get his observation report; but we should also have to ask that gentleman: 'What is the source of your knowledge that the voice you heard came from an official in the Prime Minister's office?', and so on.

There is a simple reason why this tedious sequence of questions never comes to a satisfactory conclusion. It is this. Every witness must always make ample use, in his report, of his knowledge of persons, places, things, linguistic usages, social conventions, and so on. He cannot rely merely upon his eyes or ears, especially if his report is to be of use in justifying any assertion worth justifying. But this fact must of course always raise new questions as to the sources of those elements of his knowledge which are not immediately observational.

This is why the programme of tracing back all knowledge to its ultimate source in observation is logically impossible to carry through: it leads to an infinite regress. (The doctrine that truth is manifest cuts off the regress. This is interesting because it may help to explain the attractiveness of that doctrine.)

I wish to mention, in parenthesis, that this argument is closely related to another—that all observation involves interpretation in the light of our theoretical knowledge,[43] or that pure observational knowledge, unadulterated by theory, would, if at all possible, be utterly barren and futile.

The most striking thing about the observationalist programme of asking for sources—apart from its tediousness—is its stark violation of common sense. For if we are doubtful about an assertion, then the normal procedure is to test it, rather than to ask for its sources; and if we find independent corroboration, then we shall often accept the assertion without bothering at all about sources.

Of course there are cases in which the situation is different. Testing an *historical* assertion always means going back to sources; but not, as a rule, to the reports of eyewitnesses.

Clearly, no historian will accept the evidence of documents uncritically. There are problems of genuineness, there are

[43] See my *Logic of Scientific Discovery*, last paragraph of section 24, and new appendix *x, (2).

problems of bias, and there are also such problems as the reconstruction of earlier sources. There are, of course, also problems such as: was the writer present when these events happened? But this is not one of the characteristic problems of the historian. He may worry about the reliability of a report, but he will rarely worry about whether or not the writer of a document was an eyewitness of the event in question, even assuming that this event was of the nature of an observable event. A letter saying 'I changed my mind yesterday on this question' may be most valuable historical evidence, even though changes of mind are unobservable (and even though we may conjecture, in view of other evidence, that the writer was lying).

As to eyewitnesses, they are important almost exclusively in a court of law where they can be cross-examined. As most lawyers know, eyewitnesses often err. This has been experimentally investigated, with the most striking results. Witnesses most anxious to describe an event as it happened are liable to make scores of mistakes, especially if some exciting things happen in a hurry; and if an event suggests some tempting interpretation, then this interpretation, more often than not, is allowed to distort what has actually been seen.

Hume's view of historical knowledge was different: '... we believe', he writes in the *Treatise*,[44] 'that Caesar was kill'd in the Senate-house on the *ides of March* ... because this fact is establish'd on the unanimous testimony of historians, who agree to assign this precise time and place to that event. Here are certain characters and letters present either to our memory or senses; which characters we likewise remember to have been us'd as the signs of certain ideas; and these ideas were either in the minds of such as were immediately present at that action, and receiv'd the ideas directly from its existence; or they were deriv'd from the testimony of others, and that again from another testimony ... 'till we arrive at those who were eye-witnesses and spectators of the event.'[45]

[44] David Hume, *A Treatise of Human Nature*, Book I, Part III, Section iv; Selby-Bigge, p. 83.
[45] See also Hume's *Enquiry*, Section x; Selby-Bigge, pp. 111 ff.

It seems to me that this view must lead to the infinite regress described above. For the problem is, of course, whether 'the unanimous testimony of historians' is to be accepted, or whether it is, perhaps, to be rejected as the result of their reliance on a common yet spurious source. The appeal to 'letters present to our memory or our senses' cannot have any bearing on this or on any other relevant problem of historiography.

XIV

But what, then, are the sources of our knowledge?

The answer, I think, is this: there are all kinds of sources of our knowledge; but *none has authority*.

We may say that *The Times* can be a source of knowledge, or the *Encyclopaedia Britannica*. We may say that certain papers in the *Physical Review* about a problem in physics have more authority, and are more of the character of a source, than an article about the same problem in *The Times* or the *Encyclopaedia*. But it would be quite wrong to say that the source of the article in the *Physical Review* must have been wholly, or even partly, observation. The source may well be the discovery of an inconsistency in another paper, or say, the discovery of the fact that a hypothesis proposed in another paper could be tested by such and such an experiment; all these non-observational discoveries are 'sources' in the sense that they all add to our knowledge.

I do not, of course, deny that an experiment may also add to our knowledge, and in a most important manner. But it is not a source in any ultimate sense. It has always to be checked: as in the example of the news in *The Times* we do not, as a rule, question the eyewitness of an experiment, but, if we doubt the result, we may repeat the experiment, or ask somebody else to repeat it.

The fundamental mistake made by the philosophical theory of the ultimate sources of our knowledge is that it does not distinguish clearly enough between questions of origin and questions of validity. Admittedly, in the case of historiography, these two questions may sometimes coincide. The question of the validity of an historical assertion may be testable only, or mainly, in the light of the origin of certain sources. But in general the two questions are different; and in general we do not test the validity of an assertion or information by tracing its sources or its origin, but we test it, much more directly, by a critical examination of what has been asserted—of the asserted facts themselves.

Thus the empiricist's questions 'How do you know? What is the source of your assertion?' are wrongly put. They are not formulated in an inexact or slovenly manner, but *they are entirely misconceived*: they are questions that beg for an authoritarian answer.

XV

The traditional systems of epistemology may be said to result from yes-answers or no-answers to questions about the sources of our knowledge. *They never challenge these questions, or dispute their legitimacy*; the questions are taken as perfectly natural, and nobody seems to see any harm in them.

This is quite interesting, for these questions are clearly authoritarian in spirit. They can be compared with that traditional question of political theory, 'Who should rule?', which begs for an authoritarian answer such as 'the best', or 'the wisest', or 'the people', or 'the majority'. (It suggests, incidentally, such silly alternatives as 'Who should be our rulers: the capitalists or the workers?', analogous to 'What is the ultimate source of knowledge: the intellect or the senses?') This political question is wrongly put and the answers which it elicits are paradoxical.[46] It should be replaced by a completely different question such as '*How can we organize our political institutions so that bad or incompetent rulers* (whom we should try not to get, but whom we so easily might get all the same) *cannot do too much damage?*' I believe that only by changing our question in this way can we hope to proceed towards a reasonable theory of political institutions.

[46] I have tried to show this in ch. 7 of my *Open Society*.

The question about the sources of our knowledge can be replaced in a similar way. It has always been asked in the spirit of: 'What are the best sources of our knowledge—the most reliable ones, those which will not lead us into error, and those to which we can and must turn, in case of doubt, as the last court of appeal?' I propose to assume, instead, that no such ideal sources exist—no more than ideal rulers—and that *all* 'sources' are liable to lead us into error at times. And I propose to replace, therefore, the question of the sources of our knowledge by the entirely different question: '*How can we hope to detect and eliminate error?*'

The question of the sources of our knowledge, like so many authoritarian questions, is a *genetic* one. It asks for the origin of our knowledge, in the belief that knowledge may legitimize itself by its pedigree. The nobility of the racially pure knowledge, the untainted knowledge, the knowledge which derives from the highest authority, if possible from God: these are the (often unconscious) metaphysical ideas behind the question. My modified question, 'How can we hope to detect error?' may be said to derive from the view that such pure, untainted and certain sources do not exist, and that questions of origin or of purity should not be confounded with questions of validity, or of truth. This view may be said to be as old as Xenophanes. Xenophanes knew that our knowledge—the knowledge of mortals—is guesswork, opinion—*doxa* rather than *epistēmē*—as shown by his verses:[47]

> In the beginning the gods did not grant us a glimpse of their secrets;
> Yet, in time, if we seek we shall find, and shall learn to know better.

> But as for certain truth, no man has known it,
> Nor will he know it; neither of the gods,
> Nor yet of all the things of which I speak.
> And even if by chance he were to utter
> The final truth, he would himself not know it;
> For all is but a woven web of guesses.

[47] DK, Xenophanes, B 18 and 34. (Cp. also note 14, above.)

Yet the traditional question of the authoritative sources of knowledge is repeated even today—and very often by positivists and by other philosophers who believe themselves to be in revolt against authority.

The proper answer to my question 'How can we hope to detect and eliminate error?' is, I believe, 'By *criticizing* the theories or guesses of others and—if we can train ourselves to do so—by *criticizing* our own theories or guesses.' (The latter point is highly desirable, but not indispensable; for if we fail to criticize our own theories, there may be others to do it for us.) This answer sums up a position which I propose to call 'critical rationalism'. It is a view, an attitude, and a tradition, which we owe to the Greeks. It is very different from the 'rationalism' or 'intellectualism' of Descartes and his school, and very different even from the epistemology of Kant. Yet in the field of ethics, of moral knowledge, it was approached by Kant with his *principle of autonomy*. This principle expresses his realization that we must not accept the command of an authority, however exalted, as the basis of ethics. For whenever we are faced with a command by an authority, it is for us to judge, critically, whether it is moral or immoral to obey. The authority may have power to enforce its commands, and we may be powerless to resist. But if we have the physical power of choice, then the ultimate responsibility remains with us. It is our own critical decision whether to obey a command; whether to submit to an authority.

Kant boldly carried this idea into the field of religion: '... in whatever way', he writes, 'the Deity should be made known to you, and even ... if He should reveal Himself to you: it is you ... who must judge whether you are permitted to believe in Him, and to worship Him.'[48]

In view of this bold statement, it seems strange that in his philosophy of science Kant did not adopt the same attitude of critical rationalism, of the critical search for error. I feel certain that it was only his acceptance of the authority of Newton's

---

[48] See Immanuel Kant, *Religion Within the Limits of Pure Reason*, 2nd edition, 1794, Fourth Chapter, Part II, § 1, the first footnote (added in the 2nd edition).

cosmology—a result of its almost unbelievable success in passing the most severe tests—which prevented Kant from doing so. If this interpretation of Kant is correct, then the critical rationalism (and also the critical empiricism) which I advocate merely puts the finishing touch to Kant's own critical philosophy. And this was made possible by Einstein, who taught us that Newton's theory may well be mistaken in spite of its overwhelming success.

So my answer to the questions 'How do you know? What is the source or the basis of your assertion? What observations have led you to it?' would be: 'I do *not* know: my assertion was merely a guess. Never mind the source, or the sources, from which it may spring—there are many possible sources, and I may not be aware of half of them; and origins or pedigrees have in any case little bearing upon truth. But if you are interested in the problem which I tried to solve by my tentative assertion, you may help me by criticizing it as severely as you can; and if you can design some experimental test which you think might refute my assertion, I shall gladly, and to the best of my powers, help you to refute it.'

This answer [49] applies, strictly speaking, only if the question is asked about some scientific assertion as distinct from an historical one. If my conjecture was an historical one, sources (in the non-ultimate sense) will of course come into the critical discussion of its validity. Yet fundamentally, my answer will be the same, as we have seen.

XVI

It is high time now, I think, to formulate the epistemological results of this discussion. I will put them in the form of ten theses.

(1) There are no ultimate sources of knowledge. Every source, every suggestion, is welcome; and every source, every suggestion, is open to critical examination. Except in history

[49] This answer, and almost the whole of the contents of the present section xv, are taken with only minor changes from a paper of mine which was first published in *The Indian Journal of Philosophy*, 1, No. 1, 1959.

we usually examine the facts themselves rather than the sources of our information.

(2) The proper epistemological question is not one about sources; rather, we ask whether the assertion made is true—that is to say, whether it agrees with the facts. (That we may operate, without getting involved in antinomies, with the idea of objective truth in the sense of correspondence to the facts, has been shown by the work of Alfred Tarski.[50]) And we try to find this out, as well as we can, by examining or testing the assertion itself; either in a direct way, or by examining or testing its consequences.

(3) In connexion with this examination, all kinds of arguments may be relevant. A typical procedure is to examine whether our theories are consistent with our observations. But we may also examine, for example, whether our historical sources are mutually and internally consistent.

(4) Quantitatively and qualitatively by far the most important source of our knowledge—apart from inborn knowledge—is tradition. Most things we know we have learned by example, by being told, by reading books, by learning how to criticize, how to take and to accept criticism, how to respect truth.

(5) The fact that most of the sources of our knowledge are traditional condemns anti-traditionalism as futile. But this fact must not be held to support a traditionalist attitude: every bit of our traditional knowledge (and even our inborn knowledge) is open to critical examination and may be overthrown. Nevertheless, without tradition, knowledge would be impossible.

(6) Knowledge cannot start from nothing—from a *tabula rasa*—nor yet from observation. The advance of knowledge consists, mainly, in the modification of earlier knowledge. Although we may sometimes, for example in archaeology, advance through a chance observation, the significance of the discovery will usually depend upon its power to modify our earlier theories.

---

[50] See A. Tarski, *Logic, Semantics, Metamathematics*, 1956, ch. viii; also 'The Semantic Conception of Truth', in *Philosophy and Phenomenological Research*, 4, 1944, pp. 341–76.

(7) Pessimistic and optimistic epistemologies are about equally mistaken. The pessimistic cave story of Plato is the true one, and not his optimistic story of *anamnēsis* (even though we should admit that all men, like all other animals, and even all plants, possess inborn knowledge). But although the world of appearances is indeed a world of mere shadows on the walls of our cave, we all constantly reach out beyond it; and although, as Democritus said, the truth is hidden in the deep, we can probe into the deep. There is no criterion of truth at our disposal, and this fact supports pessimism. But we do possess criteria which, *if we are lucky*, may allow us to recognize error and falsity. Clarity and distinctness are not criteria of truth, but such things as obscurity or confusion *may* indicate error. Similarly coherence cannot establish truth, but incoherence and inconsistency do establish falsehood. And, when they are recognized, our own errors provide the dim red lights which help us in groping our way out of the darkness of our cave.

(8) Neither observation nor reason is an authority. Intellectual intuition and imagination are most important, but they are not reliable: they may show us things very clearly, and yet they may mislead us. They are indispensable as the main sources of our theories; but most of our theories are false anyway. The most important function of observation and reasoning, and even of intuition and imagination, is to help us in the critical examination of those bold conjectures which are the means by which we probe into the unknown.

(9) Never quarrel about words. Philosophical problems should not and need not be verbal problems. Verbal problems are unimportant and should always be avoided, though unfortunately they are rarely avoided by philosophers.

(10) Every solution of a problem raises new unsolved problems; the more so the deeper the original problem and the bolder its solution. The more we learn about the world, and the deeper our learning, the more conscious, specific, and articulate will be our knowledge of what we do not know, our knowledge of our ignorance. For this, indeed, is the main

source of our ignorance—the fact that our knowledge can be only finite, while our ignorance must necessarily be infinite.

We may get a glimpse of the vastness of our ignorance when we contemplate the vastness of the heavens: though the mere size of the universe is not the deepest cause of our ignorance, it is one of its causes. 'Where I seem to differ from some of my friends', F. P. Ramsey wrote in a charming passage of his *Foundations of Mathematics*,[51] 'is in attaching little importance to physical size. I don't feel in the least humble before the vastness of the heavens. The stars may be large but they cannot think or love; and these are qualities which impress me far more than size does. I take no credit for weighing nearly seventeen stone.' I suspect that Ramsey's friends would have agreed with him about the insignificance of sheer physical size; and I suspect that if they felt humble before the vastness of the heavens, this was because they saw in it a symbol of their ignorance.

I believe that it would be worth trying to learn something about the world even if in trying to do so we should merely learn that we do not know much. This state of learned ignorance might be a help in many of our troubles. It might be well for all of us to remember that, while differing widely in the various little bits we know, in our infinite ignorance we are all equal.

XVII

There is a last question I wish to raise.

If only we look for it we can often find a true idea, worthy of being preserved, in a philosophical theory which must be rejected as false. Can we find an idea like this in one of the theories of the ultimate sources of our knowledge?

I believe we can; and I suggest that it is one of the two main ideas which underlie the doctrine that the source of all our knowledge is super-natural. The first of these ideas is false, I believe, while the second is true.

The first, the false idea, is that we must *justify* our knowledge, or our theories, by *positive* reasons, that is, by reasons

[51] F. P. Ramsey, *The Foundations of Mathematics*, 1931, p. 291.

capable of establishing them, or at least of making them highly probable; at any rate, by better reasons than that they have so far withstood criticism. This idea implies, I suggested, that we must appeal to some ultimate or authoritative source of true knowledge; which still leaves open the character of that authority—whether it is human, like observation or reason, or super-human (and therefore super-natural).

The second idea—whose vital importance has been stressed by Russell—is that no man's authority can establish truth by decree; that we should submit to truth; that *truth is above human authority*.

Taken together these two ideas almost immediately yield the conclusion that the sources from which our knowledge derives must be super-human; a conclusion which tends to encourage self-righteousness and the use of force against those who refuse to see the divine truth.

Some who rightly reject this conclusion do not, unhappily, reject the first idea—the belief in the existence of ultimate sources of knowledge. Instead they reject the second idea—the thesis that truth is above human authority. They thereby endanger the idea of the objectivity of knowledge, and of common standards of criticism or rationality.

What we should do, I suggest, is to give up the idea of ultimate sources of knowledge, and admit that all knowledge is human; that it is mixed with our errors, our prejudices, our dreams, and our hopes; that all we can do is to grope for truth even though it be beyond our reach. We may admit that our groping is often inspired, but we must be on our guard against the belief, however deeply felt, that our inspiration carries any authority, divine or otherwise. If we thus admit that there is no authority beyond the reach of criticism to be found within the whole province of our knowledge, however far it may have penetrated into the unknown, then we can retain, without danger, the idea that truth is beyond human authority. And we must retain it. For without this idea there can be no objective standards of inquiry; no criticism of our conjectures; no groping for the unknown; no quest for knowledge.

THE METAMORPHOSIS OF METAPHYSICS

BY JOHN WISDOM

I speak of the metamorphosis of metaphysics because I want to trace a change in identity and an identity in change in the development of metaphysics. People sometimes speak as if the metaphysician were a pretentious and really very silly old man who is now dead, and has been replaced first by the logical analyst, and later by someone still more on the spot, the linguistic philosopher. It seems to me misleading to talk like this. True when someone whom we know very well changes very profoundly we may say, 'He is no longer the same person.' And saying this we combat the deadly inertia of our minds which makes us dismiss as a mere pretence anything in what a man says or does which does not fit the picture of him which the past has given us. Jack, who never misses a party and 'always has some new crack', is suddenly serious and insists that he would like to throw it all up and grow roses. Even if we do not say 'Nonsense', we still cannot help a smile which shows him that we do not take seriously what he is saying. It's this inertia in our awareness of each other which is one of the things which often makes a person unable to talk to someone who knows him well in the way he can to a stranger. For a stranger will not laugh when he says what is out of character, or rather, what does not fit the model of him which the past has presented to others and even to himself. But, on the other hand, a stranger may be misled if he takes present appearance as the sole clue to a person's real nature. The last phase of a man's life may show us something in him which never appeared in his youth, but it may also conceal from us something which once showed plain enough though now it never shows except in some flicker of word or manner, significant only to one who knew him long ago. He has now, perhaps, sat for years at a window gazing at a landscape in suburbia. This too, it is true, shows his nature. But the secret of this inanition may elude us until we learn of something that went before, never forgotten but never recalled.

All this reminds us of the laborious, intricate, subtle process by which, alive to the variety in perpetual change, we yet in that variety detect a unity, in the obvious, the hidden, in appearance reality. It is something we never cease from doing, whether in everyday life, in poetry, in drama, in history, in science, in philosophy, and even in metaphysical philosophy which also, so it has been commonly said, is somehow concerned with appearance and reality.

So in the hope of gaining a better grasp of the real nature of metaphysical philosophy or, as one might call it, the philosophy of the schools, let us look back at how it once appeared and at what came after. And in doing this let us look at three things: first at what metaphysical philosophers said about philosophy; second, at how they formulated metaphysical questions; third, at what they did in order to answer these questions.

2. About 1920 Dr. J. Ellis McTaggart was still lecturing at Cambridge and he might be called the last of the 'speculative' philosophers at Cambridge or even in England. Although he knew Russell and Moore he still put metaphysical philosophical questions in the traditional forms 'Is time real?' 'Does matter exist?' 'Philosophy,' he used to say, 'is the systematic study of the ultimate nature of reality.' The scientist, he said, studies systematically the nature of reality but not its ultimate nature. The poet, he said, does not study the nature of reality systematically, but he does study its ultimate nature. This last remark is an important clue to what he meant by the mysterious phrase 'the ultimate nature of reality'. For it appears that this phrase refers to something which at least some poets do which scientists do not do or do much less. But what is this? Which poets do it and when do they do it most? So far as I know, McTaggart said little or nothing in further explanation of this reference to poetry. Why not? What did he mean? What made him say that poets study the ultimate nature of reality? On the

face of it it would seem that a metaphysical philosopher is much more like a scientist than he is like a poet, and surely the scientist does in some sense study the ultimate nature of matter and even of mind. One would not be surprised to hear a scientist say that it has been discovered that objects which seem to us solid are not really solid, that our flesh and bones, and chairs and tables, and even stones, are ultimately not solid, that ordinary experience makes us think they are solid but extraordinary experience enables us, if not to observe at least to infer that they are not. All this reminds us at once of metaphysical philosophers who have said that though things seem large and round and soft or hard, small and angular, they are not; that though they seem to come and go they do not; that though they seem to be in space and time they are not. It reminds us of philosophers who have said that what seems to us physical and material is not, that our bodies and even chairs and tables and stones are not material but are really collections of ideas, impressions, sensations, in our minds, or in the mind of some timeless being. The metaphysical philosopher seems for a moment to differ from the scientist only in that he goes further. The editor of *British Contemporary Philosophy* at the end of the preface to the second volume of this collection of philosophers' writings speaks of their common purpose of 'exploring the frontier provinces of human experience and perchance bringing back authentic tidings of what lies beyond'. But now is it characteristic of the philosopher to explore the frontier provinces of human experience? Is it not much less Aristotle, Descartes, Hume, Kant, and much more Flaubert, Dostoievsky, Kafka, Lawrence, Freud, who 'travel to the bounds of human experience'? And do these explorers attempt to bring back tidings of anything that lies beyond human experience? Surely it is the human experience itself that they are concerned. What they write about may be as imaginary as the frictionless planes and perfect pulleys of the engineer, but this leaves it true that what they are concerned with in the end is the wide but well-known world.

But we must leave this matter for the moment and ask what

questions McTaggart and the traditional metaphysical philosophers asked themselves. They asked, 'Is time real?' 'Does matter exist?' 'Does mind exist?' 'Does evil exist?' 'These things', they said, 'appear to be real but are they? After all what seems to be so is sometimes shown by further experience to be an illusion. Perhaps what all experience *superficially* suggests is so, more fundamental thought may show to be an illusion too, to be appearance and not ultimately real.'

These are traditional questions in their traditional form.

3. What a change then, what a shocking change, came over the scene when in 1918 Moore wrote: 'The questions whether we do ever know such things as these, and whether there are any material things seem to me, therefore, to be questions which there is no need to take seriously: they are questions which it is quite easy to answer, with certainty, in the affirmative.'[1] What a change when Moore, in lecturing on the soul, the self, the mind, the ego, declared that he would not concern himself with the question 'Does the soul exist?' but with the question 'What do we mean when we say such things as "I see this", "I did see that".' What a change when in 1914 Russell said that he believed that the problems and the method of philosophy had been misconceived by all schools,[2] that philosophical problems all reduce themselves, in so far as they are genuinely philosophical, to problems of logic.[3] For instance, the traditional philosophers had troubled themselves with the question 'How can such beings as Zeus, the horses of the gods, and Mr. Pecksniff, not have being, not exist? For how can what does not exist be thought of or talked, of, how can it entertain or annoy us? How can what does not exist have any property?' Russell showed that this old riddle vanishes under logical analysis as surely as does the riddle 'What happens when an irresistible force meets an immovable object?' He then turned his attention to those philosophers who prove, not that things which do not exist do, but that things which do exist do not, or

---

[1] Quoted by Professor Morris Lazerowitz in 'Moore's Paradox' in *The Philosophy of G. E. Moore*.
[2] *Our Knowledge of the External World*, p. 3.   [3] Ibid., p. 33.

at least that there is no real reason to think they do. For instance, McTaggart[4] at the end of a discussion as to the existence of matter concludes that there is no more reason to think that the causes of our sensations are coloured, warm, large, round, or heavy than there is to think that the face of one who boils a lobster red must itself be red. He says, 'The result is that matter is in the same position as the Gorgons or the Harpies. Its existence is a bare possibility to which it would be foolish to attach the least importance since there is nothing to make it at all preferable to any other hypothesis however wild.' Other philosophers felt that this was going rather far. And Russell, remembering the sophistical performance in which philosophers had made it appear that Gorgons and Harpies do exist, now ventured a suggestion to those who were purporting to prove that chairs and tables do not exist.

Look here, [he said],[5] surely what you really mean is not that chairs and tables are fictions like the Gorgons and the Harpies, but that they are *logical* fictions like force or the economic man or the average Englishman. You do not really mean that everyone who says anything about chairs and tables is hopelessly mistaken or irrational. What you mean is that just as statements about the average Englishman can be analysed without remainder into statements about individual Englishmen whom we see everyday, so statements about chairs and tables can be analysed without remainder into statements about what we can expect to see and feel.

There was something attractive about this suggestion. But it was revolutionary. It was not that no one had suggested before that to speak of material things is to speak of bundles of impressions or sensations. What was so unpleasantly revolutionary was the suggestion that metaphysical philosophers who had seemed to be concerned not with any merely logical question but with whether matter exists were really concerned with a logical question. Philosophers of the old school stood aghast yet unable to check the rapid metamorphosis of a subject

---

[4] *Some Dogmas of Religion*, section 73.
[5] See, for instance, *Our Knowledge of the External World*, especially Lecture III.

which had been a study of the nature of reality and now seemed no more than the purely logical investigation of the structure of propositions, the minute analysis of the meanings of words. But we who were the bright young things of the logico-analytic era welcomed the change from the absurdity of exploring the universe in an armchair to the pleasure of a dance beneath the brilliant lights of *Principia Mathematica*. We even joined hands in a party with the pragmatists amid the ruins of tradition.[6]

Even after the revolution certain difficulties beset us. Logical fictions, logical constructions, seemed to be everywhere. We did not mind that. But exactly how were they constructed and out of what? Chairs and tables, Russell had taught us, were no 'part of the ultimate furniture of heaven and earth'. But on what then could we rest? Sense data perhaps, the constituents of the ultimate atomic facts corresponding to the atomic propositions into which all other propositions can be analysed. But now what is it to analyse a proposition? It is to analyse the meaning of a sentence. But then what is the meaning of a sentence and what is it to analyse it? However to this we soon had an answer. To analyse a class of propositions, we said, is to translate a class of sentences. For instance, to analyse propositions about material things into propositions about sense data or sensations is to translate sentences about chairs and tables into sentences about sense data or sensations, to analyse propositions about good and evil into propositions about our feelings is to translate sentences of the sort 'This is good', 'That is bad', into sentences of the sort 'I like this' or 'We disapprove that'.

With this advance we did not *deny* that philosophy is a matter of the logical analysis of propositions, but we *supplemented* this account of philosophy with the explanation 'And the analysis of propositions is the translation of sentences.' This advance has sometimes been referred to as a change from 'the material mode of speech' to 'the formal mode'. It is the change from a mode of speech in which a speaker appears to refer to a logical,

[6] Here remember James's camping party and what he calls a metaphysical dispute about a squirrel: *Pragmatism*, Lecture II.

abstract, entity, such as a proposition, into a mode of speech in which he apparently refers to a word or a sentence.

Although this change from the logical to the linguistic mode of formulating philosophical questions was not adopted by all philosophers of the logico-analytic group one must not forget its importance. For with it went a change in what philosophers did in answering philosophical questions. While one speaks of 'analysing propositions' one speaks of 'trying to see their structure', 'trying to see whether one thing is or is not part of another'. When one speaks of translating sentences one speaks of inquiring into a plain matter of fact, namely whether people would or would not always be prepared to substitute a certain expression for another.

This change was indeed important. It cleared away, or seemed to clear away, or in part cleared away, the exasperating hesitancy one felt as to what to do when philosophers disagreed as they sometimes still did even after the logico-analytic reformation. An appeal to the self-evident, to the intuitively obvious, leads sometimes to unpleasant hints of blindness or of seeing what is not there. What a relief to turn instead to the plain facts of linguistic usage! But this change must not be thought of as a change from a logical phase in which one asked *only* questions as to the interrelations between such timeless entities as propositions and predicates, and *never* asked 'What would we say?' to a linguistic phase in which one asked *only* 'What would we say?' No, the change was not so sharp as this. In the logical phase questions were put in the form 'What is the analysis of propositions of the sort so and so?' But no one who remembers, for instance, Moore's lectures of that time will forget the frequent appeals to what one would in ordinary language say. The change was more like this: In the logical phase we thought of recalling the usage of words as a *means* to insight into the structure of the abstract entities, the propositions and the properties for which those words stood. In the linguistic phase the usage of words appears to be itself the ultimate object of study. Imagine someone concerned with the relations between blocks made of ice or glass so transparent as to be almost invisible. He may sometimes find it difficult to answer a question as to whether one block does or does not extend beyond another. But if each block is enclosed in a coloured frame which in most cases fits it pretty well then he may as a first step answer questions about the relations between the frames and so reach indirectly answers to questions about the relations between the blocks. How much more boldly though, how much more freely, will he give his attention to the frames if we tell him that we are no longer interested in their contents, if they have any contents at all. In the same way, or so it seemed, when we describe philosophy no longer as the physics of the abstract to which the usage of words may provide useful clues but as itself the study of the usage of words then we are freed from trying to see those meanings which seem to grow more hazy as we gaze at them and may turn with relief to a task anyone who is patient can do, namely that of recalling the usage of words.

And this advance to the boldly, not to say blatantly, linguistic phase led to another important change. It showed a way out from an impasse produced by an obsession with definition and exact equivalence. Russell before our fascinated gaze had, as I have said, dispatched the inhabitants of the world of fiction and of legend, such as unicorns and the ram which flew or swam from Greece to Colchis, those bewildering beings which have never existed and yet, it seems, must linger somewhere in the realms of being, if they are to be so much as the subjects of a conversation. He had dispatched them by providing a rule for analysing the propositions which seem to be about such beings into equivalent propositions which no longer seem to be about such beings because they are plainly only about descriptions of these beings. It was no wonder that, slightly inebriated by this success, we supposed that the same procedure must be at once sufficient and necessary to dissipate such philosophical disputes as those about the existence of material things, or of mental things.

Alas the exact analyses were not forthcoming, or rather at one moment it seemed as if they were and at the next as if they

THE METAMORPHOSIS OF METAPHYSICS

were not. Russell would suggest in the *Analysis of Matter* or the *Analysis of Mind* the lines on which with a little care the requisite analyses could be found. But Moore would produce some objection to the correctness of the suggested equations.

While philosophical problems were put in the form 'What are the propositions which together make up the ultimate parts of what we mean when we speak of things of sort X?' it seemed essential to find parts which made up exactly that of which they formed the parts. And when the philosophical problems were recast in the linguistic mode 'Can sentences of sort X be translated into sentences not of sort X?' it seemed essential to find sentences not of sort X which meant neither more nor less than sentences of sort X. But these translations could not be found. And this was not because of an accidental paucity of the English, French, or German language. It was no accident at all. The most typical tough old metaphysical puzzles are just those which arise when, pressing a question of the form 'What ultimately are our reasons for statements of sort X?', we come at last to reasons which though they are all we have are *not* such that statements of sort X can be deduced from them whether singly or in combination. The difficulty would be removed if we could say that statements of sort X are reducible to those upon the truth of which our confidence in statements of sort X is ultimately based. But the difficulty is that statements of sort X are not deducible from those on which they are ultimately based and therefore not reducible to them, not analysable into them; in other words a typical metaphysical difficulty about what is expressed by sentences of sort X cannot be met by translating those sentences into others. Remember the pattern of metaphysical trouble. For instance, someone says, 'Has anything happened before this moment? Has there been a past? Do we know what we claim to know about the past?' You are amazed at such a crazy question. However, you reply perhaps, 'Well I know I wound my watch this morning.' But the sceptic asks, 'How do you know you did?' You are again amazed but still you perhaps reply, 'I always wind it when I get up and I certainly got up this morning.' The sceptic replies, 'If you knew these two statements to be true you could indeed deduce that you wound your watch this morning. But both these statements are statements about the past and are therefore included in those about which I am asking how you know them to be true.' You reply perhaps, 'I remember getting up this morning and for that matter I remember winding my watch.' The sceptic says, 'When you say that someone remembers an incident do you not imply that that incident took place?' You reply, 'Certainly. I could not remember winding my watch this morning if I did not wind it.' The sceptic says, 'So your claim to remember winding your watch this morning includes the claim that you wound it. It therefore includes a claim about the past. And I am therefore asking how you know that you do not merely seem to remember but do remember winding your watch this morning.' You reply, 'Well I certainly seem to remember winding it. I can see now a mental picture of the watch in my hand as I wind it. I do not need to know the past in order to know that I now see this mental picture. Besides here is the watch ticking away. If you now take a watch that is not going you will find that it will not go unless someone winds it and if you ask people whether they wound my watch this morning you will find that they all reply that they did not.' The sceptic says, 'But you can not deduce from all this about the present and the future that you wound your watch this morning nor anything else about the past.'

The position is becoming clear. Any statement from which a statement about the past can be deduced is or includes a statement about the past. And therefore to reduce the latter to the former is not to translate a sentence about the past into one which is not about the past. Any statement which is not about the past and does not openly or covertly include one, is not a statement from which a statement about the past can be deduced, and therefore not one to which a statement about the past can be reduced, and therefore the sentence which expresses it is not one into which a sentence about the past can be translated.

The position is the same for any typical metaphysical question.

How then, it may be asked, did it come about that Russell did meet a metaphysical difficulty by means of an analysis, a translation? The answer is that difficulty about how a classical scholar's statement such as 'The ram swam' can be true although there was no such ram is in an important respect like typical metaphysical difficulties but is also in an important respect unlike them. Suppose someone says: 'If a man marries the daughter of a daughter of his father's parents then he marries his cousin.' For a moment you may feel it difficult to be sure whether this is true or false. However you soon say, 'Well now this just means that if a man marries the daughter of a paternal aunt then he marries his cousin, and that of course is true.' Here reformulation has helped. But then the difficulty was not at all metaphysical.

Suppose now that a classical scholar says, 'The ram swam', and suppose that though usually you are quite sensible and well able to make sure whether such statements are right or wrong, you now suddenly feel a difficulty and say in a puzzled way, 'Surely this could be true although there was no such ram and yet how could it be?' This difficulty hardly hinders you in your grasp of the actual world as does a failure to realize that seven half-crowns is the right change from a pound when you have bought a two-and-sixpenny cake. The difficulty is like a metaphysical difficulty in that the question 'Surely this statement can be true and yet it cannot be' evinces at the same time an increased apprehension of the logical character of the statement and a misapprehension of its character. When suddenly one puts this question to oneself one is noticing more explicitly than one had done before a difference between the scholar's statement 'The ram swam' and the farmer's statement 'The ram swam.' At the same time this first expression of sharper apprehension is confused. It evinces a failure to see the peculiarity of the statement for what it is—an unusual, temporary, failure to keep its logical character firmly in mind.

On the other hand your question 'How can all these statements about what does not exist be true?' is not expressing mixed apprehension and misapprehension which extends to *all* statements equivalent to those you refer to. In your case there are statements equivalent to those you refer to about which you are not bewildered. Consequently your bewilderment can be removed by reminding you of this equivalence, by reformulating the statements which trouble you in statements which do not, by translating the sentences which temporarily mislead you as to the verification appropriate to what is asserted by those who utter them into sentences which make this plain, and, in particular, make plain how it is that what is expressed by them may be true although they are about things which do not exist.[7]

With a typical metaphysical statement or question the situation is different. Here the mixed apprehension and misapprehension extends to *all* statements equivalent to any member of the class of statements to which the metaphysician refers. In his case there are no statements which both (1) are equivalent to those to which he refers and (2) do not bewilder him. Consequently no translation will bring out and disentangle his apprehension and his misapprehension, no translation will transform his bewilderment into insight without distortion.

Does this mean that nothing can be done for the metaphysician because he is absurdly asking that statements exposed to certain risks of error shall be shown to be inevitable consequences of, deducible from, reformulatable in terms of, statements not exposed to those risks? It does not. It means that that is not what the metaphysician is asking for. Does this mean that the unsuccessful attempt to reformulate the metaphysician's question in the form 'Can sentences of sort X be translated into sentences of sort Y and not of sort X?' in no way helped us to understand what the metaphysician does ask for? It does not. On the contrary the question 'How can we translate sentences of sort X?' suggests the question 'How may we define sentences of sort X?' and this suggests the question 'How do we define the expression "is a sentence of sort X"?' and this suggests the question 'How shall we define the expression "is using a sentence of sort X" or "is using a sentence

[7] See W. E. Johnson, *Logic I*, p. 166.

in the way X"?' And this suggests the questions 'How shall we explain, *whether by definition or not*, what it is to use a sentence in the way X?' 'How shall we describe a man who is using a sentence in the way X?'

There is a double change here. First there is a change from asking for a rule for translating sentences of sort X, for instance sentences about abstractions, such as the average man, the Indian elephant, to asking for a rule for translating sentences of the sort 'A is using a sentence of sort X', for instance, 'A is using a sentence about an abstraction.' This change is of importance because although any rule for translating sentences of sort X provides a rule for translating sentences of the sort 'A is using a sentence of sort X', the converse is not true. For instance, it is absurd to ask for a rule for translating sentences which attribute a property or relation to something into sentences which do not. But this does not mean that it is absurd to ask for a rule for translating sentences of the sort 'A is using a sentence which attributes a property or relation to something.' The definition 'A *is attributing a property*' means 'A *is marking an affinity between something and other things real or imaginary*' is not far wrong.

The second change is a change from asking for a definition to asking for a description. We ask now *not for a definition* of what it is to use an expression, for instance, the world 'cold', to put a question as to the external world as opposed to a question as to how someone feels, but for some *explanation*, some *description*, of the differences between one who uses the expression to ask about the weather and one who uses it to ask someone how he feels.

This change too is important. Often when someone asks 'What is a so and so?' it is impossible to answer with a definition and often even when this is possible it is useless. Faced with this situation people sometimes say, 'We do not really know what it is for a thing to be a so and so' or, more moderately, 'We cannot say what it is, cannot put into words what it is, for a thing to be a so and so.' But this is because without knowing it they have become wedded to the idea that one does not know what it is for a thing to be of a certain sort unless one can give a definition of what it is to be of that sort, or to the more moderate but still false idea that one cannot put into words, explain, bring before the mind, what it is to be a thing of a certain sort except by a definition. The moment these ideas are formulated and so brought under the light of reason they disappear. Of course we know that the meanings of words are not taught only by definition in terms of other words, that is an absurd idea. And no doubt just as sometimes the meaning of a word is taught, introduced to the mind, not by definition but by examples real or imaginary and painted or described, so its meaning may be revived before the mind sometimes by definition but also sometimes by examples. But though the ideas that we do not know or cannot say what it is for a thing to be of a certain sort unless we can define it are rejected when plainly stated, they may continue to lurk in the mind. In order to *realize* their falsity as opposed to merely *knowing that* they are false let us look at one or two examples in which definition is impossible or futile while explanation by description and sample is possible and valuable. When someone asks, 'What is schizophrenia?' one may reply, 'A schizophrenic person is a person with a split mind.' This answer *may* satisfy the inquirer. But it may not. He may ask, 'But what is it to suffer from a split mind?' One may perhaps provide a definition of this expression too, but one may instead immediately employ what one may call 'mother's method' for explaining what things are. A child asks, 'What is a greyhound?' His father replies, 'A greyhound is a dog of a certain sort.' 'I know', says the child, 'but what sort?' 'Well', his father says, 'a greyhound is a dog in which the power to weight ratio. . . .' But his mother interrupts. 'Look', she says, 'that's a greyhound, and you remember your uncle's dog, Entry Badge, well that was a greyhound. But now that', she says, pointing to a Borzoi, 'is not a greyhound, and even that', she says, pointing to a whippet, 'is not.' Or perhaps she recalls the rhyme

A foot like a cat, a tail like a rat,
A back like a rake, a head like a snake

and so on. In short the mother replies with instances of what is and what is not a greyhound or by comparing greyhounds with what they are not, and these two procedures merge into one. Asked 'What is the feminine nature?' we may reply with a definition, 'It is the nature of a female human being.' But somehow what we wanted is not contained in this easy and correct answer. Shakespeare takes longer to reply with his long stories of Juliet, of Desdemona, of Cressida, of Lady Macbeth, of Portia, of Orlando. And yet of course, his longer, less neat answer may show us as we had not yet seen it the unity in infinite variety which is the feminine nature, or, for that matter, human nature.

All this reminds us of how an answer to a 'What is a so and so?' question may be none the worse because it is not a definition, and may indeed be the better, because, more explicitly than any definition, it compares things of the sort with which we are concerned with other things, things which, though like, are different.

Remembering this we are no longer under a compulsion to provide a definition when someone asks, 'What is a poet?' 'What is a mathematician?' 'What is it to make a statement about mental things, about material things?' We are free to answer the questions 'Does matter exist?' 'What is matter?' not in the form of a definition of statements about material things but in the form of an account of what it is to make a statement about a material thing such as 'It's cold' or 'There are bees in that hive' as opposed to statements about things in the mind such as 'There are bees in his bonnet', or 'I am cold', or 'He has a warm heart.' And this account need not take the form of a definition provided it brings out by hook or by crook the unity within variety which marks on the manifold of possible statements those which are about material things in contrast to the rest.

How satisfactory to pass from a phase in which philosophical questions seemed to call on us to explore some country we could never reach, to see behind some veil we could never penetrate, to open some door we could never open, to a phase in which no such demand is made of us but, instead, only the demand that we should analyse a class of propositions we often assert, translate a class of sentences we often utter. And then when it seems that we are being asked to translate the untranslatable, how satisfactory it is to find that this too is not being insisted upon, that we are being asked only to bring before the mind, by hook or by crook, the role these sentences perform, the procedure appropriate to ascertaining whether one who has pronounced such a sentence has spoken the truth or not, the logical character of a type of inquiry. For such a task though difficult and laborious is not impossible.

4. But now, just when all seems well, something seems to have been lost, and not merely something but too much. While we put our questions in the traditional form they were indeed intractable, but at least we seemed to be engaged on some task which somehow contributed to our apprehension of reality, of the facts, and this did not mean merely facts about how people would use words. Was this all a mistake?

Let us look back and I think we shall find that the first philosophical phase, properly understood, was not so unlike the last and then that the last, properly understood, is not so unlike the first.

Although the traditional philosophers described philosophy so differently, and formulated their questions so differently, did they proceed so differently from the way philosophers proceeded later? Take their attempts to show that matter does not exist. These attempts were of two sorts. There were attempts to show that matter, involving as it does time and space, involves a contradiction. Now one cannot prove statements self-contradictory except by a purely logical procedure; statements as to what is so though it might not have been and statements as to what is not so though it might have been, are beside the point. Consequently those philosophers who argued on these lines that there are no material things no more proceeded in a matter of fact manner than does one who proves that there are no equilateral triangles with unequal angles. Second, there were those philosophers who in considering the question 'Does matter

THE METAMORPHOSIS OF METAPHYSICS 229

exist?' proceeded as for instance McTaggart did in *Some Dogmas of Religion*. What does he say? He says (section 66), 'What reason can be given for a belief in the existence of matter? I conceive that such a belief can only be defended on the ground that it is a legitimate inference from our sensations.' 'It is evident', he says (section 68), 'that the sensations are not themselves the matter in question.' And as to the causes of the sensations, he says there is no reason to believe that they resemble the sensations in such a way that they, the causes, are entitled to the name of matter. At the end of section 73 he says,

> A man who boils a lobster red may have a red face—there is nothing to prevent it. But his action in causing the redness of the lobster gives us no reason to suppose that his face is red.
>
> The result is that matter is in the same position as the Gorgons or the Harpies. . . .

At first it may appear that McTaggart is saying that though it is conceivable that we should have had reason to believe in the existence of matter we in fact have not. But careful examination of his argument reveals that at no point does it depend upon a statement which could have been false. His conclusion that we have no reason for our statements about material things is derived from the premiss (1) that if we have then those statements are legitimate inferences from our sensations and (2) that they are not legitimate inferences from our sensations—they are not legitimate *inductive* inferences, like conclusions as to what is behind one based on reflection in a mirror, nor are they legitimate *deductive* inferences, like conclusions as to the existence and nature of the honey bee based on premisses about innumerable honey bees.

If at this point someone were to say that McTaggart is really concerned with a question of logic, one might agree on the ground that though he makes some show of being concerned with something which might have been otherwise he is not. One might agree further that he is concerned with whether statements about material things are deducible from statements about our sensations. One could not agree that McTaggart is saying that statements about material things are reducible to statements about our sensations since he insists that the existence of matter is not deducible from such statements. On the other hand one might hesitate to say that he denies that statements about material things are reducible to statements about sensations. For in section 62 he says it is certain that my body influences myself, and in section 63 he says that I cannot change into bread the stone I see and touch, and in section 74 he says,

If we ask then of what reality the vast mass of knowledge holds true which science and everyday life give us about matter, we must reply that it holds true of various sensations which occur to various men, and of the laws according to which these sensations are connected, so that from the presence of certain sensations in me I can infer that, under certain conditions, I shall or shall not experience certain other sensations and can also infer that, under certain conditions, other men will or will not experience certain sensations.

The fact is McTaggart, like Berkeley and others, is not sure which of two pictures of our knowledge of the material world he wishes to present. According to the first picture we are like prisoners confined in separate cells and never allowed to look out of the windows of their cells at the outside world nor to hear any sound of it. Each has a mirror, sound reflector, and other instruments which he believes reproduces faithfully what goes on outside his cell including what is reflected in the instruments of other prisoners. When a prisoner says something about the outside world, perhaps that the sun is shining, he does not mean merely that his instruments show the sun as shining nor even that his instruments and those of the other prisoners show the sun as shining. Not at all. He can remember other days, when he relied upon no mirrors or radio sets, and were he now given his freedom he would discard them all and say, 'The sun is shining' or 'The sun is not shining' no matter what might be the programme on the apparatus on which he is now obliged to rely. Indeed it is because when he speaks of the sun and the outside world he refers to something beyond what he can observe, the reflections in his instruments, that we must say that his knowledge of the outside world is indirect and not what it might be. According to McTaggart's first picture our knowledge of the material world is like the prisoner's knowledge of the world outside his cell except that we are even worse off in that we have never known better days when we could turn from the shadow show of our sensations to the reality they reflect, nor can we dream that better days will come.

According to the second picture we are like prisoners who have been imprisoned so long that now when any of them seems to speak of the outside world and says, perhaps, 'The sun is shining' he means only that in his mirror the sun shines, that his sound machines will give a sound as of voices saying, 'Yes, the sun is shining.' In such a case each prisoner has direct knowledge of what he claims is so when he says, for instance, that the sun is shining. For now he means only something about what his mirrors and other instruments show, will show, or would show. According to McTaggart's second account of our knowledge of the material world we are like the prisoners in the second case. When we say, 'This is champagne not vinegar' what we mean is something about the programme of sensations we may expect.

But now what is this second account of our knowledge of the material world? Is it not the same as that which Russell offers us when he says that material things are logical constructions out of sense data,[8] is it not the same as that which the logical analyst offers us when he says that when we speak of material things and say, for instance, 'This is champagne not vinegar' what we mean can be analysed into a complicated statement about what sensations we may expect.

McTaggart it is true does not come down firmly in favour of this account; indeed I should say that upon the whole he gives the impression that statements about sensations are not related to conclusions about material things as statements about individual men are related to conclusions about the statistical construction, the average man. Upon the whole he gives the impression that premisses about sensations or sense-

[8] Russell, *Our Knowledge of the External World*, p. 101.

data are related to conclusions about material things as premisses about pictures in a mirror are related to conclusions about what is pictured except that we have never turned to what is pictured. But this leaves it true that he is concerned with the same question as that which concerned the logical analysts, namely, 'Are statements about material things reducible to statements about our sensations or do they refer to something over and above our sensations?'

It is not my aim to discuss which of these models of the logical character of statements about material things is correct, nor to wonder whether perhaps they are both unsatisfactory and, perhaps, both helpful—as when one calls a man the wisest fool in all Christendom.

No, my aim at the moment is to say this: read over what McTaggart says. Does he at any point rely upon some premiss which though true could conceivably have been false? Does it not now appear that if we look not at what traditional philosophers said about philosophy, nor at the form of words in which they couched their questions and their answers, but at the procedure they adopted in reaching their answers then we see that what they did was after all different only in air and in guise from what is done by their logico-analytic successors. Their aim appeared to be different, but their proceedings were fundamentally the same. True they preserved the air and guise of specially cautious scientists seeking to ascertain what is actual, not merely what is possible; but this was only a disguise for a procedure as purely *a priori* as that of the purest student of the structure of the possible, the most detached analyst of the abstract. And the analytic procedure, as we have already noticed, differs from that of those who ask not for the analysis of propositions but for the translation of sentences only in the openness with which the last appeal is allowed to appear as an appeal to the usage of words. Nor is this fundamental concern with the usage of words diminished when, no longer obsessed by equation or translation, we ask at last not for the definition but for the description of the usage of words.

5. But now, alas, we seem to have lost nothing only because

we never had it, seem to have lost only an illusion, the illusion that somehow philosophy played some part in revealing the actual, and that not merely the actual use of words but the actual state of things which the use of words in everyday life, in history, in science, in law, purports to represent. That idea it now seems was all illusion.

But was it all illusion?

6. Consider a somewhat parallel case. The statements 'Two and two always make four', 'Seven and five always make twelve' may at first seem to be statements which tell us about what actually happens in nature. Indeed teachers sometimes introduce these statements in such a way that a child may naturally think that they are established by experiments with beads, marbles, and the rest, and that they would be false were these experiments not to turn out as they do. It is only later that the child learns that these mathematical statements are statements which could not have been false no matter what had happened. They are not statements which would be shown to be false were we to drop two beads into a box and then two more and then upon opening the box find seven. Such a miraculous sequence of events would show only that we had been wrong in thinking that beads never breed other beads; it would not prove that two and two do not make four. When one says 'If there are two and two then there are four' one is not saying of two possible states of affairs then whenever one is actual the other is also as one is when one says 'If you drink this you will recover.' But if one is not doing this when one says 'Two and two—that means four' what is one doing? Is one saying 'The words "Two and two" mean the same as the word "Four"'? When one says 'If there are a dozen there are twelve, if there are two dozen there are twenty-four' is one saying 'the expression "a dozen" means the same as "twelve"'? Sometimes—but only when one is teaching the meaning of the word 'dozen' to someone who does not know its meaning, not when one is making the mathematical statement 'Two dozen, that means there are twenty-four.' One is making the mathematical statement only when one is *not* teaching, or even

reminding oneself or another of the meaning of the expression 'a dozen'. It begins to seem as if one is making a mathematical statement only when one is saying nothing. What can be the point of making a mathematical statement, and in particular how can the making of it ever be of any use in apprehending the actual?

Let us think. When, in what circumstances, does one find it worth while to make a mathematical statement? Suppose someone knows that there are thirty-four guests at her party and can see set out three groups of glasses, in each group three rows with four glasses in each row. Still she is worried as to whether she has enough glasses. 'Look', you say, 'In each lot three rows of four. Three fours is a dozen. Three dozen means thirty-six. Thirty-six is thirty-four and two extra.' Her face clears. Your mathematical talk has not been useless. It has helped to set in a new light an actual situation, it has helped in reviewing an actual situation. The same effect *might* have been obtained without making any mathematical statement. You might have said: 'There are three groups and in each group there are three rows of four glasses. There are three dozen glasses. There are thirty-six glasses. There are thirty-four glasses and two extra.' Had you done this you would have made only statements which though true could have been false. Each later statement presents only what has already been presented in the one before it, but each later statement *presents differently* what has already been presented. Suppose one says, 'Indigenous, at Epsom, covered 5 furlongs in 55·0 seconds, so he travelled for more than half a mile at rather over 40 miles an hour.' The second description of this colt's performance omits part of the information provided by the first, but apart from that the second description may enable one readily to grasp the affinities and differences between his performance and that of locomotives, automobiles, cyclists, in a way in which the description in terms of furlongs may not. One may review an actual situation by redescribing it without making any mathematical or logical statement. But in fact we sometimes find it helpful to insert mathematical and logical statements which are all hypothetical and make no

THE METAMORPHOSIS OF METAPHYSICS

declaration as to what is actually the case and further are not dependent upon what actually happens in the way in which 'If you deprive rats of vitamin B they lose condition' is. For instance, one may say '5 furlongs in 55·0 seconds is over 40 miles an hour' or 'If anything covers 5 furlongs in 55·0 seconds then its average speed is over 40 miles an hour.' In saying this one prepares oneself to review actual situations, or, to put the thing another way, one reviews possible situations. One may do this with an eye to reviewing an actual situation which is already before one. But one may do it without much expecting ever to come upon a situation of the sort one reviews. For instance, I may say 'If I earned a salary of twenty thousand a year I should be earning wages of about £380 a week.' It may entertain me to review this possibility, to try to realize better what it would be like, even though I do not expect the possibility to become an actuality. In short, with such statements one reviews the possible.

Here then in mathematical statements we have statements which at first appear to be telling us about what in fact happens in nature like the statements 'There is no smoke without fire' or 'Faint heart never won fair lady', and then turn out to be independent of what actually happens in nature, turn out to be nothing but words in which we review the possible. But such review of the possible may at any time serve us in reviewing the actual, for at any time the possible may become actual.

Mathematical and logical statements review the possible only on quite conventional lines. One may review the possible upon unconventional lines. For instance, someone may say: 'Suppose that on several occasions two men dream very vividly but very differently. Suppose that no research into the past, however careful and extended, reveals a hidden circumstance sufficient to explain why the one dreams as he does and the other as he does. Suppose, however, that the dream of each exactly and vividly portrays events which happen to him the following day. In such a case would not the explanation of the dreams lie not in what went before them but in what came after? But can the explanation of an event lie in what happens after it?' This question is not one to be settled by investigating nature. One might for a moment be tempted to call it a verbal question. But it is not a question of linguistic fact as to what people would say, nor a question of linguistic policy—'Shall we call an associated but future difference an "explanation"?' It is a question in which we frame and guide our efforts to view, to review, to contrast, to assimilate, to differentiate the shocking possibility we contemplate. Hitherto whenever we have been mystified because on one occasion an event occurred and on another occasion it did not, diligent research has always revealed a difference in what went before. In the case of the dreams we have imagined this would not be so. In face of such a shock we might feel our faith in science and order tremble, and then, looking at the situation again in the light of a modified notation, we might find our faith in science and order restored in a wider form. For looking not only at what goes before events but also at what comes after we might find a justification, not for the old faith that for every difference between two states of affairs there is always a difference in their present or past surroundings, but for the wider faith that for every difference between any two states of affairs there is always a difference *somewhere* in their surroundings, present, past, or *future*. At any moment such purely fanciful and also unconventional reviews of an extraordinary possibility may be needed by those concerned with the actual. For sometimes nature pulls a rabbit from a hat and makes our dreams come true.

Again someone may review unconventionally not some extravagant possibility but some familiar possibility. Sometimes we may be concerned not so to prepare ourselves for the extraordinary that we shall not be unable to 'take it in' when it occurs but to revive or renew our apprehension of possibilities so ordinary that when they are actual we hardly bother to take them in. Christ's story of the good Samaritan was not a story of some unparalleled incident. The point of the story lay in Christ's question 'Who was neighbour to him who fell among thieves?' When dramatists, poets, novelists, present to us possible situations and give us a new view of these situations they do not assert, like historians, that such situations have actually occurred. They review the possible. But such review of the possible leads to a new view of the actual whenever and in so far as that reviewed as possible becomes actual.

So far so good. Words which make no statement as to the actual but merely review the possible may at any moment aid our apprehension of the actual.

7. Now what about metaphysical philosophy? Unquestionably metaphysics puts in a different light certain sorts of possible incidents and undoubtedly such incidents often occur. For instance, when a metaphysical philosopher says that questions as to good and evil are questions of taste, or questions as to how we feel, this puts in a new light what one does if and when one asks a moral question. Such an account of what one is doing if one asks a moral question represents a person who asks, for instance, 'Would it be wrong to go?' as more like than we had ever imagined to one who asks 'Would we feel guilty if we went?' Perhaps this account of moral questioning distorts it. Perhaps another metaphysical philosopher says, 'No, if someone asks "Would it be wrong to go?" then he is usually asking for further information as to what the present circumstances are, as to what are the facts of the case. It is only when no further question of fact remains that the words "Would it be wrong?" put to the hearers a question as to what his sentiments are towards going.' Perhaps a third philosopher says, 'No, this won't do. One who replies "It would be wrong" is not expressing his sentiments. His words are imperative and they mean "Don't go".' Perhaps a fourth philosopher says, 'No. You are all profoundly distorting the situation. The words "It would be wrong" are an answer to a question, and this question is not one which directly all the circumstances are known becomes a question of sentiment or no question at all, only a request for advice or orders. On the contrary, questions of right and wrong, good and evil are those which will be asked when we come to our last account. They will be argued before the Judge from whom no secrets are hid, they will be settled by the Great

Accountant who makes no mistakes and whose books omit no liability and no asset. When an accountant calls a man bankrupt or declares him solvent his voice may betray contempt or satisfaction; when one calls a man a sinner or declares him a saint one may be said hardly to mean what one says unless one not only grasps his affinity to a paradigm as when one calls a spade a spade, a greyhound a greyhound, but also feels towards him in a certain way. As meta-moralists we must note this; for as meta-moralists we are concerned with what is done by one who makes a moral judgement. But we must note also how, just as the question "Is he bankrupt?" may call for thought even after all the facts have been ascertained, so may the question "Is he a sinner?" An answer to the question "Is he a sinner?" commits the speaker to an attitude to reality in a way in which an answer to the question "Is he bankrupt?" does not. But this does not make it any less an instrument for apprehending reality.'

I am not concerned here to argue which account of moral questioning is right or better, nor even to argue that the whole of this piece of meta-morals leaves us with a better apprehension of what it is to be concerned with a moral question than that we had before the meta-moralists began their talk.

But I do submit that each account, for better or for worse, puts in a new light anyone who is concerned with a moral question and that the whole discussion does this too even if at the end of it one is no more and no less inclined to offer the word 'objective' or the word 'subjective' as adequate descriptions of the nature of such a question as 'Would it be wrong?' The fact that we use the same word as we did before the metaphysics began, or that we are still dissatisfied with both words, does not mean that we do not know any better whether and how such questions are subjective or objective. When counsel for the plaintiff and counsel for the defendant present conflicting views of a case, then if one listens only to one of them one may easily get a distorted view of the case. It may even happen that when one listens to both, one's view of the case is in some way less clear than it was before one had heard all the argument. But it will certainly be different. And even if one still gives the

THE METAMORPHOSIS OF METAPHYSICS 239

same answer as one gave before the case came up for consideration the apprehension which lies behind the answer is different from that which lay behind it before.

On the other hand while recognition of *a priori* truth in logic and mathematics throws light both on what happens when a statement of a certain sort is made and also on the situation described by that statement, recognition of *a priori* truth in metaphysics does not in this *double* way throw light on the actual.[1] Suppose a mathematician says, 'To say that there are

---

[1] Many people, I believe, would say something of this sort: 'Parts of mathematics, for instance the multiplication tables, are frequently of practical value but metaphysics, epistemology, is seldom of practical value.' What do they refer to and what are the circumstances, if any, in which epistemology is of practical value?

1. Most knowledge can be (and has been) achieved without a study of epistemology, without a study of the 'theory of the methods or grounds of knowledge' (*Concise Oxford Dictionary*). And much knowledge can be (and has been) achieved without a study of arithmetic, without study of a 'treatise on computation' (*Concise Oxford Dictionary*). A person can understand and know how to reach the knowledge called for by questions about things material or mental, in the present, in the past, in the future, without studying an epistemological treatise on the ways in which these sorts of knowledge are to be reached. And a person can understand and know how to reach the knowledge called for by questions of these sorts, including numerical questions such as 'How many marbles have you?', without studying arithmetic.

2. A person can show so good a practical knowledge of how one may reach the knowledge called for by questions of a certain sort that one may fairly say that he understands such questions and yet betray much weakness in his power to reach such knowledge by computation. He may betray much weakness in his practical knowledge of the arithmetic of questions of that sort. In contrast to this a person cannot show so good a practical knowledge of how one may reach the knowledge called for by questions of a certain sort that one may fairly say that he understands such questions and yet betray much weakness in his practical knowledge of the epistemology of questions of that sort. For instance, if a person understands questions about the past, then, *ipso facto*, he cannot show more than a very limited weakness in his practical knowledge of the relevance to such questions of memory, of past experience and present experience, and thought, including the power to recognize a thing as being of a certain kind, e.g. a human footprint. He cannot show more than a very limited weakness in his practical knowledge of all that about these questions which an epistemologist endeavours to describe.

3. Nevertheless, although one who understands questions of a certain sort cannot have more than a very limited weakness in his practical knowledge of the epistemology of such questions, he may *upon occasion* betray *some* weakness in his practical knowledge of the epistemology of these questions. A person who

three times twelve things of a certain kind in a certain place is equivalent to saying that there are thirty-six things of that kind in that place.' Consideration of what the mathematician draws our attention to will throw a light both on what is being done if and when someone says, for instance, 'There are three times twelve glasses here' and also on the situation which this person describes. Suppose a metaphysical philosopher says, 'To say that a thing is sweet is very like and yet profoundly different from saying that to most creatures with a sense of taste it tastes sweet.' Consideration of what the metaphysician draws our attention to will throw a light on what is being done if and when someone says, for instance, 'This sherry is sweet', but it will throw little or no light on the situation which this person describes. We need to inquire the reason for this if we are to grasp the nature of metaphysical philosophy and the difference between it and logic and mathematics. But that inquiry must be left for another time.

We must also leave for another time an inquiry into the difference and the connexion between metaphysical philosophy and another study which is also called philosophy and finds expression in such words as 'Continual disappointment can be avoided and contentment attained only by overcoming the will to live', 'Life is a tale told by an idiot', 'For goodness, growing to a plurisy, dies in his own too-much.'

---

feels uneasy about the adequacy of Newton's explanation of certain phenomena, including the depression at the centre of rotating water in a rotating bucket and the flattening of the earth at the poles, may find it useful to read what Berkeley or Mach says as to the way questions about motion are *relative*, that is, are concerned with the spatial relations between one or more bodies in space and other bodies in space (see Sciama, *The Unity of the Universe*, pp. 94–101). Again, a person who well understands questions as to whether or no a thing or person is of a certain kind, e.g. mad, may yet upon occasion show a certain weakness in his grasp of how such questions are *comparative*, and are such that the knowledge they call for may be achieved even on those comparatively rare occasions when neither the answer 'Yes' nor the answer 'No' will do. The removal of this weakness may on these comparatively rare occasions make a considerable difference to his power to recognize the position of the thing or person he wishes to place, and it may make a small difference of this sort on those much more numerous occasions when 'Yes', or 'No', is by normal standards adequate and yet perhaps leads one to neglect some light or shadow on the face of reality.

SOME PROBLEMS OF SELF-REFERENCE IN JOHN BURIDAN

BY A. N. PRIOR

In all the periods in which their subject has been in a flourishing condition, logicians have devoted considerable attention to paradoxes involving self-reference. In this preoccupation, it is easy to accuse them of pedantry and even of frivolity; but such accusations are a mistake. Some of the paradoxes of Buridan even have a certain grim relevance to our practical predicaments in this nuclear age, and as it were bring together the Russell who gave us his part of *Principia Mathematica* and the Russell who worries about world peace. But even apart from that, paradoxes about self-reference present exceptions or apparent exceptions to logical generalizations of great persuasiveness, and any logician with a scientific conscience is bound to take them seriously.

The puzzles of this sort which I shall be considering in this lecture come from the eighth chapter of Buridan's *Sophismata*.[1] This treatise, like medieval logical treatises generally, is rather unsystematic by modern standards, and we have to gather what Buridan's leading principles are as we go along; its acuteness lies in its details, and in Buridan's eye for ingenious objections to inadequate solutions. The skill of modern logicians, and indeed of some ancient logicians, in developing not only particular proofs and disproofs but large deductive systems, is something which seems to be wholly admirable; but it is useful, and I think it even makes for the construction of better systems in the end, if this activity is continually interrupted by bouts of the philosophic niggling at which the schoolmen were masters, and Buridan perhaps one of the greatest masters.

[1] I should like here to thank Mr. Peter Geach for not only drawing my attention to this chapter but sending me a copy of it when I was working on these problems in some isolation in New Zealand.

Chapter 8 of the *Sophismata* contains some twenty 'sophisms' or debatable sentences or arguments, which fall successively into a few broad groups. There are to begin with one or two which involve the notions of logical consequence and possibility; for example, he inquires into the validity of the inference 'No proposition is negative, therefore some proposition is negative'. This hinges on the question whether it is possible that no proposition should be negative, the argument against it being that if the proposition 'No proposition is negative' were ever true it would be false, since it is itself a negative proposition. Then there is a small group about propositions which occur as parts of other propositions, as in 'I say that a man is a donkey'—if a man thus says, not that a man is a donkey, but only *that he says that* a man is a donkey, is he right or wrong? After this group we have Buridan's variations on the ancient paradox of the Liar. He asks whether the proposition 'Every proposition is false' would itself be true or false if enunciated when all *other* propositions were certainly false; and again, whether Socrates and Plato speak truly or falsely if Socrates says 'What Plato says is false', and nothing else, and Plato says 'What Socrates says is false', and nothing else; whether Plato speaks truly or falsely if under the same conditions he says 'What Socrates says is *true*', and says nothing else; whether a man speaks truly or falsely if he says 'There are exactly as many true propositions as false ones' when the only other propositions are two obviously true ones and one obviously false; whether a man utters a falsehood or a truth if he simply says 'I am uttering a falsehood' and says nothing else (this is, of course, the original 'Liar' paradox); and finally, whether the conjunctive proposition 'God exists and some conjunctive proposition is false' is true or false if it is the only conjunctive proposition there is. After this we have a group involving the notions of knowledge, doubt and belief. Suppose we say that a proposition is in doubt with a person if and only if he neither knows that it is true nor knows that it is false. Then we can suppose that the proposition 'Socrates knows that the proposition written on the wall is in doubt with him' is written on a certain wall, and nothing else is written there, and Socrates sees it and wonders whether it is true or false, and knows that he is doing this. Buridan asks whether in this case the proposition on the wall would be true or false.

After some further examples of this last sort, Buridan has a final section in which he considers puzzles arising not with statements but with questions, wishes, promises, &c. He asks, for example, what we are to make of the answer 'No' to the question 'Will you answer this question negatively?' Then he considers a situation in which Plato promises to let people over a certain bridge if and only if the first thing they say to him is true, and to throw them in the river if and only if what they say to him is false, and Socrates says to him, 'You will throw me in the river'. This is a puzzle of some literary interest, since there is a very similar one in *Don Quixote*—Sancho Panza, as governor of an island, is asked to adjudicate in a case where people who cross a certain bridge are hanged if they state their purpose falsely, and let go if they state it truly, and a man announces as *his* purpose that he has come over to be hanged.[2] To finish up with, there are three puzzles about conflicting conditional wishes. For example, Socrates wishes to eat if and only if Plato wishes to eat, but Plato wishes to eat if and only if Socrates does *not* wish to eat. This is where we begin to be reminded of contemporary problems of high politics.

I shall not be discussing this last group of puzzles here, but will concentrate on some of the more elementary ones. And before examining some of Buridan's solutions in detail I want to jump the centuries and, for comparison's sake, briefly survey the treatment that such self-reflexive paradoxes have received in our own time. In the preface to the first edition of Whitehead and Russell's *Principia Mathematica* some seven 'contradictions' of this sort are listed, and there is said to be in all of them 'a common characteristic, which we may describe as self-reference or reflexiveness'.[3] F. P. Ramsey, in his 1925 paper on *The*

[2] Miguel de Cervantes, *Adventures of Don Quixote de la Mancha*, chap. li (cited in Alonzo Church, *Introduction to Mathematical Logic*, Exercise 15. 10).

[3] Alfred North Whitehead and Bertrand Russell, *Principia Mathematica*, 1st edn. vol. i (1910), pp. 63 ff.

Foundations of Mathematics, divided these into two sharply demarcated groups, of which the first 'consists of contradictions which, were no provision made against them, would occur in a logical or mathematical system itself', while those in the second group 'all contain some reference to thought, language or symbolism'.[4] Typical of the first group is Russell's paradox of the class of all classes which are not members of themselves —this class being, on the face of it, a member of itself if it is not, and not a member of itself if it is. Typical of the second group is the paradox of the Liar—the man who says 'What I am saying is false', and says nothing else, his statement being, on the face of it, true if it is false and false if it is true.

The 'provision' which Ramsey had in mind for preventing our logic and mathematics from being disfigured by paradoxes of the first sort, was the so-called 'simple theory of types'. Here the paradoxes are resolved by denying that classes of classes are classes at all in the sense in which classes of individuals are. This view is usually associated with the view that classes are in any case 'logical fictions', talk about classes being only an oblique but often handy way of talking about individuals. Thus understood, the theory of types is basically a theory of 'syntactical categories' or, in a broad sense, 'parts of speech'. To say that x is a member of the class of smokers is not really to relate two objects, x and the class of smokers, but is simply to say, approximately, that x smokes, where 'smokes' is not a name but a verb, that is an expression which forms sentences out of names. To say (no doubt falsely) that the class of smokers is a member of the class of 6-membered classes is again not to relate two objects, or even any objects, but simply to say, approximately, that exactly six individuals smoke, where the prefix 'Exactly six individuals' is neither a name nor a verb but a higher-type expression, a numerical quantifier in fact, which forms sentences out of verbs. Talk of classes being members of themselves then expands to a form in which we make some verb its own subject—a form with a bit in it like 'smokes

[4] F. P. Ramsey, *The Foundations of Mathematics and Other Logical Essays* (Kegan Paul, 1931), p. 20.

smokes'—which just does not construe, or as the logicians say is 'ill formed'.

This may seem an awful lot of grammar for dealing with paradoxes of Ramsey's first type, but remember that what is being straightened out here is our talk about individuals and classes and numbers; what has to be straightened out to get rid of the other group of paradoxes is our talk about talk. And their solution is usually understood to require not merely a hierarchy of syntactical categories or parts of speech, but a hierarchy of languages. Sentences which are true or false are always true or false in some language, and *that* they are true or false is not itself true or false in that language but in some higher one. These might not be different languages in any ordinary sense, but rather different levels or stages of a single one, but the point remains that an assertion *about* the truth or falsehood of a sentence cannot itself be true or false in the language or level or stage of a language to which the sentence itself belongs. For this reason no sentence can directly or indirectly assert its own falsehood, or for that matter its own truth. This hierarchy of languages is a very fundamental conception in, for example, Tarski's well-known monograph on Truth.[5]

Even before Ramsey wrote his paper there were known to be alternatives to the theory of types as a method of handling the strictly mathematical or logical paradoxes, and some of these alternatives have been very fully developed since. In particular it is perfectly possible to treat classes of individuals, classes of classes, &c., as nameable objects in exactly the same sense as individuals are, provided that we do not over-simplify the relations between objects of these various sorts. One may, for instance, refuse to equate simply ϕ-ing with being a member of the class of ϕ-ers, and one may hold, e.g. that the class of classes which are not members of themselves is-not-a-member-of-itself and yet is not a member of the *class* of classes-which-are-not-members-of-themselves. Zermelo's set theory and the

---

[5] Alfred Tarski, 'The Concept of Truth in Formalised Languages'. Item VIII in *Logic, Semantics and Metamathematics* (Clarendon Press, 1956).

modifications of it which have been made by von Neumann and Quine are well-known systems of this broad type.[6]

On the side of the puzzles which Ramsey has classified as linguistic rather than logical or mathematical, the most important development since his time has been the clear demonstration by Gödel, Carnap and others that there is a great deal that *can* be said within a given language or language-level about that language or language-level itself, e.g. we can talk within a language about that language's grammatical structure. What is still generally disallowed, in order to eliminate contradictions, is talk within a language about its relation to the rest of the world, and in particular about questions of the meaning and truth of expressions within it. Taking one of Buridan's examples, a modern logician would insist that the proposition that the proposition 'No proposition is negative' is *true* must belong to a higher language-stratum than that proposition itself, but the proposition that it is *negative* is one that *can* be framed within the very language-stratum in which the proposition itself is framed.

There has also been considerable interest in recent years in what are called 'pragmatic' paradoxes, involving personal attitudes like belief and knowledge. Particular attention has been given, under this head, to a puzzle which appears in the literature in a variety of dramatic guises, e.g. the story is told of a prisoner who is sentenced to be hanged on some one of a number of days, but who is told when he is sentenced that he will not know which day it is until the time comes. He works out that it cannot be the last day because then, all the other days having passed, he would know beforehand that it was going to happen that day. He then successively eliminates the other days in the same way, but is nevertheless hanged on one of them, and unexpectedly too. There is no general agreement as to how paradoxes of this sort are to be solved or classified.

It seems to me useful to bear in mind these broad features of current work when examining Buridan's treatment of the same

[6] See, e.g. W. V. Quine, *From a Logical Point of View* (Harvard University Press, 1953), Item V.

PROBLEMS OF SELF-REFERENCE IN BURIDAN 247

and allied topics, but we would be wise *not* to take it for granted that we know all the answers better than he did; and with a little open-mindedness I think we can find in him only the material for new formal exercises but also suggestions towards new solutions of our problems. And I shall devote a good deal of time to simply *discussing* Buridan's theories as if he were present and one of us—on the general principle that there is much less to be learnt from the history of philosophy as history than there is from the people we meet in it.

One of the most striking contrasts between Buridan's discussion and, for example, Russell's is the complete absence from Buridan's chapter of any puzzles falling into Ramsey's first or logico-mathematical group. In an earlier chapter of the same work there is indeed something that could be construed in this way. This is the fourth *sophisma* in Chapter 3, to the effect that there is a wider *genus* than the widest one, for the term *genus* itself covers both the widest *genus* and all the less wide ones besides. A distinction between classes of individuals and classes of classes seems clearly called for here, but Buridan's own solution is very brief and not very satisfactory—he seems to think that the secret lies in the distinction between the *word* 'genus' and what the word signifies. Ramsey could have put him right here.

In the eighth chapter, all the puzzles considered do fall into Ramsey's second or linguistic group, apart perhaps from the ones near the end about doubting, &c., which modern writers would classify as 'pragmatic'. It is significant here that Buridan almost invariably uses the term *propositio* to mean simply a bit of language, a spoken or written sentence—a particular noise or inscription. And he never forgets that the very existence of 'propositions' in this sense is a contingent matter, and speaks quite freely of the *annihilation* of propositions (asking what would be the case, for example, if all negative propositions were annihilated). There is just no trace in him of the use of the term 'proposition' to mean, not a sentence, but a supposed abstract entity of which the sentence, or the corresponding 'that' clause, is a name. Nor does he appear to believe that there *are* entities of this sort. There is, indeed, a passage in the discussion of his seventh *sophisma* in which he might seem to hold that *true* sentences do name such abstract entities but *false* sentences do not, and he even at this one point uses the word *propositio* for what does not exist when a sentence is false. He makes in this passage the strange remark *hominem esse asinum nihil est*, and the context makes it clear that he would have equally said *hominem esse animal aliquid est*. It is quite clear from what he says elsewhere, however, particularly under his sixth *sophisma*, that he would *not* have meant by this that there is an abstract entity of which the expression 'that a man is an animal' is a name. The *aliquid* that the expression *hominem esse animal* and even the sentence *homo est animal* stands for is not an abstract entity but simply a *man*, a man being an animal, and *hominem esse asinum* or *homo est asinus* in this sense stands for nothing because there is no such object as a man being a donkey.

What is really illuminating in Buridan, however, is not this rather curious material about what sentences 'stand for' but his treatment of the question as to what they *mean* or signify. What he does is not so much to answer this question as to transpose it. The transposition comes out most clearly in his account of what it is for a sentence to be true. A sentence is true if and only if *sicut significat, ita est*, or as he sometimes says if *qualiter significat, ita est*; this, though, is only a first approximation—the final version is: *qualitercumque significat, ita est*. This is not easy to put into English, but the important point is that Buridan does not say that a sentence is true if and only if *what* it signifies, or *whatever* it signifies, is so or is the case; what he says is rather that a sentence is true if and only if *however* it signifies that things are, *thus* they are. He gets rid of the suggestion of *objects* that are signified by sentences by beginning his definition not with a generalized noun but with a generalized adverb, *qualitercumque*.

What this means, in modern terms, is that the hierarchy of parts of speech is relevant not only to our talk about classes and the like, but also to our talk about meaning. Modern writers have seen this also; for example, Russell in his 1924 paper on

'Logical Atomism' says this: 'When two words have meanings of different logical types, the relations of the words to what they mean are of different types; that is to say, there is not one relation of meaning between words and what they stand for, but as many relations of meaning, each of a different logical type, as there are logical types among the objects for which they are words.'[7] By current standards even this, with its easy talk of 'objects' of different logical types and of 'relations' of meaning which hold in each case, is extremely loose and a little misleading, but I think we can put what Russell is getting at in the following way: In spite of some recent objections, I think it can be argued that what a proper name means is simply the object that it names—'Fido', the name, means or names Fido the dog. But a verb cannot have this sort of meaning, for verbs do not name anything, and if we wrote, for example, '"Runs" means runs' this would just be a senseless sentence, with two verbs and only one subject. In English and other languages we invent abstract nouns to meet this difficulty, and we could say that 'runs' means or signifies the activity of running, or more shortly that 'runs' means running. But we misunderstand the function of abstract nouns if we think that there is an object called 'running' which the verb 'runs' names, or even does something else to ('connotes' it or what have you). The fact of the matter is that here the word 'means' has no meaning in itself but is just part of the expression 'means (blank)-*ing*', which constructs a sentence not out of two names but out of a name and a verb. When we come to the meaning of *sentences*, the word 'means' is again without meaning on its own, but is part of the expression 'means *that*', which constructs a sentence not out of two names but out of a name and a sentence—'A man is a donkey' *means that* a man is a donkey. So we need not ask what is named by the clause 'that a man is a donkey'; the word 'that' does not belong here but with the 'means' that precedes it, and what is left, 'a man is a donkey', names nothing because it is not a name but a (subordinate) sentence.

After this excursion into grammar, we can re-state Buridan's

[7] Bertrand Russell, *Logic and Knowledge*, pp. 332–3.

250 PROBLEMS OF SELF-REFERENCE IN BURIDAN

definition of truth as follows: A sentence x is a true one if and only if for any p, if x means that p, then it is the case that p; or more shortly, if for any p, if x means that p, then p. This is much simpler than any of Tarski's definitions of truth for the various languages that he considers. It ought in fairness to be added that part of Tarski's aim was to avoid the use of 'intensional' conceptions like that of 'meaning'; but it is certainly worth noting that if we do not restrict ourselves in this way, and get our grammar straight, it *is* possible to define 'true' very straightforwardly.

Does Buridan's definition, however, avoid the necessity of a language-hierarchy? On the face of it, it does not, but merely traces the systematic ambiguity of 'true' to a similar ambiguity in the more basic conception of 'meaning'. And I am not now referring to the different syntactical types involved in the meaning of different types of expression, but to the ambiguity which still seems to remain when we confine our attention to the meaning of *sentences*, i.e. to the sort of meaning that is always a meaning *that* something-or-other. For suppose I utter the sentence 'The sentence I am uttering is false', and utter no other sentence; then it would appear that what this sentence means, and all that it means, is *that* the sentence I am uttering is false, and this is therefore true, by the definition of 'truth' just given, if and only if the sentence I am uttering *is* false, and we are back with the 'Liar' paradox. It therefore seems necessary to say that 'meaning that p' must always be 'meaning in a language L that p'; and *that* a sentence means in a language L that p, cannot itself be said by a sentence of the language L.

Buridan, as we have seen, was as familiar with the 'Liar' paradox, and variations upon it, as anyone has ever been, and indeed it is precisely in this context that his definition of truth appears. Language-hierarchies of the systematic type that we meet with in such writers as Tarski are a comparatively modern invention, but Buridan does consider and reject certain solutions which it would be easy to put into the language-hierarchy form. For example, when considering the proposition 'Every proposition is false', supposed to have been put forward by

Socrates after all other propositions had been annihilated but false ones, he says that we might understand the proposition of Socrates simply as a comment on everything that was being said in the time just preceding its own appearance on the scene, and then it would be quite straightforwardly true. But, he very properly asks, what happens if we *don't* understand it in this way, but understand it as referring to all propositions in being *at the time*, itself included? He tells us that according to some it just cannot be so understood, because in a proposition which contains terms which themselves stand for propositions, these terms cannot stand for that proposition itself but only for all others. This, however, Buridan says, won't do, for *quod aliquis intelligit, de illo potest loqui*, and as it is certainly possible for someone to think about all propositions whatsoever (past, present, and to come), what he thinks about them can be expressed in a proposition, which will inevitably be itself among those intended.

What else, then, can we do about these paradoxes? Buridan mentions, but rejects out of hand, the solution that some propositions can after all be true and false at once. He then mentions another, which he says that he himself formerly thought satisfactory, to the effect that every proposition, whatever else it may signify or assert, signifies or asserts, by its very form as a proposition, that it is itself true. Any proposition, therefore, which asserts or implies its own falsehood asserts both its falsehood and its truth, and is bound to be in fact false, since at least *something* that it asserts to be the case is not so. We cannot pass back from its falsehood, thus established, to the conclusion that it is after all true, since it says that it is false and things are as it says they are; for things are not *entirely* as it says they are, part of what it says being that it is true.

To this former view of his own, Buridan now objects that propositions do *not* in general signify in virtue of their very form that they are themselves true, because if you take, say, the proposition 'A man is an animal', its terms are 'of first intention', i.e. non-linguistic, while the proposition 'The proposition "A man is an animal" is true' contains terms 'of second intention', i.e. terms referring to pieces of language. Buridan is led by these considerations to distinguish between what a proposition 'formally' signifies and what it 'virtually' signifies. What it 'virtually' signifies is what follows from the proposition itself together with a proposition correctly describing the circumstances of its utterance. In particular, from a proposition x together with the proposition 'The proposition x exists' we may infer the proposition 'The proposition x is true'. And a proposition is only true if all that it signifies, formally *or* virtually, is so. From this point on the argument is very much as before, but I shall not follow it out in detail because this later position of Buridan's seems open to a quite fundamental objection. Since he employs this term 'formal signification' in such a sense that 'What I am now saying is false', for example, formally signifies that what I am now saying is false, and nothing else, we can re-state the paradox in terms of formal signification without bringing in truth and falsehood at all. We simply suppose a person to say 'What is formally signified by this sentence is not the case', and ask about this sentence, not whether it is true or false, but whether things are or are not as it formally signifies that they are, and the answer is that they are if they aren't and they aren't if they are.

This is a transformation of the paradox which suggests itself more readily to a modern logician, accustomed to the use of abstract symbolism, than it would to a medieval one. Suppose I write 'It is ϕ that p' for *any* sentence formed from the sentence 'p', for example 'It is not the case that p', 'It is possible that p', 'It is signified by the sentence x that p', 'It is feared by the person y that p', &c., I can then construct the following formula:

It is ϕ that, for any p, if it is ϕ that p, then it is not the case that p; and for no other p is it ϕ that p.

From anything of this form it is possible to deduce contradictory consequences, by quite elementary logical processes. There can therefore be no ϕ which will turn a complex of this form into a true sentence. For example, none of the following can possibly be true:

1. It is being brought about by James that whatever is being brought about by James is not the case; and nothing but this is being brought about by James.
2. It is feared by James that nothing that is feared by James is the case; and nothing but this is feared by James.
3. It is apparently feared by James that nothing that is apparently feared by James is the case; and nothing but this is apparently feared by James.
4. It is signified by x that nothing that is signified by x is the case; and nothing but this is signified by x.
5. It is signified by x (so far as x signifies anything at all) that whatever is signified by x (so far as x signifies anything at all) is not the case; and there is nothing else that is (signified by x, so far as x signifies anything at all).
6. It is conventionally (normally, formally) signified by x that nothing that is conventionally (normally, formally) signified by x is the case; and nothing else is conventionally (normally, formally) signified by x.

At least, none of these is true if the expression substituted for 'ϕ' is used in the same way throughout the sentence. (If, for example, 'signified' means 'signified in L' in one occurrence and 'signified in M' in another, it is quite a different story.) And any semantics which is to avoid inconsistency must have some means of blocking the introduction of ϕ's with which sentences of this general form are constructible and provable. Buridan's later theory, so far as I can see, fails to meet this requirement.

But what of his *earlier* theory? This it seems to me, *is* logically workable; it is, at all events, not immediately open to the above objection, since it involves no sense of 'it is signified by x that' for which a sentence of the above form would be provable. Its method of preventing this has its own repercussions, some of them perhaps not too palatable; but I fear we must reconcile ourselves to the fact that, however it is conducted, Semantics is a mess. (A theologian of some logical competence once described this as 'a sign of our creaturely status', but even God's language, if such there be, and if it is consistent, must be subject to the same limitations.) It is of some interest that the solution now proposed (the younger Buridan's) has been defended in our own period by a very great logician indeed, namely Charles Sanders Peirce.[8] Peirce did not attempt a detailed formalization of the position, and I have myself only looked at the beginnings of such a development, but I am fairly confident it can be done. In other words, a language *can* contain its own semantics, that is to say its own theory of meaning, provided that this semantics contains the law that for any sentence x, x means that x is true. To set the whole thing out in a fully formalized way, we would need to introduce a symbol, say 'M', for 'means that', and write 'Mxp' for 'x means that p', and then with this and ordinary logical symbols we could formulate, and assert as a law of the system, the sentence 'x means that for all p, if x means that p, then p', i.e. 'x signifies that, however x signifies that things are, thus they are', or 'x means that x is true'. This law is not intended as a definition of 'means that', and as such would be circular and absurd, nor does it assert that *all* that a sentence x means is that x is true, but it does say that any sentence x means this, whatever else it may mean besides. The Liar paradox could then be disposed of exactly as the younger Buridan did dispose of it.

What I am really suggesting now is that the fault of Buridan's later theory, and the source of its inconsistency, is just its half-heartedness. When Buridan, in objecting to his own earlier theory, makes so much of the distinction between sentences which do and sentences which do not contain terms of second intention, he has already sold the pass to the proponents of language hierarchies; a man who is really determined to abandon these—a whole-hearted Presbyterian in semantics, as we might say—will not attach much weight to such arguments, drawn as they are from the armoury of linguistic Prelacy. The fact seems to be that if any sentence *could* be about the semantics of its own language, then all sentences of that language to a certain extent *must* be about its semantics, though in general they will be about other things as well.

[8] *Collected Papers of C. S. Peirce*, 5. 340.

Let us not, however, be over-violent here, and replace linguistic feudalism by a new totalitarianism. We must live and let live. It would be foolish to deny that the word 'means' must be relativized to a language—words don't just 'mean' on their own; 'meaning' *is* always 'meaning in a language L'. And the language L in question *could* be one which does not itself contain the expression 'means in L', and which thereby gains various simplicities. But it could also be one which does contain this expression; for this a price must be paid, but it can be a price less than inconsistency.

I would envisage such a 'Buridanian' language as having a syntax of a broadly Russellian type, with a sharp distinction made between genuine proper names and definite descriptions. In particular, the enclosing of a sentence in quotation-marks should not be thought of as forming a genuine proper name of that sentence, but rather as an abbreviated description. ('The sentence "Grass is green"' would abridge something like 'The sentence formed by writing a Gee followed by an Ar followed by an Ay', &c., &c.) A genuine proper name would have no internal logical structure. But a 'Buridanian' language *would* contain genuine proper names of its own expressions; in fact, in the law 'x means that x is true', the variable must be thought of as one keeping a place for precisely such a proper name. (The law might, incidentally, have to be enunciated in the qualified form 'If x means-that anything'—i.e. 'For any p, if x means that p'—'x means that x is true'; since a proper name is not by its very form a name of a sentence rather than of some other object.) Such a proper name could, moreover, be a name of a sentence in which this name itself occurs, e.g. 'A' could be a name of the sentence 'A is false'. If A were not a genuine proper name but just an abbreviation of the description 'The sentence "A is false"' this would not be possible, as we would never be able to give the fully expanded form of this description; but a mere proper name would not require any such expansion.

Buridan himself frequently used letters as proper names of sentences, and described them as precisely that. He made it clear, and a modern refurbishing of his semantics would also have to make it clear, that these are proper names not of sentence 'types' but of particular utterances and inscriptions. If 'A', for example, is the proper name of the following inscription: *A is false*, then it is not the name of the following exactly similar (or as is often said 'equiform') but numerically different inscription: *A is false*. And if it is in *this* sense of 'sentence' that all sentences signify their own truth, it follows that even a pair of equiform sentences are never *quite* synonymous. '2 and 2 are 4', for instance, means that 2 and 2 are 4 and that *that* inscription back there is a true sentence; while the following: '2 and 2 are 4', means that 2 and 2 are 4 (this much meaning the two inscriptions have in common) and that *this other* inscription (the nearest one to here) is a true sentence. Further, two equiform inscriptions may not always even have the same truth-value (a consequence which Buridan quite boldly drew). For example, if 'A' is the proper name of this inscription: *A is false*, then A in fact *is* false, but precisely because of this the following inscription: *A is false*, is true. For the first inscription asserts its own falsehood (and, of course, like all inscriptions, its own truth), but the second inscription asserts, not *its own* falsehood, but the falsehood of the *first* inscription (together with *its* own truth; but now there is no contradiction, only a difference in truth-value between equiform inscriptions).

So-called structural-descriptive names of sentences (like 'The sentence formed by writing a Gee followed by an Ar', &c., &c.) will in consequence not be even genuine *descriptions* of sentences, in the sense of 'sentence' intended, but will refer rather to classes of equiform sentences; and the rules which give the meaning of particular sentences will be somewhat complicated. In many cases, nevertheless, equiform inscriptions *will* have the same truth-value, e.g. all inscriptions equiform with this one: *No proposition is negative*, are false; and their differences in meaning can in many contexts be ignored, so that no harm is done by talking about, say, 'The sentence "No proposition is negative"' when what is really intended is 'All sentences equiform with the sentence "No proposition is negative"'. (And I shall myself indulge in this harmless laxity below.)

With this particular example, we do run into a difficulty, though not an insuperable one, in connexion with the problem which we have already found Buridan raising about it. Buridan insists that the proposition 'No proposition is negative' must be classified as a 'possible' one because things could be as it signifies, even though it could not possibly be true. It cannot possibly be true because it will only be true if it exists, and if it exists there will be at least one negative proposition, namely itself. But if God were to annihilate all negative propositions there would in fact be no negative propositions, even if this were not then being *asserted* in any proposition at all. In short, *it can be that no proposition is negative, though it cannot be that 'No proposition is negative' is true*. Up to this point Buridan's reasoning seems to me quite conclusive and extremely important. Numerous modern writers have insisted that 'possibility' is in the first instance a property of sentences; there are, they say, no possibilities in things themselves, which are simply so or not so; and to say that some state of affairs is possible (that is, to say with respect to some p that it is possible that p) is just to say that the sentence which expresses this state of affairs (that is, the sentence x such that x means that p) has some property or other. What this property is supposed to be is a little obscure, but Buridan's example at least shows that it cannot plausibly be possible-truth. Buridan is still prepared, nevertheless, to use 'possible' as an adjective predicable of sentences, and attempts what one would have thought to be a more hopeful task than the converse modern one, the definition of this 'possibility' of sentences in terms of the possibility of states of affairs (not *vice versa*). A sentence x, he says in effect, is possible not only if it could be true, but also (even when it *couldn't* be true) if things could be as x says they are, or in modern formal terms, if for all p, if x means that p, then it could be that p.

If, however, we adopt the semantics of the younger Buridan, this account of 'possibility' in sentences won't quite do. For according to this semantics, one thing that is meant by any sentence x is precisely that x is true; and in particular, one thing that is meant by the proposition 'No proposition is negative' is precisely that the proposition 'No proposition is negative' is true. If we adopt Buridan's later distinction between 'formal' and 'virtual' signification, we can escape this difficulty by saying that a sentence is possible if everything that is *formally* signified by it could be the case, and since the proposition 'No proposition is negative' formally signifies only that no proposition is negative, and *not* that the proposition 'No proposition is negative' is true, we can classify this proposition as 'possible' because it could be that no proposition is negative, even if the other thing could not be. But we have already seen where this notion of 'formal signification' leads us—either back to the paradox of the Liar, or, as the only means of escaping this, back into the Babylonish captivity of a hierarchy of languages.

There are, however, ways out of this predicament which are quite simple and I think quite satisfactory. In the first place, I don't see that there *has* to be a sense of 'possible', as an adjective predicable of sentences, which is distinct from 'possibly true'. We can still say that it could be the case that no proposition is negative, *without* saying that the proposition 'No proposition is negative' is thereby classifiable as a 'possible proposition'. But if we do insist on using this language, we can define 'possible' as applied to sentences in a more indirect way, namely by saying that a sentence *x* goes into the 'possible' class if and only if the sentence formed by prefixing 'It could be that' to this sentence *x* is a true one. This does give the distinction that Buridan wanted to make. The proposition 'No proposition is negative' is 'possible' in the sense that the proposition 'It could be that no proposition is negative' is true. This longer proposition, it must be admitted, signifies not only that it could be that no proposition is negative but also that the proposition 'It could be that no proposition is negative' is true; but to say that the proposition with 'It could be' in it *is* true is a different thing from saying that the proposition without that addition *could be* true; so Buridan's distinction is still preserved.

The semantics which I have sketched might prove to be in its details (despite the Russellian character of the associated syntax) not unlike the Zermelo-Quine alternative to the theory of types, and I cannot help feeling that it is much more called for. For the simple theory of types, especially in the forms in which it is now propounded by Polish logicians such as Suszko and Borkowski, seem to me not at all burdensome, and anyway even the Zermelo-Quine logic itself has to have *some* distinctions of syntactical categories—a name, for example, is still something different from a sentence. The only gain which this logic brings is a rather technical one, a limitation of the kinds of variables that need to be bound by quantifiers, and I don't think even this advantage can be plausibly carried over into non-mathematical contexts. But a hierarchy of languages, as opposed to a hierarchy of parts of speech, really *is* a lot for us to have to carry around, and if the theories of the younger Buridan promise a way out of it, they are certainly worth looking into.

INDEX

a priori, 93, 232
 judgements, 93
 propositions, 95
 truth, 93, 239
Absolutists, 93, 111, 113
Abstract nouns, 6, 7, 113, 139, 249
Acquaintance:
 with fellow human beings, 25–39
 with things, 12–14, 23
Action:
 circumstances with obligation to *do* something, 41–64
 justification of, 95, 104
 meaning of 'an action', 42–44
 moral rules, 41–49, 53, 61, 64
 rightness or wrongness, 62–63
Activity:
 goal-directed, 96–97, 106–7, 111
 obligation to perform, 57–64
Adjectives, 7–8, 14–15, 17–19
Aesop, 26
'After-images' or 'after-sensations', 69–76, 80, 82–83
Alexander, Samuel, 35–37
Algebra, 150, 159, 162
Alternatives, 21–23
Ambiguity, 250
Analysis:
 by means of language, 147–50, 154, 164–5
 of propositions, 218–21, 223, 228, 232
Anamnēsis, theory of, 180–4, 210
Anankē, 179
Anaxagoras, 193
Animals:
 bodies 'to be met with in space', 68, 76–78
 experiences, 83
Appear or seem to exist, 11, 13
Apprehension of our fellows, 31–32, 35
Aristotle, 101, 108, 112–13, 169, 174, 189, 198, 215
 method of induction, 183–5, 188
Astrology, 145
Astronomy, 144–5
Ātman or self, 35, 39
Attention, act of, 154–6

Augustine, St., 30, 188
Augustus, 160, 166
Auteuil, philosophers of, 144, 164
Authoritarianism, 171, 173, 177–8, 182, 189, 205–6

Baal, priests of, 35–36
Bacon, Francis, 165, 190–1, 199–200
 attacks predictive policies, 105
 classical empiricism, 170, 199–200
 induction theories, 183–8
 optimistic epistemology, 173, 175, 177, 188–9
 spelling out the book of Nature, 185–7
 truthfulness of Nature, and, 175, 194–5
Bain, Alexander, 95
Balfour, Lord, 27
Behaviour-dispositions, 95–104
Beliefs, 94–95, 198–100, 102, 104, 106, 189
Berkeley, George, 8, 24, 36, 167, 170, 230
Berzelius, J. J., 159
Bible, 189
Billiard balls, particular roundness, 6–7, 10–11
Biran, Maine de, 152–3, 155, 157, 160, 162–7
Bodies, 'to be met with in space', 68–69, 76–78, 80, 82–84
Body (word), 198
Borkowski (Polish logician), 259
Bosanquet, Bernard, 5, 14
Boscowich, R. J., 157
Bovillus, C., 193
Bradley, F. H., 5, 13–14
Brain, 144
British Contemporary Philosophy, 215
British school of philosophy, 167, 170
Bruder, C. H., 169, 172
Bunge, Mario, 185
Buridan, John, 241–59

Cabanis, P. J. G., 143–4, 154–5
Calculus, 163, 165
Calvin, John, 190
Can (word), 'Ifs and *cans*', 115–42

260

Carlyle, Thomas, 31
Carnap, R., 246
Cartesianism (*see also* Descartes, René), 171, 173, 181–2, 190
Causality, 94–5
Cervantes, Miguel de, 243
Characters, 6–10, 12, 14–17, 19, 23
Chemistry, language of, 150–1, 158–9
Cherniss, Harold, 180
Children, self-consciousness, 31
Choose or *chosen*, use of, 115–28
Church, Alonzo, 243
Cicero, 193
Class of all classes paradox, 244–5, 247
Class or kind, unity of a, 5–24
Collingwood, R. G., 54
Colour, 9, 13, 16–20
Common character, 6–8, 16–17
Communication of thoughts and emotions, 28–30, 38
Condillac, Étienne B. de, 145–67
Conditionals, 119–21, 125–8, 130–1, 138
Conditioned reflex experiments, 96
Conspiracy theory of ignorance, 170, 175–7
Constable, John, 195
Continental school of philosophy, 170
Contradictions, *see* Paradoxes
Copernicus, N., 145
Could or *could have*, use of, 115–39
Cratylus, 192
Critias, 176
Crowd-psychology, 33

Daumas, M., 150
Decomposition, 147–8, 151, 154–5
Definitions, 196–9, 225–7, 232
Degérando, Joseph, 152–64, 167
Del Litto, V., 153
Democritus, 189, 193, 210
Descartes, René, 115, 169, 177–83, 185, 187–91, 198, 215
  consciousness of self, and, 30, 32
  doubt, 188, 190
  external things, and, 67, 90
  intellectualism, 170–1, 173, 178–80, 182–3, 191, 207
  optimistic epistemology, 173, 175, 177, 181, 188
Desire, 61
Determinables, 6, 16–20
Determinism, 116–18, 128–9, 147
Dewey, John, 99

Diels-Kranz, 179–80, 183, 192–3, 206
Dikē (goddess), 179
Dionysius Thrax, 141
Disagreement, 143, 152, 160–1
Distributive unity, 6–9, 17, 20–21
Divine natures, 38–39, 181, 188
Dostoievsky, F. M., 173, 215
Double image, 71–73, 75
Doubt, 32, 188, 190
Dreams, 80, 82, 90, 235–6
Duty:
  and ignorance of fact, 41–64
  duties of special obligation, 102–3, 111

Economics, 111
Einstein, Albert, 112, 208
Emotive meaning, 94, 160
Empedocles, 192–3
Empiricism, 93–95, 101, 162, 194, 199–200, 205, 208
  classical, 170–1
  empirically external objects, 68–69, 78–79
  linguistic, 151, 153, 165
  Lockean, 151, 170, 173
  moral decisions, 93–94, 113
  propositions, 93
Encyclopaedia Britannica, 200, 204
Epicharmus, 192
Epicureans, 161
Epicurus, 194
'Epistemic' (Epistemonic), 18, 20
Epistemology, 171–83, 188–90, 205–10
Erasmus, 190–1
Error, 169, 175, 190–2, 195, 206–7, 210
Essentialism, 197–9
Ethics, 93–95, 99, 102, 104, 109–10, 171, 207
Experience, 13, 93, 101–3, 215
  philosophic use of 'having an experience', 81–85
'External things', existence of, 67, 75–80, 83–91 (*see also* under Things)
External world:
  perception, 25–26, 28–33, 35–37
  proof of existence, 65–91

Fact, duty and ignorance of, 41–64
Fallibility, doctrine of, 190–1
Falsehood, 175–6, 180, 195, 210, 242, 244–5, 251–2

Far East faiths, 39
Flaubert, Gustave, 215
Foster, Sir Michael, 69
France, Revolutionary, philosophy of language in, 143–67
Free Will, 115–17, 128–9
Freedom, 107, 172, 191
Freud, Sigmund, 215

Galileo, 185
Games, theory of, 109–10
Garat, J. Joseph, 162
Geach, P. T., 122, 241
Genius, philosophical, 115
Genus (word), 247
Gestures, use of, 148–9
God, 35–36, 38–39, 144, 146, 175, 178, 188–90, 206
Gödel, K., 246
Goethe, 36
Gombrich, E. H., 195
Goodness, 112–13
Grammar, 249–50
  logical, 141
Greek poets, 178
Greeks, 194, 207
Guthrie, W. K. C., 179, 192

Hallucinations, 75
Handford, S. A., 125
Happiness, 112–13
Hartley, David, 167
Hegel, G. W. F., 188
Helvétius, C. A., 164
Helvétius, Madame, 144
Heraclitus, 178–80, 192
Hesiod, 178–9, 192
Hippias, 195
Historical assertion, 202–5, 208–9
Hobbes, Thomas, 198
Homer, 178–9, 192
Humboldt, Alexander von, 159
Hume, David, 95, 162, 167, 169–71, 199, 203, 215

Ideas, sensations and, 143–57, 162–3, 166
Idéologues, the, 153, 155, 163, 165–6
Ideology, 145–6
If (word), '*Ifs* and *cans*', 115–42
Ignorance:
  conspiracy theory of, 170, 175–7
  sources of, 169–212
Imagination, 210
Impotence of all philosophy, 171–2

'in' my mind, metaphorical uses of, 79–83
Indeterminacy, 6, 18–20
Indian faiths, 35, 39
Indian Journal of Philosophy, 208
Induction theories, 183–8
Inductive policies, 94–95, 101; moral principles and, 93–114
Inferential theory, 30
Innate ideas (see also *Anamnēsis*), 148, 180
Institut National des Sciences et Arts, 143–4, 146, 151–4, 158–63, 166
Intellectualism, 170–1, 173, 178, 180, 183, 191–4, 207, 210
Interpretation, 185–7, 194, 202–3
Intuition, 93, 170, 173, 178, 210
Invariance, 107, 113

James, William, 218
Jeans, Sir James, 55
Johnson, W. E., 5–6, 9–10, 16–20, 224
Jordan, Camille, 153
Joseph, H. W. B., 32
Joyau, E., 144
Justice, 172

Kafka, Franz, 215
Kant, Immanuel, 32, 93, 99, 171, 198, 207–8, 215
  and 'the existence of things outside of us', 65–69, 74, 78–79, 86, 88, 90
Kaufmann, Felix, 103
Kepler, Johannes, 145
Keynes, J. M., 138
Kind, *see* Class or kind
Kirk, G. S., 192
Kneale, William, 105
Know (verb), 140
Knowledge:
  an end in itself, 106–7
  analysis and, 147–9
  based upon experience, 93
  by acquaintance, 12–14, 23–24
  expressing, 47
  language and, 159, 164
  of one another as persons, 25–39
  sources of, 153–4, 169–212

Lancelin, P.-F., 153
Land, J. P. N., 169, 172
Language:
  analysis and, 148–50
  authority of, 194

INDEX

Language (*contd.*):
  hierarchy of languages, 245, 250, 254, 258–9
  in expressing moral judgements, 93–94
  linguistic dictatorship, 160, 165–6
  philosophy of, in Revolutionary France, 143–67
  puzzles, 244, 246–7
  science and, *see under* Science
  science of, 142
  to describe inductive action, 95
  universal, 159, 165
Latin language, 125, 160
Lavoisier, Antoine, 150–1, 159
Lawrence, D. H., 215
Lazerowitz, Morris, 161, 216
Leibniz, G. W., 115, 159, 161, 165, 170
LeRoy, G., 147, 156
Lewis, Sinclair, 109
Liar paradox, 242, 244, 250, 254, 258
Liberalism, 173–6
Libido, 33
Locke, John, 145–7, 162–7, 187, 191
  and language, 147, 154, 159–60, 162–7
  empiricism, 151, 170, 173
  on truth, 169, 172
Logical fictions, 217–18, 244
Logico-analytic group, 218–19, 231–2
Logico-mathematical puzzles, 244–7
Love-relationships, 33
Luther, Martin, 190

McKie, D., 150
McTaggart, J. Ellis, 5, 9–11, 15–16, 214, 216–17, 229–32
Magee, Bryan, 180
Manley, T., 186
Marx, Karl, 188
Marxism, 176
Material things, 32, 38, 68, 227–32
Materialism, 144
Mathematics, 150, 162, 233–5, 239
Matter, existence of, 214–17, 227–30
May (word), use of, 122–3, 127, 129
Meaning, 163, 250
  and truth, 195–9
  of words, 160–1, 166, 226, 248–9, 254–5
Mental activity, 57, 61, 81, 154–5
Metaphysics, 145, 161
  metamorphosis of, 213–39
Might or *might have*, use of, 129–30

Mill, J. S., 100–1, 112, 114, 170, 191
Milton, John, 176, 191
Mind (journal), 32
Mind (word), use of, 79–83
Mirabeau, Comte de, 144
Modal phrases, 129
Montaigne, M. de, 190–1
Moore, G. E., 12, 112–21, 124–31, 138, 214, 216, 219, 221
Moral:
  judgements, 93–95, 99
  philosophy, 93, 103, 112, 167
  policies, 102–3, 107, 111
  principles and inductive policies, 93–114
  questioning, 237–8
  reflection, 30
  rules, 41–49, 53, 61, 64
  truths, 162
Morgenstern, Oskar, 109
Morveau, Guyton de, 150
Murray, Gilbert, 178
Muses, the, 178, 182
Mutual recognition of persons, 25–39

Names:
  proper, 197, 249, 255–6
  system of, 148–51, 158–9
Narcissus, legend of, 26
Naturalists, 93
Nature, 98, 109–11, 148, 150, 188–9
  spelling out the book of Nature, 185–7
  truthfulness, 175, 194–5
Negative, propositions, 242, 246–7, 256–8
Neumann, John von, 109, 246
Newton, Sir Isaac, 112, 207–8
Nicolas of Cusa, 190–1
Nisbet, R. M., 125
Nominalism, 8–9
Non-predictive policies, 99, 101–3
Nowell–Smith, P. H., 129–39

Obligations (*see also* Duty), special, 102–3, 111
Observation (*see also* Perception), as source of knowledge, 170–1, 191, 199–204, 210
Origin, and factual truth, 195–9, 205–6
Orphic theology, 39
Otto, Rudolf, 34, 37
'Outside of us', *see* 'Things outside of us'

INDEX

Pains:
  'in my mind', 80–83
  'presented in space', 72–76
Pantigraphia, 159
Paradoxes (contradictions), 241–7, 250–2
Parents, moral rules regarding, 43–44, 46–47
Parmenides, 178–83, 192–5
Parts of speech, 244–5, 259
Pascal, Blaise, 165
Pasigraphie, 159
Past, statements about the, 221–2
Pavlov, I. P., 96
Peirce, Charles Sanders, 95, 105–6, 254
Perception, 101, 154–5, 157
  of the external world, 25–26, 28–33, 35–37
Phaedo, 180
Phenomenalists, 194
Physical objects, 68–70, 80, 84
'Physical realities', 73
Physical Review, 204
Picavet, 153
Pindar, 192, 195
Plants, 'to be met with in space', 68, 76–77
Plato, 16–17, 30, 176, 178–83, 185, 188, 192–3, 195, 242–3
  cave story, 181–2, 210
  epistemology, 178, 182–3
  philosophical genius, 115
Poets:
  and ultimate nature of reality, 214–15
  source of knowledge, 178, 180
Polish logicians, 259
Politics, 171, 174, 205
Positivists, 111, 194, 200, 207
Possibilities, 22
Pragmatic paradoxes, 246–7
Pragmatists, 218
Predictive policies, 99–103, 105–7
Prejudices, 174–6, 187–9, 191, 194
Preparedness-dispositions, 96–102, 106–7
Prévost, Pierre, 152, 157–8, 165, 167
Probabilities, 55, 110
Promises, 102, 243
Propositions, 112, 147, 197–8
  analysis, 218–21, 223, 228, 232
  empirical, 93
  nature of, 20–24
  negative, 242, 246–7, 256–8
  true or false, 242–3, 250–2

Protagoras, 192–3
Protestants, 176
Psychology, 145
  'new psychology', 33
Puzzles, 243, 246–7
Pythagoras, 181

Qualities, 5–18, 20, 23
Questions, puzzles about, 243
Quine, W. V., 246, 258–9

Ramsey, F. P., 211, 243–7
Rationalism, 177, 173–4, 182, 207–8
Raven, J. E., 192
Reality, nature of, 214–15
Reason:
  as source of knowledge, 171, 174, 191
  practical and theoretical, 94
Reasoning, art of, 149–50, 210
Reflections in mirrors, 75–76
Reid, Thomas, 167
Reinhardt, Karl, 182–3
Relations, 5–10, 13–16, 23
Religion, 33–39, 143–4, 146, 176, 188–9, 207
Renaissance, 172
Resemblance, 8–9, 18, 81
Richter, Jean Paul, 31
Right and wrong, 115–16
Roederer, P. L., 164
Roman Church, 176
Ross, Sir W. David, 102–3, 111
Russell, Bertrand, 180, 191, 214, 247, 255, 258
  characters, and, 12
  epistemology, and, 171
  logical analysis, and, 216–18, 220–1, 223, 231
  paradoxes, 241, 243
  relations of meaning, on, 248–9
  truth, on, 212
  universals, and, 5, 23

St. Pierre, Bernardin de, 144, 146
'Scandal' to philosophy, 65–67, 88
Schlick, Moritz, 198
Science; scientific:
  abstract, 162
  decisions, 101
  epistemology and, 171–2
  hierarchy, 112
  inductive policy, 109–10
  judgements, 99
  knowledge, 110, 113, 170

INDEX

Science; scientific (*contd.*):
　language and, 146–7, 150–2, 158–63
　methodology, 99, 101
　nature of reality, and, 114–15
　necessity for, 107
　procedure, 103
Selby-Bigge, L. A., 199, 203
Self-consciousness, 25–28, 30–32, 35, 37–38
Self-reference, 241–59
Semantics, 253–5, 257
Sensations and ideas, analysis of, 143–5, 151–7, 162–3, 166, 229–32
Senses, 147, 173, 188–9, 191–4, 199
Sentences, 247–9, 255–8
　translation of, 218–19, 221–5, 228, 232
　true or false, 245, 250–8
Serkin, Rudolf, 185
Sextus, 179
Shadows, 'to be met with in space', 68–69, 74, 76–77, 84
Shakespeare, 227
Shall (word), use of, 121, 123–4, 127–8, 133
Shape, 6–8, 17–19, 21–22
Should or *should have*, use of, 116–19, 124–5, 127–30
Sicard, Abbé, 164
Signs, use of, 147–9, 152–6, 161, 164–6
Size, physical, 211
Sky, and space, 75–76
Smith, Kemp, 65
Soap-bubble, existence of, 84–85
Social relations, 25–29, 32–33, 36, 38, 111, 113, 143–4
Socrates, 113, 181, 184–5, 187–90, 242–3, 251
Solipsism, 26–27, 32
Sophisms, 242, 247–8
Space:
　things 'met with' in, 68–80, 83–85, lists, 68, 76–77
　things 'presented in', 69–75
Spinoza, Benedictus de, 36, 161, 169–70, 172, 183
Spirits, communication by incorporeal, 28–30
Statistical hypotheses, 107–11
Stendhal, 153
Stevenson, C. L., 94, 113
Stoics, 161, 194
Stout, G. F., 69

Substances, 9–12, 14–15, 17–18
Super-natural, 211–12
Suszko (Polish logician), 259
Syntactical categories, 244–5, 250, 259

Tarán, L., 179, 192–3
Tarski, Alfred, 209, 245, 250
Tautologies, 161
Teleology, 103–5, 111, 113
Telepathy, 29
Terms, 5–7, 9
'Things external to our minds', 67, 71–72, 74–80, 83–85
'Things external to us', 67
'Things outside of us', 65–69, 74, 78, 85–86 (*see also* External world)
'Things presented in space', 69–75
'Things which are to be met with in space', 68–80, 83–85; lists, 68, 76–77
Thomas, St., 194
Thought, 152, 156–7, 192–3
Times, The, 200–2, 204
Tisserand, Pierre, 155, 164–5
Tolerance, 176, 191
Tooke, Horne, 147
Totalitarian idea, 171
Tracy, Destutt de, 144–6, 151, 157, 159–60, 162–3, 166–7
Traditionalism, 173–4, 182, 189, 209
Transcendental sense, 68, 78
Translation of sentences, 218–19, 221–5, 228, 232
Truth, 162, 171, 174–83, 190–1, 206, 210, 242–5, 251–3, 256
　above human authority, 212
　abstract, 162
　definition, 250
　doctrine that truth is manifest, 169, 172–8, 182, 184, 188, 190–1, 202
　origins and factual truth, 195–9
Types, theory of, 244–6, 258–9

United States, empiricism, 170
Unity, forms of, 5–7
Universals, nature of, 5–24
Utilitarianism, 104–5, 110

van Vloten, J., 169, 172
Verbs, 7, 249
　peculiar, 120, 140
　requiring conditional clause, 126–7, 130

Volney, Constantin, Comte de, 143–4
Voltaire, 191

Wald, Abraham, 109
Watkins, J. W. N., 176
Whitehead, Alfred North, 243
Wilkins, 159
Will (word), use of, 127, 130–1, 133, 135–8
Wilson, Cook, 19
Wishes, puzzles about, 243
Wittgenstein, Ludwig, 93
Wondering, state of, 61

Words:
  never quarrel about, 210
  origins and truth, 195–9
  usage of, 219–20, 232–3 (*see also* Meaning)
Wordsworth, William, 34–35, 180
Would or *would have*, use of, 129–31, 133–4, 137–8

Xenophanes, 182–3, 189, 192, 206

Zermelo, E., 245, 258–9
Zeus, 179, 216